If Someone Speaks,
It Gets Lighter

Dreams and the Reconstruction of Infant Trauma

Lynda Share

THE ANALYTIC PRESS

1994   Hillsdale, NJ   London

BF
175.5
D74
S48
1994

Published by
The Analytic Press, Inc.
365 Broadway
Hillsdale, New Jersey 07642

Typeset by Sally Ann Zegarelli, Long Branch, NJ

Library of Congress Cataloging-in-Publication Data

Share, Lynda, 1944-
    If someone speaks, it gets lighter : dreams and the reconstruction
    of infant trauma / Lynda Share
        p. cm.
    Includes bibliographical references and index
    ISBN 0-88163-182-5
    1. Dreams. 2. Psychoanalysis. 3. Childbirth—Psychological aspects.
    4. Memory in infants. 5. Psychic trauma in children. I. Title.
BF175.5.D74S48 1994
154.6'3—dc20   94-20530
                                                              CIP

Printed in the United States of America
10 9 8 7 6 5 4 3 2 1

To Bernard Bail, M.D
With profound gratitude
For the foundations of this work

and

To Evan
Whose infancy brought me anew the meaning of
Babies and memory, dreaming,
And love

Contents

Acknowledgments

*T*o my patients, those who are presented in this book and those who are not, I would like to express my gratitude and especially my respect. With courage, they bring me their dreams and, in so doing, allow us the privilege of discovering anew in each hour the wonders of the inner universe and the remarkable power of the unconscious mind. I hope that our work together will be of great benefit to them in the years to come.

My deep gratitude to Drs. Jane Van Buren, Annie Kramer, and Jeanette Gadt, my colleagues at the Psychoanalytic Center, who heard the eight clinical examples of birth and infant trauma that I had reconstructed from adult dream analysis many years before coming to the Institute. With determination and unrelenting persistence, they eventually convinced me that this material needed to become a book. They spent time and interest over the past number of years listening to early ideas about the structuring of the work and critiquing an initial paper as well as various sections of the book itself.

A similar debt of gratitude goes to Dr. James Grotstein. I presented him with the clinical examples and an initial research paper on the topic. His enthusiasm and support were unbounded. He generously offered many reference materials and theoretical avenues to pursue. He reviewed the manuscript thoroughly on its completion and personally introduced it to Dr. Paul Stepansky, Editor-in-Chief of The Analytic Press. Dr. Grotstein's conviction about the importance of this work for analytic theory and technique and his interest in being a part of it have been quite special.

My thanks to other colleagues who contributed their support as well as criticisms to the initial research paper: Drs. Bonnie Engdahl, Fred Vaquer, Richard Alexander, Erna Osterweil, Sharon Sterne, and especially Marianne and David Young.

My appreciation to Yvonne Hansen for her contribution to my understanding of Jean Piaget's work as it relates to the central issues presented by my clinical findings. My thanks to Drs. Judith Broder and Irene Harwood for their commentaries on this work and their contributions to my understanding of self psychology's "organizing principle." My thanks to Dr. Jean Sanville for her suggestions regarding presentation of the clinical material. My appreciation to Dr. James Gooch for numerous discussions of neonatal trauma and psychoanalytic theory. Special appreciation to Dr. Erna Osterweil for sharing her findings and ideas from her prenatal research, so helpful to me in my own work. The same for Dr. Louis Weisberg, who consulted with me regarding the various medical conditions of my patients and their effects on the mind and body of neonates.

My thanks as well to colleagues who read and critiqued all or parts of the final manuscript: Ms. Carolyn Okazaki and Drs. Irene Harwood, Louis Weisberg, and Susan Williams. My very special appreciation goes to Dr. Williams, who spent a great deal of time reviewing and critiquing each chapter of the manuscript. Her support, criticism, and encouragement through this process were invaluable.

I would like to speak for a moment about John Kerr, my editor at The Analytic Press. He had a very special role in this project. He not only edited the manuscript with enormous skill, he nurtured its development in every possible respect. He spent countless hours; his absorption in the development of the material was truly exceptional. My thanks as well to Eleanor Starke Kobrin (Lenni) for her fine manuscript editing, to Joan Riegel for her thorough attention to this project, and to Paul Stepansky for his gracious and warm welcome to TAP. Much appreciation, too, to Jamie Robinson for her scrupulous proofreading.

Untold appreciation goes as well to Colleen Edwards-Bridges, who typed and retyped every version of this project from its inception. Her help over these years has been invaluable to me. I also wish to acknowledge Lee Freeling, Chief Librarian, Reiss-Davis Child Study Center Library, who helped me gather various reference materials throughout the development of this work.

My absorption in psychoanalysis has spanned some three decades. I would like to mention two individuals who were instrumental in nurturing my interest very early on: Dr. Rocco Motto, former Director of the Reiss-Davis Child Study Center, who encouraged me, when I was a young student working on the Reiss-Davis research staff, to pursue my interest in psychoanalytic learning and provided me with many opportunities for such learning at Reiss-Davis; also Barbara Carr, who provided many years of child analytic supervision in the tradition of the Hampstead Clinic.

My interest, beginning 13 years ago, in pursuing formal research in the area of dreams and infant trauma was encouraged while I was in clinical consultation with Dr. Lorraine Gorlick, a colleague at the time of Dr. Bernard Bail. Dr. Gorlick's astute understanding of how the unconscious processes of the infant were manifesting in my adult patients' material was most compelling. I am deeply appreciative to her for this contribution to the inception of the work and specifically for her valuable consultation on the first two clinical examples presented in the book.

With respect to the effects of early trauma, I would also like to acknowledge Gail Abarbanel and the Santa Monica Hospital Rape Treatment Center. I provided some clinical supervision to the staff some time ago, and as a result I gained first-hand experience with the devastating effects of sexual assault and early incest on the total personality. I believe this experience helped me to develop a feeling of conviction about the reality and impact of early trauma that I would not have had without the Rape Treatment Center involvement.

I would like to offer special appreciation to Annie Reiner, whose poetic intuition into the infantile unconscious and particularly how that unconscious intuits the unconscious of the analyst has influenced my later thinking about the clinical material presented in the book.

I wish to thank my family for their support, encouragement, and *unimaginable patience* through the long years of psychoanalytic training, research, and writing. Also to my colleagues and very good friends, all of whom have supported and encouraged me during the development of this work, I am most appreciative.

And, finally, I would like to thank my analyst, Dr. Bernard Bail, to whom this work is dedicated and without whom this work could not possibly have been done. My appreciation to Dr. Bail: for his willingness to explore the whole of a life--from its very beginnings in the womb to its very end; for his unwavering commitment to knowing the truth of the unconscious; and for his most remarkable detailing of that unconscious through dream analysis. For the benefit his ideas and methods have been to me personally and especially to my patients, I extend my profound gratitude.

While I was in the next room, I heard a child who was afraid of the dark call out: " Do speak to me, Auntie! I'm frightened!" "Why, what good would that do? You can't see me," said the aunt. To this the child replied: "If someone speaks, it gets lighter."—Freud (1917b, p. 407)

1
Introduction

We cannot take the newborn child as a tabula rasa but must consider the possibility that emotional experiences, their symbolic representation in dream-thought, and their impact on the structuring of the personality, may commence in utero. . . . Similarly the impact of interferences such as prematurity, incubation, early separation, failures of breast feeding, physical illness in mother or baby reveal themselves in character development as unmistakably as the "shakes" in a piece of timber mark early periods of drought [Meltzer, 1988, pp. 8, 25].

*I*t began with the dream. The basis of this work originated with a single dream of a single patient seen in psychoanalytic treatment. The dream, dreamt on my patient's birthday, seemed to bring to us her entire manner of being in the world, her constant way of bringing herself to a life and death struggle. This "way of being" appeared to be at least in some part a reenactment of her actual "birth day": her life at its very beginning. Both the patient and her dream are reported in detail in chapter 9 (clinical example #1), but I will state the essentials here. In the course of relating a dream whose meaning was initially quite opaque, the patient noted a single perplexing detail: she was given three baskets in the dream, the middle one of them was blue. When she tried to associate to this element in the dream, nothing emotionally significant came to mind.

As the dream had been dreamed on her birthday, and as other lines of inquiry seemed to go nowhere in particular, I finally wondered aloud if this element of her dream might be trying to tell us something about her birth. Specifically, I wondered whether during or shortly after her birth she might have turned "blue" due to asphyxiation. The patient was struck by this suggestion, but she had no knowledge that there ever had been any such complication surrounding her delivery. Nevertheless, she was sufficiently curious to ask her mother in the interval before her next session. She discovered

1

that her mother had had two previous miscarriages, that her mother's pregnancy with her had, indeed, been complicated, and that she had been delivered early by caesarian section. The specific hypothesis concerning the threat of asphyxiation during delivery, though it was plausible given the specific medical complications involved, could not be confirmed. Nor did my patient have an "ah hah" experience of self-recognition. My patient's mother was a rather closed individual, who did not talk in any great detail about such matters. We did not have birth records. There was much room for doubt. Nonetheless, I began to elaborate for her my thinking that complications surrounding her birth had contributed to her particular sense of the human dilemma and were still informing her difficulties existing in the world. Following these interpretations, there was a striking shift in my patient's behavior. One could almost feel an ease in the pressure to enact a variety of life-and-death scenarios. Her propensity for risky, even dangerous acting-out diminished. The change was palpable in the room in the weeks that followed, as though the air was slowly withdrawing from a dangerously overinflated balloon. I found it astonishing. How could this be? How could a dream "know" about this? How could the unconscious have "remembered" such information, stored it, and produced its continuous enactment throughout the patient's 40 some odd years of life? The nature of the trauma, the way it had become an organizing force for her whole personality, and how it was being enacted in the analytic transference all became apparent from the analysis of a single dream. Was this possible? Was it just a fluke or perhaps a fantasy?

This experience led me to reflect further on the scope of the unconscious mind in an individual and the possibility of making contact with it through dream interpretation. By virtue of my work with Bernard Bail, I had already become interested in the power of dream analysis to make contact with a patient's deeper anxieties and unconscious meaning-making, and in the possibility that earliest experience can be stored in the unconscious mind. In fact, the dream analyses reported later in this book are based on an approach to dream interpretation that did not originate with me, but with Bail. My patient's dream and her response to interpretation intersected with this general approach, however, in a way that piqued my curiosity about the possibility that dreams might enable a reconstruction of the earliest traumas. A few more cases followed in which traumas either at birth or during early infancy were reconstructed from a patient's dream. These patients, unlike my initial patient, *had* been informed of the particular traumatic events many years before so that the facts were not new. What did seem to be new, however, was the often dramatic recognition of how these traumatic "facts" were still alive in the personality and how they were being enacted in the present in exquisite, and exquisitely painful, detail.

As I considered these cases, the issue was thus put squarely before me: *how do the earliest experiences of life etch their mark on the human character?* Accordingly, in addition to compiling my own cases, I began delving both into the psychoanalytic literature on the limits and possibilities of reconstruction and into the scientific research literature on infant potentialities in relation to early memory. Does a neonate have a sufficiently well-developed psyche such that it is capable of meaningful psychological experience? If the neonate does, in fact, have such a capacity for meaningful psychological experience, is it also able to store its experiences in some form of memory? And if the infant can have and store such experiences, how would they be manifest later in life? Is it possible to resurrect the meaning of such experiences through reconstruction during the course of psychotherapy and psychoanalysis? If so, what would be the best avenue for pursuing such reconstruction? In reconstructing, what criteria should we use for supposing that we are on the right track? And so forth.

This book is the result of my meditations on questions like the foregoing. As I have come to realize in the course of writing it, the selection of trauma as a point of departure for reflecting on the sequelae of very early experience, though it presents certain pitfalls, also possesses some advantages. Likewise, as I have also come to realize, there is a reason to suppose that dreams may provide unusually potent access to the meaning of such early traumas to the individual. That is to say that traumatic early experiences, whether physical or emotional, may reveal themselves more distinctly in later life than other average expectable experiences. And though it is by no means the sole avenue of investigation, dream analysis may constitute a privileged means for unearthing how these traumas inform the beginning of life and how they live on in the present.

TRAUMA AND RECONSTRUCTION

Psychoanalysis was founded within the context of trauma. Initially Freud (Breuer and Freud, 1893–1895) postulated that hysterical states were the result of unmentalized, "traumatic," unbearable ideas, usually unacceptable sexual wishes. The influence of trauma remained even when Freud replaced his theory of externally imposed trauma with his concepts of unconscious fantasy and psychic reality. Reconstruction of oedipal and postoedipal psychic reality became a fundamental procedure in the psychoanalytic method. Reconstructions of pre-oedipal and earlier preverbal states are, however, relatively scarce and are often considered very questionable. Freud's (1918) analysis of the Wolf Man dream (1918), in which he retrieved an 18-month-old's view of the primal scene, a memory that became a trauma retroactively during the oedipal period, was the first attempt at a detailed reconstruction of a very early experience and its meaning to the patient.

Reconstruction from the preverbal period was quite rare in the classical psychoanalytic literature and remains so today. As interest grew in treating more disturbed patients psychoanalytically (borderline, psychotic, and narcissistic disorders), however, analysts began to explore the nature of primitive states of mind and their foundations in a patient's early history (Valenstein, 1989). Thus, Melanie Klein (1975a, b) and her followers from the English school investigated the infant's internal world. Donald Winnicott (1958), Masud Khan (1964a, b) and Michael Balint (1968, 1969), from the Middle school, were noted for their attention to the mother–infant relationship and the consequences of the mother's misattunement to the baby. Classical analysts Phyllis Greenacre (1941, 1945, 1952) and Margaret Mahler (Mahler, Pine, and Bergman, 1975) focused on birth and pregenital patterning and the separation-individuation phase of development respectively. And, finally, the Italian analyst Alessandra Piontelli (1987, 1989), in her fetal ultrasound studies, pioneered the observation of "life before life."

It has been assumed that the earliest phase of life is characterized by a "vague and amorphous" state of mind (Bernstein and Blacher, 1967; see also Anna Freud, 1969; Rubinfine, 1981; Dowling, 1982b; Fajardo, 1987; Arlow, 1991). Thus it was thought that discrete experience, even when traumatic in nature, would not be stored and retained as such in the infant (infancy defined as birth through three years). On the basis of this assumption, a significant controversy still remains as to whether or not the earliest preverbal states (or traumas) can be reconstructed in the course of an analysis; and if they can, how these states would manifest themselves in the patient's material. Anna Freud (1969) typifies the view that such reconstruction is not really feasible.

> There is further the question whether the transference really has the power to transport the patient back as far as the beginning of life. Many are convinced that this is the case. Others, myself among them, raise the point that it is one thing for preformed object-related fantasies to return from repression and be redirected from the inner to the outer world (i.e., to the person of the analyst); but that it is an entirely different,

almost magical expectation to have the patient in analysis change back into the prepsychological, undifferentiated, and unstructured state, in which no division exists between body and mind or self and object [pp. 40–41].

Roy Schafer (1976), Paul Ricoeur (1977), and Donald Spence (1982) see reconstructing a veridical account of the past as impossible and thus advocate the use of the narrative technique in psychoanalysis (cited in Wetzler, 1985). Ernst Kris (1956) suggested that we can reconstruct only the general "patterns" of childhood, since our view and memory of the past are colored and modified by the present. In addition, he points out that traumatic events are infused with fantasy and consequent defenses. They take on different meanings as development progresses and are reinterpreted from these new perspectives.

Even if one supposes that reconstruction of earliest life is possible, the further question remains whether the resulting material reflects a fantasy[1] of the patient about that period of life or the reality as he experienced it. Some commentators have insisted that there must be detectable differences between the sequelae of actual trauma and the sequelae of fantasized scenes. Harold Blum (1980) states the point bluntly: "There are significant differences between primal scene fantasy versus actual exposure, between fantasied desertion and actual object loss" (pp. 45–46). In a similar vein Greenacre (1981) notes:

> The opinion is sometimes expressed that the effects of an actually experienced trauma may be no different from those of one that has been only fantasized. I have come to doubt that this is usually true. Awareness of the actual trauma may be repressed at the time of its occurrence, when the impression of it is broken up into bits, as described by Freud. These bits find their way into various screen memories, where they contribute to the intensity. They also appear repetitively in dreams, sometimes with a double denial. They are prone to reappear in bizarre physical symptoms either in sleep or in half-wake states. In other words, the meaning of an actual trauma is disguised but tenacious [p. 44].

Greenacre (1941) writes with conviction of the possibility of the reconstruction of events from the beginning of life:

---

[1]In this book, I am using *fantasy* to refer to both conscious and to unconscious processes. *Phantasy* is used by some authors to distinguish unconscious processes from conscious ones.

As patients speak of their own birth injuries, their earliest illnesses, accidents, the attitudes of their mothers toward and during pregnancy, I reconstruct for them the possible effects of such experiences on a young child, and indicate the inevitable contribution to the general tension and amorphous anxiety of the later adult. In this connection, it is interesting that one can in the course of such interpretation pretty well reconstruct what has been the specific experience of the given patient. He does not recover clear memories or confirmatory evidence which he can convert into words, but he reacts with wincing, increase of tension, or the appearance of confirmatory somatic symptoms when the old sensitive areas are touched, even when this has to do with events of the very earliest weeks and months of life [p. 67].

Similarly, Winnicott (1949a) writes sympathetically of a colleague that he was "quite willing to believe that the psychology of an individual is something which can be studied prenatally and at the time of birth" and then added, "I do find in my analytic . . . work that there is evidence that the personal birth experience is significant, and is held as memory material" (pp. 176–177).

More recent studies in child psychiatry, neurobiology, and psychoanalytic infant observation support the notion that an early memory system exists, and that, therefore, a later reconstruction of infantile events may be possible.

From child psychiatry, Lenore Terr (1988, 1990, 1991) has studied verbal and behavioral memories of traumatized children under the age of five, and compared these memories with documentation of the same events. She found that at age two-and-a-half to three, most children retain and can later retrieve some type of verbal memory of trauma. At that time, children can articulate verbally what has happened to them. But a most significant finding concerns trauma that is inflicted between birth and two years, a time when no verbal memory exists. Traumatized children from this group showed *behavioral* memory of their traumas. They reenacted in play or other behaviors at least a part of their traumatic experiences. An example was a child who had been sexually abused from birth to six months in a day care setting from which she was removed at six months. She played out the exact details of her abuse when she was interviewed at two years, 11 months as verified in photographs confiscated by the police. Terr (1988) states, "What is striking is how literal their behavioral memory is, how early it comes into operation, how accurate the details are" (p. 98). Of the duration of terrifying experiences, she writes "If one could live a thousand years, one might completely work through a childhood trauma by playing out the terrifying scenario until it no longer terrified. The lifetime allotted to the ordinary person, however, does not appear to be enough [time]" (Terr, 1991, p. 13).

Evidence as to the physiological underpinnings of Terr's findings comes from recent research in neurobiology. Joseph LeDoux (1989; LeDoux, Romanski, and Xagoraris, 1989) has demonstrated that some centers of primitive emotional reaction in the brain are developed in the first year of life, before the infant's cognitive capacities have matured. LeDoux's findings regarding the indelibility of subcortical emotional learning suggest that emotions experienced before they are processed cognitively may be registered in earliest infancy and persist through time. As a consequence, emotional memories, fears, and resentments from the beginning of life may be formed, stored, and acted on throughout life (Goleman, 1989).

And, finally, Piontelli (1986, 1987, 1989) has studied the possibility that mental life, ego functioning, and awareness already exist in the fetus and has explored the consequent bearing of this possibility on the mental functioning of babies. Using ultrasound, she observed individual fetuses and twins monthly, beginning in the fourth month of pregnancy. Observing the children over a period of two years, she found early markers of individual temperament and behavior beginning in the womb and continuing in the same direction during infancy. For example, a very sensual fetus who continually licked and stroked the placenta and the umbilical cord, licked and stroked everything in sight during her first two years of life.

Piontelli (1988) also analyzed a two-year-old psychotic child who had stopped moving in the womb at five months and who was born with the umbilical cord wound tightly around her neck. This child had undergone painful medical procedures during hospitalization in her first month of life. In all her actions and autistic "play," she seemed to live out the *memories* of her past entangled life inside the womb. She wore a huge, heavy, double-knotted chain around her neck and refused to part with it. She continually pressed an object horizontally across her navel. Playing with the cord and curtain in Piontelli's office, she wrapped herself up like a mummy, excluding the rest of the world, and by these various means recreated her past life inside the womb.

The evidence from these studies can be comprehended by clinical work with adult patients. The contention of this book is that there now exists sufficient clinical case material, some of it previously reported and some of it reported for the first time here, to warrant the assumption that birth and infant experiences, and the emotional meaning of these experiences, are stored in the unconscious from the beginning of life; and that they can be symbolized, and thus utilized for dream-thought and retrieved in dreams much later in life in the therapeutic setting. Moreover, it appears that dreams can reveal in symbolic form not only the memories of actual traumatic events but also a metaphorical expression of the meaning of these events to the patient. Through an understanding of such material, we as analysts have an important opportunity to touch patients emotionally in a very profound way—to bring alive for them how their earliest experiences have shaped the very essence of personality and how they affect the analytic interaction at a given moment in time.

One could say that a number of "royal roads" exist to retrieve such infantile material. There are behavioral manifestations and symptoms. And certainly the analysis of transferential manifestations is very important. The dream, however, seems an especially promising avenue of investigation because of its pictorial form and its ability to "tell a story" about one's unconscious emotional experience. Understanding the dream can also help the clinician make sense of behavioral manifestations and symptoms and clarify the nature and meaning of the transference. As Blum (1976) has written, "The dream may facilitate the recovery of repressed childhood memories, and may provide particular access to early infantile experiences relatively unavailable from other data" (p. 319). Nor is Blum alone in stressing the investigative value of the dream. Ralph Greenson (1970) sees dreams as having an "exceptional position" (p. 519) in psychoanalysis: "No production of the patient occurs so regularly and reveals so much so graphically about the unconscious forces of the mind as the dream" (p. 522). And Paul Sloane (1979) has written, "Dreams convey authentic messages from the unconscious; they are free of artifacts and express thoughts over which the dreamer has no control. . . . The correct interpretation of a dream carries greater conviction to the patient than do interpretations of any other material" (pp. 13–14).

A few of the early analysts had already elaborated on Freud's view that early childhood experiences could be represented in dreams. Otto Rank (1929), Nandor Fodor (1949, 1951), and Calvin Hall (1967) all attempted to investigate birth dreams and provided some convincing examples of birth imagery revealed in dream material. Dream analysis seemed to go out of fashion, so to speak, beginning in the 1930s, when the study of the ego and the mechanisms of defense became prominent. (See Sharpe, 1937; Altman, 1969; and Greenson, 1970 for a discussion of this historical trend.) Thus, little has been done since the efforts of these early writers to explore dreams as a vehicle for reconstructing birth and early infant experience (or trauma) and for reconstructing how such experience or trauma may be lived out in the core of a person's personality. This book thus represents a resumption of a line of inquiry that had been discontinued. Interestingly, just as it once seemed unreasonable on scientific grounds to search for very early memories, more recent research suggests that it may be time to renew the quest.

2

Freud

Trauma, Reconstruction, and Memory

*L*et us begin where psychoanalysis began, with Freud and hysteria. What follows is a summary of the evolution of Freud's concepts regarding psychic trauma, beginning with the seduction theory: sexual experiences directly inflicted on a child that may have effects (hysterical symptoms) at a later point in time by way of "deferred action." Next, we shall discuss Freud's notions of the primal scene as trauma (what of a sexual nature is seen and heard by the child). Trauma is then reconceptualized in Freud's thinking as "psychic reality," a mixture of fantasy and reality combining sexual constitutional factors and defenses against one's own sexual activity. We will focus on Freud's struggle to determine the nature of the data he was reconstructing: real experience or unconscious fantasy. Freud later returned to actual experience again as it emerged in the war neuroses, traumas involving overwhelming experiences too great to be mentally processed. The individual attempts to master the experience through the repetition compulsion. Finally, we take up the birth trauma in the context of the initial organization of anxiety, foreshadowing the infant's separation anxiety from the mother and the resultant helplessness of the infant's ego. We also briefly examine Freud's concept of psychoanalytic reconstruction and some of his ideas regarding early memory as they may be relevant to the retrieval of infant trauma.

TRAUMA THEORY

Freud's Early Formulations

Elizabeth Von M, one of Freud's first patients (Breuer and Freud, 1893–1895), had spent long hours nursing her sick father and continued to care for him after her sister married a young handsome suitor. When her sister lay dying in childbirth, Elizabeth was called to her bedside. As she stood by the bed next to her brother-in-law she had the unbearable thought, "Now he is free again and I can be his wife!" (p. 156). The thought immediately vanished from her conscious mind, but leg pains and difficulty walking (abasia) appeared. These hysterical symptoms symbolized both her wish to walk to her brother-in-law and her intense mental prohibition against such a wish.

"Hysterics," wrote Breuer and Freud, "suffer from reminiscence" (p. 7), that is, from memories of "trauma" that are unacceptable to the conscious mind. At first, Freud and Breuer proposed that traumas could consist of "any experience which generated distressing affects such as those of fright, anxiety, shame or physical pain" (p. 6). Trauma could be created by a single experience or, more often, by a number of "partial traumas" forged from a group of provoking causes. These multiple conditions and experiences exercised their traumatic effects by generating a strong enough force to create hysterical symptoms. (Masud Khan, 1964a, b, and Joseph Sandler, 1967, later developed the partial trauma concept into the concepts of cumulative trauma and strain trauma, respectively.)

Breuer and Freud indicated that normally the affect accompanying a traumatic experience will be discharged through various verbalizations, gestures, and ideas and will "join in the chain of associations" belonging to other experiences. Joining the chain of association helps to put the trauma into perspective and facilitates the "fading away" of its memory and affects. With hysterics, however, the affect of the trauma remains "strangulated," and the traumatic idea, unacceptable to the conscious mind, becomes cut off from consciousness and repressed. The repressed memories and affects do not then go through the normal fading away process; rather, they remain fresh and alive in the unconscious and act like foreign bodies in the mind, affecting the personality for years to come. The trauma becomes mentally *unrememberable*, while concurrently somatically and behaviorally *unforgettable* (see Frank, 1969; Dorpat and Miller, 1992). As in the case of Elizabeth Von M's abasia, hysterical symptoms are a result of a "conversion" of the intense affect accompanying the trauma into a physical form or, as Breuer and Freud described it, into a "mnemic symbol" (p. 90). For Elizabeth, this symbol served as a "compromise formation" between the unacceptable wish (marrying her about-to-be-widowed brother-in-law) and the mental forces prohibiting that wish. It demonstrated to the world her internally conflicted feeling and experience—a story of unrequited longing and desire.

The cure for her hysterical neurosis involved the cathartic method, in which the traumatic ideas were brought into consciousness *in detail* along with the full strength of the accompanying affect. The technique used initially was hypnosis, then the "pressure technique," and, finally, free association. The process of abreacting the emotional experience allowed the traumatic ideas and affects to join the normal chain of associative connections and thus begin the fading away process. (For a contemporary version of the bifurcation of the mind evident in traumatic experience and its treatment, see Dorpat and Miller, 1992.)

Initially, Breuer and Freud postulated two sources of hysteria, both traumatic in origin: (1) experiences and ideas themselves that are unacceptable to the conscious mind and therefore have to be repressed; and (2) the particular state of mind (described as the "hypnoid state") into which experiences and ideas are received. The hypnoid state of mind occurred in Breuer and Freud's cases when the patients were particularly exhausted or frightened and underwent split or dissociated states, characterized by trancelike, half-sleep/half-wake states or daydreaming. Such a "constricted" state of mind, in which "the ideas which emerge . . . are cut off from associative communication with the rest of the content of consciousness" (p. 12), precludes appropriate processing of experiences. (For a contemporary description of the hypnoid state as an infantile state of mind relevant to infant trauma see Loewald, 1955.) Later and perhaps somewhat unfortunately, Freud disregarded the hypnoid concept and with it the workings of split-off, dissociated mental states as both consequences of and contributors to emotional disturbances. Concentrating instead on a unitary mind in conflict, he postulated repression as a central defense.

Freud's theorizing about the source of trauma narrowed and became more specific as his work with patients progressed. Thus, he soon specified that hysteria was due exclusively to traumas of a sexual nature. Early in his thinking, he saw the sexual content as simply involving *sexual wishes* and sexual ideas that were unacceptable to the patient's conscious mind, as in the case of Elizabeth Van R. He then went on to develop a genetic/historical perspective. He stated that the original cause involved an actual sexual *experience* in early childhood: *"these sexual traumas must have occurred in early childhood (before puberty), and their content must consist of an actual irritation of the genital (of processes resembling copulation)"* (Freud, 1896c, p. 163). Thus, Freud came to believe that trauma consisted in some kind of prepubertal sexual incident that in time gives rise to hysterical symptoms. This is a significant step from his and Breuer's original notions, which were quite general.

Freud thought that the incident was not experienced as traumatic at the time it occurred because of the sexual immaturity of the child, but became so when it was revived in memory with experiences of excitation following puberty, that is, when more mature mental and sexual development allowed the person to comprehend the meaning of the earlier victimization. Freud considered this to be trauma by "deferred action" (p. 212). He did not specify how the initial trauma had been reacted to by the infant or young child, but seemed to imply that no, or only a very slight reaction had occurred initially. The experience remained stored in the unconscious, untouched until a later point in time. Modern analytic research indicates that early experience can be reorganized and reworked into more mature forms as development proceeds (see Schur, 1966; Paul, 1981; Dowling, 1985; Terr, 1988). It remains doubtful, however, that trauma inflicted on an infant is not experienced as such at the time. In this respect, Freud may have been blinded by prevailing views of infancy—that infants do not see, feel, hear. (See Terr, 1988, for clinical research demonstrating that trauma is not deferred, that the baby lives out traumatic experience from the beginning.)

Freud outlined his findings regarding the extent of the traumatization and the variety of perpetrators. His descriptions of the types of perpetrators and the dynamics of child perpetrators are consistent with contemporary research findings on actual child abuse (Finkelhor, 1984). He emphasized as well the "grave" nature of the events.

> My thirteen cases were without exception of a severe kind; in all of them the illness was of many years' duration, and a few came to me after lengthy and unsuccessful institutional treatment. The childhood traumas which analysis uncovered in these severe cases had all to be classed as grave sexual injuries; some of them were positively revolting [Freud, 1896b, p. 164].

> In none of these cases was an event of the kind defined above missing. It was represented either by a brutal assault committed by an adult or by a seduction less rapid and less repulsive, but reaching the same conclusion [Freud, 1896a, p. 152].

> Foremost among those guilty of abuses like these, with their momentous consequences, are nursemaids, governesses and domestic servants, to whose care children are only too thoughtlessly entrusted; teachers, moreover, figure with regrettable frequency. In seven of the thirteen cases, however, it turned out that blameless children were the assailants; these

were mostly brothers who for years on end had carried on sexual relations with sisters a little younger than themselves. No doubt the course of events was in every instance similar to what it was possible to trace with certainty in a few individual cases: the boy, that is to say, had been abused by someone of the female sex, so that his libido was prematurely aroused, and then a few years later, he had committed an act of sexual aggression against his sister, in which he repeated precisely the same procedures to which he himself had been subjected [Freud, 1896b, pp. 164–165].

If one were a victim of sexual abuse, then *hysterical symptoms* would develop. If, however, one were a perpetrator of seduction (for example, a brother who seduced a younger sister), then *obsessional symptoms* (i.e., self-reproaches) would emerge. These perpetrators, however, had themselves been victims of seduction at an earlier time (Freud, 1896b).

As Freud had previously narrowed the cause of trauma from a range of frights and experiences to sexual abuse in childhood, so gradually he narrowed the types of perpetrators from a variety of caretakers to the father almost exclusively. Such a narrowed understanding then subsequently contributed to his conviction that a theory of actual abuse as the cause of hysteria must be faulty. If fathers were the sole perpetrators, then the widespread nature of hysteria meant that a huge number of fathers were molesting their daughters, an untenable idea at best. In his May 2, 1897 letter to Fliess, Freud wrote of a conversation with a patient:

"Well then, let us speak plainly. In my analyses the guilty people are close relatives, fathers or brothers."—"Nothing has gone on with my brother."—"Your father, then." And it then turned out that her supposedly otherwise noble and respectable father regularly took her to bed when she was from eight to twelve years old and misused her without penetrating ("made her wet," nocturnal visits). She felt anxiety even at the time. A sister, six years her senior, with whom she talked things over many years later, confessed to her that she had had the same experience with their father. A cousin told her that when she was fifteen she had had to fend off her grandfather's embraces [Masson, 1985, p. 238].

In emphasizing the role of the father as perpetrator, Freud (1896b) made it a point to state that the child's own sexual activity was not a cause of hysteria:

Active masturbation must be excluded from my list of sexual noxae in early childhood which are pathogenic for hysteria. Although it is found so very often side by side with hysteria, this is due to the circumstance that masturbation itself is a much more frequent consequence of abuse or seduction than is supposed [p. 165].

Later, Freud (1908) reversed this position: sexual fantasy of seduction is put in place to defend against memories of one's own masturbatory activity and attendant reverie.

How early in the child's life did the father's seductions take place? As far back as infancy: "as far back as memory itself . . . to the tender age of one and a half or two years" (Freud, 1896b, p. 165). Freud noted having two cases of this kind. In a letter to Fliess (January 24, 1897), Freud suggested that such traumas may occur at an even earlier age:

The early period before the age of 1½ years is becoming ever more significant. I am inclined to distinguish several periods even within it. Thus I was able to trace back, with certainty, a hysteria that developed in the contexts of a periodic mild depression to a seduction, which occurred for the first time at 11 months old [Masson, 1985, p. 226].

And in his letter of April 6, Freud wrote, much to the consternation of those surrounding him:

What I have in mind are hysterical fantasies which regularly, as I see it, go back to things that children overhear at an early age and understand only subsequently. The age at which they take in information of this kind is, strangely enough, from six to seven months on! [Fliess's] brother-in-law Oscar [Rie] implored me to drop this one point (probably he has been charged with this mission) and repeatedly asked me what you have to say about this novelty [Masson, 1985, p. 234].

In reference to the case in which the seduction occurred at 11 months, Freud described the early traumatic interactions with significant objects as so specifically and concretely internalized that they appeared to be "stamped" in the infant's mind and replayed as if in a phonograph recording: "[I could] hear again in the words that were exchanged between two adults at that time! It is as though it comes from a phonograph. The temporal determination of epilepsy [hysterical] and hysterical psychosis therefore lies further back" (Masson, 1985, p. 226).

Freud was for a time thoroughly convinced of the veracity of these experiences as reconstructed in his work with patients. He described the great resistance of the patients to look at the painful issues involved and the forcefulness, therefore, with which he had to apply his technique. Freud appeared to have to bring his patients to a "conviction of the truth," rather than their having arrived at such a conviction spontaneously. He saw their incredulity as proof of the reality of their experience: they would not be making up something they themselves found so painful to believe. In all these respects, one gets, as well, a feeling for the significant emotional impact these "stories of suffering" had on Freud.

> Doubts about the genuineness of the infantile sexual scenes can, however, be deprived of their force here and now by more than one argument. In the first place, the behavior of patients while they are reproducing these infantile experiences is in every respect incompatible with the assumption that the scenes are anything else than a reality which is being felt with distress and reproduced with the greatest reluctance. Before they come for analysis the patients know nothing about these scenes. They are indignant as a rule if we warn them that such scenes are going to emerge. *Only the strongest compulsion of the treatment can induce them to embark on a reproduction of them.* While they are recalling these infantile experiences to consciousness, they suffer under the most violent sensations, of which they are ashamed and which they try to conceal; and even after they have gone through them once more in such a convincing manner, they still attempt to withhold belief from them, by emphasizing the fact that, unlike what happens in the case of other forgotten material, they have no feeling of remembering the scenes.
>
> This later piece of behavior seems to provide conclusive proof. Why should patients assure me so emphatically of their unbelief, if what they want to discredit is something which—from whatever motive—they themselves have invented? [Freud, 1896c, p. 204, italics added].

Freud understood the patients' "reluctance to believe" as "proof" that his reconstructions were of real experiences, as opposed to fantasy. He outlined other indications of truth:

> There are, however, a whole number of other things that vouch for the reality of infantile sexual scenes. . . . there is the

uniformity which they exhibit in certain details, which is a necessary consequence if the preconditions of these experiences are always of the same kind. . . . patients sometimes describe as harmless events whose significance they obviously do not understand, since they would be bound otherwise to be horrified by them. Or again, they mention details, without laying any stress on them, which only someone of experience in life can understand and appreciate as subtle traits of reality [p. 205].

From Freud's description of his therapeutic process, these seduction traumas were deeply unconscious and very difficult to unearth because of their painful nature. They were put together by Freud through reconstructive technique, using fragments of dreams, associations, visual images and fantasies.

Looking back from a later period of an analysis to an earlier one, we are often astonished to realize in what a mutilated manner all the ideas and scenes emerged which we extracted from the patient by the procedures of pressing [Freud's pressure technique]. Precisely the essential elements of the picture were missing—its relation to himself or to the main contents of his thoughts—and that is why it remained unintelligible.

. . . For instance, the patient sees the upper part of a woman's body with the dress not properly fastened—out of carelessness, it seems. It is not until much later that he fits a head to this torso and thus reveals a particular person and his relation to her. Or he brings up a reminiscence from his childhood of two boys. What they look like is quite obscure to him, but they are said to have been guilty of some misdeed. It is not until many months later and after the analysis has made great advances that he sees his reminiscence once more and recognizes himself in one of the children and his brother in the other [Breuer and Freud, 1893–1895, pp. 281–282].

One cannot help but be struck by the contrast between this description of a piecemeal reconstructive process of deeply unconscious experiences resisted with great force by his patients and Freud's (1925a) discussion of the same issue. In the later paper, Freud attempted to explain his change of thinking regarding the cause of hysteria from actual experience to unconscious fantasy. His description implies that his patients' verbalizations of abusive experiences were not arrived at through a reconstructive process but instead were told to him directly by his patients and were fully conscious to them. He also suggested an alternative understanding: his own forceful technique may have brought about "scenes by suggestion." "When, however, I was at last obliged to recognize that these scenes of seduction had never taken place, and that *they were only fantasies which my patients had made up* or which I myself had perhaps forced on them, I was for some time completely at a loss" (p. 34, italics added). (See Schimek, 1987, for a further discussion of this issue.)

We see, then, that Freud's thinking about the source of neurotic symptoms shifted in those early years from his initial view of real traumatic experience that caused fright, to actual child abuse, and finally to the child's inner world, his fantasy life, as the source of the difficulty. (See Caper, 1988, for a discussion of the development of Freud's concept of unconscious fantasy.) Despite this progression away from actual experience, it is clear from reading the body of Freud's work that he never assumed that real sexual abuse (and other real traumatic experiences) did not occur nor that, when they did occur, they created serious and long-lasting consequences for the development of the personality. His revised thesis, rather, was that trauma was not the sole cause of hysteria.

Psychic Reality: Trauma as Fantasy

As Freud began to change his emphasis from abusive acts inflicted on the child to the strength of unconscious fantasy as the source of neurotic symptoms, he focused more on trauma related to the primal scene. This was still trauma of a sexual nature, but one step removed from the child: the child observed what was happening between others and was excessively and inappropriately stimulated by what he observed. Initially, Freud considered that fantasy was used defensively against the *actual memories* and awareness of overstimulating experiences and observations. Thus he wrote to Fliess on May 2, 1987:

> Everything goes back to the reproduction of scenes. Some can be obtained directly, others always by way of fantasies set up in front of them. The fantasies stem from things that have been *heard* but understood *subsequently* (deferred action) and all the material is of course genuine. . . . [Masson, 1985, p. 234]

> For fantasies are psychic facades *produced in order to bar access to these memories.* Fantasies simultaneously serve the tendency toward refining the memories, toward sublimating them. They

are manufactured by things that are *heard* and utilized *subsequently* and thus combine things experienced, heard, past events (from the history of parents and ancestors), and things that have been seen by oneself. They are related to things heard as dreams are related to things seen [Masson, 1985, p. 240, first italics added].

Once Freud gave up the seduction theory and moved to mental life and the vicissitudes of infantile sexuality as the cause of neurotic symptoms, sexual abuse became a fantasied *projection of the child's impulses* directed at the parents. Though these fantasies took their form partly from "material reality"—from early interactions between parent and child—the interactions were no longer considered in reality of a traumatic kind. Thus, in Freud's description to Fliess, the nature and purpose of fantasy had changed.

In the first place, a small bit of my self-analysis had forced its way through and confirmed that fantasies are products of later periods and are projected back from what was then the present into earliest childhood; the manner in which this occurs also emerged—once again by a verbal link.

To the question, *"What happened in earliest childhood?"* the answer is, *"Nothing, but the germ of a sexual impulse existed "* [Masson, 1985, letter of January 3, 1899, p. 338, italics added].

The father, instead of being the seducer, is now seen in some sense as the victim of the little girl's newly awakened sexual desire.

It is found in the fantasy encountered in most female patients—namely, that the father seduced her in childhood. This is the later reworking which is designed to cover up the recollection of infantile sexual activity and represents an excuse and an extenuation thereof. The grain of truth contained in this fantasy lies in the fact that the father, by way of innocent caresses in earliest childhood, has actually awakened the little girl's sexuality (the same thing applies to the little boy and his mother). It is these same affectionate fathers that are the ones who then endeavor to break the child of the habit of masturbation, of which they themselves had by that time become the unwitting cause. And thus the motifs mingle in the most successful fashion to form this fantasy, which often dominates a woman's entire life (seduction fantasy): one part truth, one part gratification of love, and one part revenge [Freud, 1912, pp. 24–25].

In 1906, Freud introduced the idea publicly that neurosis was related to a person's sexual fantasies rather than to actual sexual experience. Fantasy would be created to defend against awareness of *one's own* sexual activity (infantile masturbation). One's own sexual activity now became the "unacceptable idea." Psychic reality, universal infantile sexuality, and hereditary (sexual) disposition become central issues. Sexual constitution (the instincts and their components), fixations, and regressions to different developmental phases, as well as the universally bisexual nature of man were now considered the significant forces in symptom formation. Thus "accidental influences derived from experience having thus receded into the background, the factors of constitution and heredity necessarily gained the upper hand once more"(p. 275). The most important factor was not what happened to the child but how he reacted to his experiences—whether he employed repression or could keep his experiences within the mental realm to be thought about and understood.

Freud (1914b) described this new consideration of the interaction between experience and constitution as such:

> For *disposition* exaggerates impressions which would otherwise have been completely commonplace and have had no effect, so that they become traumas giving rise to stimulations and fixations; while *experiences* awaken factors in the disposition which, without them, might have long remained dormant and perhaps never have developed [p. 18].

Neurosis was now also the result of *psychical reality* rather than material or factual reality—a mixture of fantasy and reality that dominates the mind and behavior of the individual. Moreover, Freud proposed that psychic reality or fantasy could exert as significant an influence on symptom formation and character development as actual physical seduction could.

The shift in Freud's view from real traumatic experience to unconscious fantasy was the culmination of a long development, and its beginnings can be seen in his famous letter to Fliess of September 21, 1897, in which he announced the demise of the seduction theory.

> I no longer believe in my *neurotica* [theory of the neuroses]. . . . I will begin historically [and tell you] where the reasons for disbelief came from. The continual disappointment in my efforts to bring a single analysis to a real conclusion; the running away of people who for a period of time had been most gripped [by analysis]; the absence of the complete

success on which I had counted; the possibility of explaining to myself the partial successes in other ways, in the usual fashion—this was the first group. Then the surprise that in all cases, the *father*, not excluding my own, had to be accused of being perverse—the realization of the unexpected frequency of hysteria with precisely the same conditions prevailing in each, whereas surely such widespread perversions against children are not very probable. . . . Then, third, the certain insight that there are no indications of reality in the unconscious, so that one cannot distinguish between truth and fiction that has been cathected with affect. . . . Fourth, the consideration that in the most deep-reaching psychosis the unconscious memory does not break through. . . . [Masson, 1985, pp. 264–265].

I will remark here on two of Freud's reasons as he related them to Fliess. First, despite intensive analysis, "the unconscious memory does not break through." Freud thought at this time that an actual trauma at even a very early age could be remembered if properly reconstructed, as subsequently he told the Wolf Man (Freud, 1918) in regard to the patient's observation of the primal scene at 18 months. One of the Wolf Man's later complaints about Freud's treatment was that he never remembered the trauma of the primal scene as Freud had told him he would (Obholzer, 1982). Actual verbal recall does not appear to be a realistic criterion for proof that trauma took place in earliest infancy. Freud (1914a) seemed to acknowledge this difficulty and again suggested using the criterion of the "conviction of truth" as operating in a fashion equivalent to a memory. This criterion is in itself problematic, however, since one may have a conviction about something that is not true. Other criteria, such as a diminishment of the repetitive enactments of the trauma, would seem to be more substantial indicators of the veracity of a reconstruction.

A second reason Freud gave Fliess he described as "the certain insight that there are no indications of reality in the unconscious so that one cannot distinguish between truth from fiction that has been cathected with affect." This statement began what became a lifelong series of questions, evident at various times throughout Freud's writings: Which criteria establish evidence of real experience in the unconscious? Can reality be distinguished from fantasy in the unconscious? If so, how does one make such a differentiation? Is such a differentiation necessary for therapeutic result, or is psychic reality the only important issue to be addressed? He stated at this point—at the height of his disillusionment with the seduction theory—that there are *no* indications of reality in the unconscious. Earlier, as noted, he had tried to develop criteria to serve as evidence of "material" or factual reality as opposed to fantasy. Later, in the Wolf Man case, Freud (1918) again suggested a criterion for distinguishing real experience: A lasting sense of reality of the dream. Freud stated in reference to the Wolf Man's dream:

> We know from our experience in interpreting dreams that this sense of reality carries a particular significance along with it. It assures us that some part of the latent material of the dream is claiming in the dreamer's memory to possess the quality of reality, that is, that the dream relates to an occurrence that really took place and was not merely imagined. It can naturally only be a question of the reality of something unknown . . . The dream seemed to point to an occurrence the reality of which was very strongly emphasized as being in marked contrast to the unreality of the fairy tales [p. 33].

Here Freud also treated particular types of dreams as equivalent to memories of scenes in infancy.

> I am not of opinion, however, that such scenes must necessarily be fantasies because they do not reappear in the shape of recollections. It seems to me absolutely equivalent to a recollection, if the memories are replaced (as in the present case) by dreams the analysis of which invariably leads back to the same scene and which reproduced every portion of its content in an inexhaustible variety of new shapes. Indeed, dreaming is another kind of remembering, though one that is subject to the conditions that rule at night and to the laws of dream-formation [p. 51].

In his struggle with the issue of determining the importance of psychic reality over material reality, Freud (1917b) at one point took the position that the truth or falsity of experiences did not matter:

> It will be a long time before he can take in our proposal that we should equate fantasy and reality and not bother to begin with whether the childhood experiences under examination are the one or the other. Yet this is clearly the only correct attitude to adopt toward these mental productions. They too possess a reality of a sort. It remains a fact that the patient has created these fantasies for himself, and this fact is of scarcely

less importance for this neurosis than if he had really experienced what the fantasies contain. The fantasies possess *psychical* as contrasted with *material* reality, and we gradually learn to understand that *in the world of the neuroses it is psychical reality which is the decisive kind* [p. 368].

Perhaps the clearest description of the difficulties that this issue of distinguishing fantasy from reality presented for Freud is condensed in his discussion of the Wolf Man's primal scene material. Freud (1918) published this case largely in response to criticism from Adler and Jung regarding the central role of sexuality in the production of neurosis. Freud reconstructed from the Wolf Man's dream an observation of the primal scene at 18 months of age. He then tried to demonstrate how this observation had become a trauma by deferred action with far-reaching consequences for personality development and symptom formation. Freud again struggled with the veracity of such a reconstruction: it is true; it is a fantasy; it does not matter whether it is truth or fantasy; it is phylogenetic inheritance; and, finally it is undecided. Thus, he stated:

> I should myself be glad to know whether the primal scene in my present patient's case was a fantasy or a real experience [p. 97]. . . . the primal scene, which may in other cases be a fantasy, was a reality in the present one [p. 96]. . . . These scenes of observing parental intercourse, of being seduced in childhood, and of being threatened with castration are unquestionably an inherited endowment, a phylogenetic heritage, but they may just as easily be acquired by personal experience [p. 97]. . . . All that we find in the prehistory of neuroses is that a child catches hold of his phylogenetic experience where his own experience fails him. He fills in the gaps in individual truth with prehistoric truth; he replaces occurrences in his own life by occurrences in the life of his ancestors. . . . I intend on this occasion to close the discussion of the reality of the primal scene with a *non liquet* [it is not clear] [p. 60].
>
> I admit that this is the most delicate question in the whole domain of psychoanalysis. I did not require the contributions of Adler or Jung to induce me to consider the matter with a critical eye, and to bear in mind the possibility that what analysis puts forward as being forgotten experiences of childhood (and of an improbably early childhood) may on the

contrary be based upon fantasies created on occasions occurring late in life. . . . No doubt has troubled me more; no other
uncertainty has been more decisive in holding me back from
publishing my conclusions. I was the first—a point to which
none of my opponents have referred—to recognize both the
part played by fantasies in symptom-formation and also the
"retrospective fantasizing" of late impressions in childhood
and their sexualization after the event [p. 103n].

Clearly, Freud considered the matter of distinguishing reconstruction of real experience from fantasy to be crucial, a matter upon which
the credibility of psychoanalysis stood. It is also clear that he did not
wish to relinquish the importance of actual early traumatic experience
and its effects on the personality, even though unconscious fantasy
had become central to his theory of neurosis and was extremely
important to the understanding of mental life. Thus, he stated, "The
significance of infantile experiences should not be totally neglected. . . .
They are all the more momentous because they occur in times of
incomplete development and are for that reason very liable to have
traumatic effects" (Freud, 1917, p. 361). To the end of his life, he
retained his belief in the central role of reconstruction of actual
experience and memory recovery, as is evident in "Constructions in
Analysis" (Freud, 1937) and in "Moses and Monotheism" (Freud,
1939).

Freud (1937) suggested that actual infantile experience is at the
core of some delusions and hallucinations. He specified this historical
truth as primarily something experienced in infancy and then
forgotten. He then used such an understanding to provide a further
criterion for determining reality in the unconscious: an expectation of
catastrophe in the future represents a memory of a terrible occurrence
in the past (see chapter 9, clinical example #2). Thus, he stated, "Often
enough, when a neurotic is led by an anxiety state to expect the
occurrence of some terrible event, he is in fact merely under the
influence of a repressed memory; something which was at that time
terrifying *did really happen*" (p. 268, italics added). He concluded that
constructions are effective precisely because they recover a fragment
of lost experience, and he noted that those who experience delusions,[1]

---

[1]William Niederland's (1980) research on Schreber's (Freud, 1911) early punitive
childhood experiences with his father and the manner in which these served as the
"kernel of truth" in Schreber's later delusions provides a stunning clinical example of
early traumatic experience as it is lived out in later symptoms, thought, phantasy, and
behavior.

rather than those with hysterical symptoms, are "suffering from their own reminiscences" (p. 268).

Thus, over 40 years after his dismissal of the seduction theory, Freud returns to aspects of his original formulations: infantile trauma and its memories are taken up and reactions to real experience and observation are emphasized. The conflict in Freud's mind, lasting for so many years, about the issue of trauma as reality versus fantasy remains the source of considerable controversy even now. It contributes to the debate over the feasibility of psychoanalytic reconstruction (see chapter 4) and only in recent years have we been sufficiently attentive to real sexual abuse. It is as if it was difficult for Freud, and those who followed, to consider a place for both psychical reality and material reality *at the same time*. This was particularly the case with regard to childhood sexual abuse. We see in "Moses and Monotheism" Freud's (1939) final statements regarding early trauma. His continued belief, first voiced in the 1890s, in the role of actual infantile traumatic experience as a source of psychopathology, is evident.

> We give the name of *traumas* to those impressions, experienced early and later forgotten to which we attach such great importance in the aetiology of the neuroses. . . . the genesis of a neurosis invariably goes back to very early impressions in childhood. . . . Impressions from the time at which a child is beginning to talk stand out as being of particular interest; the periods between the ages of two and four seem to be the most important; it cannot be determined with certainty how long after birth this period of receptivity begins. (b) The experiences in question are as a rule totally forgotten, they are not accessible to memory and fall within the period of infantile amnesia, which is usually broken into by a few separate mnemic residues, which are known as "screen memories." (c) They relate to impressions of a sexual and aggressive nature, . . . *The traumas are either experiences on the subject's own body or sense perceptions, mostly of something seen and heard—that is, actual experiences or impressions* [pp. 72–74, last italics added].

Freud's Two Models of the Mind

Underlying all of Freud's discussion of trauma are at least two divergent theoretical models, one or the other emphasized at different times throughout his writings: (1) an energic model based on 19th-century Newtonian physics and (2) a model of the mind that makes meaning of experience (Van Buren, 1989). In the former model, the mental apparatus was seen as an energy system whose purpose was to "keep the quantity of excitation present in it as low as possible, or at least to keep it constant" (Freud, 1920a, p. 9). This energic model provided a theoretical explanation of trauma:

> Every event, every psychical impression is provided with a certain quota of affect . . . of which the ego divests itself either by means of a motor reaction or by associative psychical activity. If the subject is unable or unwilling to get rid of this surplus, the memory of the impression attains the importance of a trauma and becomes the cause of permanent hysterical symptoms [Freud, 1893, pp. 171–172].

In clinical terms, this understanding translates as follows in the case of a man with a paralysis: *"The arm will be paralyzed in proportion to the persistence of this quota of affect or to its diminution by appropriate psychical means . . . and it can be shown that the arm is liberated as soon as this quota is wiped out"* (p. 171).

Freud had a second model of the mind, however, which was certainly evident in his rich clinical data and more significantly in some of his later theoretical writings (Freud, 1914c, 1917a, 1923). This model, which became the basis for the later work of the object relations theorists, involves a mind that contains feeling, meaning, and an "inner world." The baby creates this inner world from internalizations and identifications, experiences with and fantasies of, the significant objects on whom its very life depends.

As early as 1896, and despite his concurrent insistence on an energic model, Freud was already understanding trauma in relation to the existence of an internal world. Thus, he described a symptom evident in adult life as a dramatization of a real interaction between a patient in his infancy and his mother. This interaction now dominates the patient's adult fantasy life and creates a symptom—fits of weeping. The baby's manner of "reaching his mother," who was lost to him at a very early age, continues to live on:

> Attacks of dizziness and fits of weeping—all these are aimed at *another person*—but mostly at the prehistoric, unforgettable other person who is never equaled by another later. Even the chronic symptom of a pathological desire to lie in bed is explained in the same way. One of my patients still whimpers in his sleep as he did long ago (in order to be taken into bed by his mother, who died when he was 22 months old.) Attacks

never seem to occur as an "intensified expression of emotion" [Masson, 1985, letter of December 6, 1896, p. 213].

The Stimulus Barrier and the Protective Shield

Freud's energic model was particularly prominent in his conceptualization of trauma during the war years. Here Freud was observing the effects of World War I on combat soldiers who were dealing with overwhelming, terrifying experiences and the continuous threat of death. This type of trauma was very real and very conscious; its effects immediate as opposed to by "deferred action." Freud (1917b) focused on the intensity of the stimulus in his definition of trauma and added a time dimension: overwhelming experiences that take place within a short period of time create profound effects. His conceptualization along these lines became pertinent to what future authors described as "shock traumas" (see Kris, 1956; Sandler, 1967; Terr, 1991). He stated, "We apply it [the term trauma] to an experience which within a short period of time presents the mind with an increase of stimulus too powerful to be dealt with or worked off in the usual way, and thus must result in permanent disturbances of the manner in which energy operates" (p. 275). He noted further that these traumas are repeated in dreams and hysterical attacks: "It is as though these patients had not finished with the traumatic situation, as though they were still faced by it as an immediate task which has not been dealt with" (p. 275).

Freud (1920a) began to emphasize not just the force of the stimuli that created trauma but how the individual protected himself from such stimuli: "*Protection against* stimuli is an almost more important function for the living organism than *reception* of stimuli" (p. 27).

Freud described traumatic effects as a result of both the nature of the traumatic stimulus and the person's inability to deal with the stimulus. Part of the latter involved the extent to which the "stimulus barrier" was prepared for overwhelming anxiety. He stated: "It would seem, then, that preparedness for anxiety and the hypercathexis of the receptive systems constitute the last line of defence of the shield against stimuli" (p. 31). Freud saw the lack of preparedness, particularly in the traumatic war neurosis connected to fright, as "a state a person gets himself into when he has run into danger without being prepared for it; it emphasizes the factor of surprise" (p. 12). A break in the protective shield leads to regression to earlier modes of functioning. His formulation of fright and surprise resembles his and

Breuer's (1893–1895) initial conceptualization of trauma: "anything that creates fright, anxiety, shame" (p. 6).

Traumatic Dreams: The Repetition Compulsion

Freud (1920a) enunciated the role of traumatic dreams. In fact, he revised his theory of dream formation at this point. Where originally he saw the sole purpose of dreaming as fulfillment of an infantile wish, he now described a second, earlier, and more fundamental role for dream formation, namely, the mastery of trauma: "though it does not contradict the pleasure principle, [it] is nevertheless independent of it and seems to be more primitive than the purpose of giving pleasure and avoiding unpleasure" (p. 32). Freud developed the concept of the repetition compulsion here. What is reexperienced under the compulsion to repeat includes past events that have no possibility of bringing pleasure, nor could they ever have brought satisfaction. Trauma cannot not be processed in the usual way; it must be continuously reenacted. Freud believed that when the protective shield is broken and the mind is flooded with excessive amounts of excitation, the repetition compulsion is set in motion. The repetition compulsion is employed to master the excessive amount of stimulation.

Anxiety States: Separation Anxiety

Freud (1923) began to take up trauma as it related to the earliest mother–infant relationship, although in an attenuated fashion. In his discussion of melancholia he indicated that the ego gives itself up because it feels hated by the superego instead of loved; he drew a parallel to a time when there is a real danger and to a time even further back, to infancy. Freud stated that when the ego finds itself in such real danger that it cannot overcome by its own means, it draws the same conclusions as in melancholia. It sees itself as deserted by all protecting forces and lets itself die. He added: "Here, moreover, is once again the same situation as that which underlay the first great anxiety—the state of birth—and the infantile anxiety of longing—the anxiety due to separation from the protecting mother" (p. 58).

But what if the mother does not provide a protective force? What if, instead, she (or the parents) is the very *source* of danger? How can we make use of Freud's description for understanding trauma involving unconscious hostile projections and other ongoing mother–infant interactions of a destructive nature? Such would have the potential to lead to a "death," so to speak, of the baby's mind, in that the baby would feel itself deserted by the mother's protective forces and therefore could not exist (see Reiner, 1993a, b for a description of this concept). We might see later ramifications of this process, including difficulties thinking (see author's clinical example #3, chapter 9) and developing a personality (Balint, 1969); or the development of a false self-structure (Winnicott, 1958; Khan, 1964a, b); or, identification of the ego with the abandoned hostile object (Freud, 1917a). Such experiences and ramifications may be different from traumas with an external source. The effects may also be more pervasive in terms of the person's ability to live a life. Freud (1914c) had alluded to some of the difficulties in the early mother–child interaction when he stated that some people with perverse character development took as a model not their mothers, but themselves. This implies that there was a "turning away from the mother" early on. Why and how did such a turning away happen? Unfortunately Freud chose not to examine the issues involved. He stated only that this was "an important field of work that still awaits exploration" (p. 92).

The Birth Trauma

Otto Rank (1929) published *The Trauma of Birth*, (written in 1923 and known to Freud), wherein he saw the pivotal source of neurotic formation as due to the birth trauma rather than to the oedipal conflict. Freud objected to Rank's theories. "Inhibitions, Symptoms, and Anxiety" (1926) was the result. Beginning to address the birth situation, Freud equated the baby's first cry with the first expression of anxiety:

> We assume, in other words, that an anxiety-state is the reproduction of some experience that contained the necessary conditions for such an increase of excitation and a discharge along particular paths, and that from this circumstance the unpleasure of anxiety receives its specific character. In man, birth provides a prototypic experience of this kind, and we are therefore inclined to regard anxiety-states as a reproduction of the trauma of birth [p. 133].

Discussing his view that birth has no psychical content, Freud went on to say:

> The danger of birth has as yet no psychical content. We cannot possibly suppose that the foetus has any sort of knowledge that there is a possibility of its life being destroyed. It can only

be aware of some vast disturbance in the economy of its
narcissistic libido. . . . It is not credible that a child should
retain any but tactile and general sensations relating to the
process of birth [p. 135].

In trying to ascertain which aspects of the birth experience the
baby uses to determine a danger situation, Freud wrote:

Unfortunately far too little is known about the mental make-
up of the newborn to make a direct answer possible. . . . It is
easy to say that the baby will repeat its affect of anxiety in
every situation which recalls the event of birth. The important
thing to know is what recalls the event and what it is that is
recalled. . . . All we can do is to examine the occasions on
which infants in arms or somewhat older children show
readiness to produce anxiety [p. 135].

In rejecting Rank's theories, Freud acknowledged that man's first
and prototypical experience of anxiety is birth. At the same time, and
in a somewhat contradictory manner, he emphasized that birth anxiety
could not be reproduced in later anxiety experiences, since the
situation of birth has no psychic content and the fetus does not know
that its life is in danger. During these years, Freud was attempting to
consolidate a universal theory of psychopathology. He saw neurosis
as based in the Oedipus complex, with castration anxiety as the central
affective issue. Rank's theories, which focused in an entirely different
direction, did not fit Freud's model. Freud had difficulties widening
his scope of serious inquiry to the depths of unconscious mental life
earlier in development than the oedipal period. At times, he touched
on preoedipal issues but usually reframed them in terms of regressions
from oedipal problems. Therefore, the possibility of birth memories
and neonatal mental life was not investigated, and the earliest
mother–infant interactions were addressed in an attenuated fashion
only. Thus, Freud (1926) stated in relation to the birth experience:

But we must not forget that during its intra-uterine life the
mother was not an object for the foetus, and that at that time
there were no objects at all. [See Osterweil, 1990, for medical
and psychoanalytic evidence supporting the existence of prenatal mental life and the view that the umbilical cord is the
first object relation.] It is obvious that in this scheme of things,
there is no place for the abreaction of the birth trauma. We

cannot find that anxiety has any function other than that of being a signal for the avoidance of a danger-situation [p. 138].

Trauma as a Situation of Helplessness

Freud (1926) also distinguished between a traumatic situation (which Freud now defined as a state of helplessness) and expectation of danger. The feeling of helplessness is considered the trauma, and anxiety is the signal that calls the person into action to ward off the impending danger.

Freud then distinguished between "automatic anxiety" and "signal anxiety." Automatic anxiety originates in the situation of birth. It is a reaction to an actual, experienced state of danger and then is reproduced whenever a similar danger recurs. The original experience at birth has an adaptive purpose; it leads to the initiation of necessary functions such as cardiorespiratory activity. In future years, such a response to danger is maladaptive. Signal anxiety, rather than automatic anxiety, needs to be initiated. Signal anxiety is a response to the *expectation* of danger and helps the individual to initiate defensive maneuvers to ward of the approaching threat. But, "the infant makes the transformation of automatic anxiety to signal anxiety when on the basis of experience, he learns that the presence of his *mother serves as a protection against danger*" (Furst, 1967, p. 13, italics added). This formulation of necessity assumes that, from infancy, the baby perceives a relationship with the mother and has awareness, memory, and a capacity to learn from experience.

> This change [from automatic to signal anxiety] constitutes the first great step forward in the provision made by the infant for its self-preservation, and at the same time represents a transition from the automatic and involuntary fresh appearance of anxiety to the intentional reproduction of anxiety as a signal of danger [Freud, 1926, p. 138].

Freud pointed to the displacement involved in the transformation from one type of anxiety to another. The original displacement sets in motion a pattern for later displacements. All are variations of the original anxiety regarding separation from the mother: birth (loss of the mother's womb), loss of the mother (with separation), loss of the penis, loss of the mother's love, and loss of the superego's (internalized mother's) love. Clearly, this sequence leaves open the possibility that primal forms of anxiety (birth, early loss of mother's love) continue to inform, or to be manifest in, later forms of anxiety.

Trauma: Positive and Negative Effects

Just before the end of his life, Freud (1939) reiterated his views concerning the importance and characteristics of trauma, as well as its effects:

> (a) The effects of traumas are of two kinds, positive and negative. The former are attempts to bring the trauma into operation once again—that is, to remember the forgotten experience or, better still, to make it real, to experience a repetition of it anew, or, even if it was only an early emotional relationship, to revive it in an analogous relationship with someone else. We summarize these efforts under the name of "fixations" to the trauma and as a "compulsion to repeat." They may be taken up into what passes as a normal ego and, as permanent trends in it, may lend it unalterable character-traits, although, or rather precisely because, their true basis and historical origin are forgotten. . . .
>
> The negative reactions follow the opposite aim: that nothing of the forgotten traumas shall be remembered and nothing repeated. We can summarize them as "defensive reactions." Their principal expression are what are called "avoidances," which may be intensified into "inhibitions" and "phobias." These negative reactions too make the most powerful contributions to the stamping of character. Fundamentally they are just as much fixations to the trauma as their opposites, except that they are fixations with a contrary purpose. . . .
>
> (b) All these phenomena, the symptoms as well as the restrictions on the ego and stable character-changes, have a *compulsive* quality: that is to say that they have great psychical intensity and at the same time exhibit a far-reaching independence of the organization of the other mental processes, which are adjusted to the demands of the real external world and obey the laws of logical thinking. They (the pathological phenomena) are insufficiently or not at all influenced by external reality, pay no attention to it or to its psychical representatives. . . . They are, one might say, a State within a

State, an inaccessible party, with which co-operation is impossible. . . . [pp. 75–76].

PSYCHOANALYTIC RECONSTRUCTION

The importance Freud placed on trauma and pathological interactions experienced by children in their early years necessitated a therapeutic means that could reach these early experiences. If one retained distorted ideas and fantasies about these experiences, then these too had to be understood and corrected. Reconstruction, therefore, became a central aspect of analytic work—helping to put together early unconscious experiences, fantasies, and thoughts and bringing them to the patient's conscious mind.

Reconstruction, or "construction" (Freud used the terms interchangeably), was an integral part of psychoanalysis from its inception. Freud (1937) differentiated a "construction" from an "interpretation." He indicated that "interpretation applies to something that one does to some single element of the material, such as an association or a parapraxis. But it is a 'construction' when one lays before the subject of the analysis a piece of his early history that he has forgotten" (p. 261). Analysts construct lost memories from various materials presented by patients, such as dream fragments, free associations, repetitive behaviors, and transference material. He thought of construction as an archeological excavation and noted that, unlike destroyed ruins, analysts have the advantage of working with "something that is still alive" (p. 259). Freud's proposals regarding reconstruction are based on the assumption that the dynamic unconscious preserves the past and that the past remains alive in the present. He considered it a matter of the skillfulness of our technique whether or not we can find the past.

> All of the essentials are preserved; even things that seem completely forgotten are present somehow and somewhere, and have merely been buried and made inaccessible to the subject. Indeed, it may, as we know, be doubted whether any psychical structure can really be the victim of terrible destruction. It depends only on analytic technique whether we shall succeed in bringing what is concealed completely to light [p. 260].

Freud pointed out that constructions do not always lead to the patient's direct recall, even when the patient is at an age when conscious memory could apply. Particularly in regard to preverbal reconstructions, Freud (1914a) proposed that a conviction of truth has the status of a discrete memory—a problematic criterion, as noted earlier. He then suggested that the patients' current enactments provide a criterion for discerning early experience.

> The patient does not *remember* anything of what he has forgotten and repressed, but *acts* it out. He reproduces it not as a memory but as an action; he *repeats* it, without of course, knowing that he is repeating it. . . . As long as the patient is in the treatment he cannot escape from this compulsion to repeat; and in the end we understand that this is his way of remembering [Freud, 1957, p. 150].

Although he attempted to provide these criteria for the validity of a reconstruction, Freud did not neglect the manifold difficulties of attempting to reconstruct past events, feelings, and fantasies in work with patients in the present.

As early as 1901, he began to address the issue, and in his Leonardo paper, Freud (1910) highlighted the problem of establishing the veracity of early memories in attempting to construct a true account of the past:

> Quite unlike conscious memories from the time of maturity, [childhood memories] are not fixed at the moment of being experienced and afterwards repeated, but are only elicited at a later age when childhood is already past; in the process they are altered and falsified, and are put into the service of later trends, so that generally speaking they cannot be sharply distinguished from fantasies. . . . The memories that [an individual] has of his childhood correspond, as far as their origins and reliability are concerned, to the history of the nation's earliest days, which was compiled later and for tendentious reasons [pp. 83–84].

Considering the nature of Freud's (and later authors') concerns regarding the difficulties of accurate reconstruction based on memory distortion, it may be helpful to note some of Freud's theories regarding early memory and to see, in particular, what is helpful to us in the reconstruction of infant trauma.

MEMORY

Freud was well aware of the problem of establishing the veracity of early memory. He also held the view, however, that the perceptual system lays down discrete and permanent, though alterable, *memory traces* that correspond to reality—a "trace theory" of memory (Freud, 1925b). In 1896, he wrote to Fliess that changes in memory are due to the normal tendency toward hierarchical arrangement as development becomes more complex (see also Schur, 1966; Terr, 1988).

> As you know, I am working on the assumption that our psychic mechanism has come into being by a process of stratification; the material present in the form of memory traces being subjected from time to time to a *rearrangement* in accordance with fresh circumstances—to a *retranscription*— . . . memory is present not once but several times over, that it is laid down in various kinds of indications. . . . I should like to emphasize the fact that the successive registrations represent the psychic achievement of successive epochs of life. At the boundary between the two such epochs a translation of the psychic material must take place [Masson, 1985, letter of December 6, 1896, pp. 207–208].

In 1901, Freud stated that memory impressions can be retained in both the original form in which they were obtained *and* in all subsequent forms derived from further development.

> It is highly probable that there is no question at all of there being any direct function of time in forgetting. . . . In the case of *repressed* memory-traces it can be demonstrated that they undergo no alteration even in the course of the longest period of time. The unconscious is quite timeless. The most important as well as the strangest characteristic of psychical fixation is that all impressions are preserved, not only in the same form in which they were first received, but also in all the forms which they have adopted in their further developments. . . . Theoretically, every earlier state of the mnemic content could thus be restored to memory again, even if its elements have long ago exchanged all their original connections for more recent ones [pp. 274–274n].

His assertions became more modest over time. Thus, in 1930 Freud wrote:

Perhaps we are going too far in this. Perhaps we ought to be content with asserting that what is past in mental life *may* be preserved and is not *necessarily* destroyed. . . . We can only hold fast to the fact that it is rather the rule than the exception for the past be preserved in mental life [pp. 71–72].

Freud's (1900, 1925b) trace theory of memory, often referred to as a "copy theory" of memory (see Dorpat and Miller, 1992), proposed that perceptions are registered and stored in a veridical manner. In other words, the actual perception is an exact and true account, copy, or trace of the object or experience. "Our mental apparatus . . . has an unlimited receptive capacity for new perceptions and nevertheless lays down permanent—even though not unalterable—memory traces of them" (p. 228). Freud compared this memory process to the mystic writing pad: "the Pad provides not only a receptive surface that can be used over and over again, like a slate, but also permanent traces of what has been written" (p. 230).

Freud (1900) remarked upon the unconscious nature of our memories and the pervasive impact they can have in their unconscious form.

Our memories—not excepting those which are most deeply stamped on our minds—are in themselves unconscious. They can be made conscious; but there can be no doubt that they can produce all their effects while in an unconscious condition. What we describe as our "character" is based on the memory-traces of our impressions; and moreover, the impressions that have had the greatest effect on us—those of our earliest youth—are precisely the ones which scarcely ever become conscious [p. 539].

Thus, in Freud's system, perceptions and memories can be retained veridically, both consciously and unconsciously. Freud also acknowledged that memory material could be distorted, condensed, and forgotten. As for forgetting, Freud saw early experience up to latency as being repressed (infantile amnesia). At the same time, he noted, children can have distinct memories from the third and fourth years. He integrated these disparate views with his concept of "screen memory" (Freud, 1899), a conscious form of memory with significant unconscious components. Here, affectively charged childhood memories are hidden behind indifferent ones. They must be reached through analysis of the condensations and displacements involved, just as an image in the manifest content of a dream must be unraveled through knowledge of dream mechanisms and association (see chapter 8).

Freud (1901) subsequently distinguished among three types of screen memories. In the retroactive or *retrogressive screen memory*, the screening memory is from an earlier period, and replaces an event in later development. In *displacement forward*, an indifferent, disguised material from a recent experience serves as a screen for an earlier event. In the contemporary or *contiguous screen*, a current memory covers a more disturbing experience from the same period of time. (See also Abraham, 1913; Glover, 1929; and Lansky, 1991, who described traumatic memories as having screening functions in which one trauma screens another. Greenacre, 1949, also described the intensity of the screen memory or its "ultra clear quality," as establishing its origin in the preverbal period.) Freud (1914a) stated of these memories:

> In some cases, I have had an impression that the familiar childhood amnesia, which is theoretically so important to us, is completely counterbalanced by screen memories. Not only *some* but *all* of what is essential from childhood has been retained in these memories. It is simply a question of knowing how to extract it out of them by analysis. They represent the forgotten years of childhood as adequately as the manifest content of a dream represents the dream-thoughts [p. 148].

More recent memory research raises a host of objections to the trace, or copy theory of perception and memory. Memory is thought to be reconstructive in nature, forming "schemas" into which current experience and perceptions are integrated (see, e.g., Bartlett, 1932; Paul, 1967; Schimek, 1975; Loftus and Loftus, 1980; Slap, 1987; Dorpat and Miller, 1992). In a general psychology of memory, exact veridical accounts of the past are considered unlikely. Does *traumatic memory*, however, operate like *normal memory*? Some have suggested that it does not (Terr, 1990; Dorpat and Miller, 1992).

I propose that traumatic perceptions and memories—particularly those in infancy and those never made conscious—are registered in the unconscious in a veridical manner, perhaps even in an *indelibly* veridical manner, and are subsequently enacted in detail through the repetition compulsion. As Terr (1990) stated:

> Traumatic remembrance is far clearer, more detailed, and more long-lasting than is ordinary memory. As with matters of perception, it appears that overwhelming excitation creates

a different state of thinking—in the case of memory, a clearer, more detailed picture with little chance of gradual wipeout [p. 171].

Because of their traumatic nature so early in life, traumatic memories may in fact *also* serve as the basis for memory schemas, as templates, so to speak, that organize fantasy and that shape new perceptions, ways of thinking about and perceiving the world (see clinical examples in Yorke, 1968, and Frank, 1969).

In the case of early traumatic experiences, then, Freud's veridical memory trace theory—a 19th-century model of cognition—may be applicable. In fact, aspects of his concept of the pathogenic memory structure (Breuer and Freud, 1893–1895), from the seduction theory, may be particularly useful. A contemporary critic, MacMillan (1992), has described Freud's notion of pathogenic memory structures with unusual clarity:

> Memories in the pathogenic memory structure were arranged around a nucleus in a tridimensional way. The first dimension was chronological; memories closest to the nucleus were the earliest laid down, the later material being furthest away. A concentric stratification in terms of the degree of consciousness, or of resistance to retrieval, characterized the second dimension; memories nearest the nucleus were the most difficult to recover and recognize; those more peripherally organized were more readily recalled. The most important dimension was third [p. 115].

This "third dimension," according to MacMillan's description, is at the center of the pathogenic memory structure. It was considered by Freud to be the "purest manifestation" of the trauma, consisting of the actual sensory content of the experience. One might think of this pure sensory content as analogous to Freud's (1915b, 1923) description of a "thing presentation" (the sensory data of the unconscious) before it is connected to a "word-presentation" in the preconscious (where it may become available for language and conscious thought). Another analogy would be to Freud's (1923) "perceptual image," which, according to Lewy and Rapaport (1944), is a raw sensory image. It would be this "nucleus," or "purest manifestation of the trauma," that becomes a veridical, unconscious trace memory.

Freud (1896a) first suggested that the earliest traumatic memories (of seduction) are the nucleus around which other ideas are drawn in.

Together, they form a "grouping" withdrawn from the conscious mind. This grouping attracts further related ideas, and so on. Such a process can be considered analogous to the creation of a "schema" in contemporary memory theory. Thus, a memory is formed from an initial perception/sensation/experience. This memory draws in further analogous perceptions/sensations/experiences. Together they create a constellation through which later memories, perceptions, fantasies, and experiences are filtered. If trauma occurs at the beginning of life, then such an experience becomes the *initial* traumatic one. This initial traumatic perception/experience is stored veridically and draws later perceptions/sensations/experiences to it, forming a "trauma schema." Thus, veridical memory and memory schemas are both involved in a complex mental process. We can see, then, that portions of Freud's earliest trauma theories can merge with contemporary memory theory to help us decipher the nature and impact of infant trauma.

SUMMARY

Freud gave us a beginning, an array of often opposing "ways" to think about trauma. Trauma is about sexual abuse; trauma can be developed from psychic reality. Trauma can be an overwhelming, terrifying, real experience of immediate threat to one's life; trauma can be deferred. Trauma can begin with birth and organize only a general pattern of anxiety; trauma can be about the vicissitudes of separation from the mother. Trauma is about the nature of noxious stimuli; trauma is about what one possesses to protect oneself from such stimuli. Trauma is a matter of quantity and force; trauma is a matter of ongoing pathological interactions with significant objects taken inside one's mind and contributing to the development of an inner world. Each of these "ways" has been explored over the last 100 years by different authors and theorists, arriving at often equally diverse conclusions.

Consequently, Freud left us with a host of problems and questions also debated and explored over the past 100 years. Most of the debate remains today a source of unsettled controversy. We focus on some of this debate in the balance of this book. Are the earliest real traumatic experiences of life so important? Can we know about them, and do they have more of a psychic content than we had supposed? Can they be stored in the mind and have real effects in terms of later symptoms, behavior, and characterological manifestations? Can earliest experience/trauma be reconstructed in psychoanalysis, and does it impact the transference? If so, is such reconstruction useful or necessary in analytic work? If necessary, then how can real experience be distinguished in the unconscious? What are some of the criteria? What is the nature of memory formation in trauma? Does it differ from general memory in regard to its veridical storage and reconstruction?

Arguably, Freud was hampered in two or three major ways in thinking about these questions. First, he continuously tried to fit his very rich clinical data and understanding into a mechanistic, quantitative model of the mind. Second, he tried to develop a theory of mental functioning encompassing all of psychopathology within a universal understanding of the neurosis based on castration anxiety and the role of the father. Finally, he tried to develop a general psychology encompassing all mental phenomena of ordinary life (i.e., general memory, dreams, slips of the tongue, as well as commentaries in the arts, literature, history, and the humanities). Thus, Freud's theorizing about specific pathological processes and their unique and specific characteristics needed to "fit into" these overriding conceptual schemas. The results were at times awkward and cumbersome and did not always fit his intuitive grasp of observations. In particular, his oedipal theories of neurosis hampered him from exploring and elaborating further the details of the early mother–infant relationship and its internalizations in the creation of pathology. To be sure, as noted from some of his poignant vignettes, at times he appeared to see and understand the nature of the infant–mother relationship and of its living out in the inner world, but he had great difficulty focusing in detail on these observations and developing his theory from these particular and specific data. Later authors would not be so encumbered.

We shall continue, then, where Freud left off.

3
Infant and Childhood Trauma

W hy trauma? Would not any type of infant experience do as the topic for this work? Most likely. Psychic trauma and its sequelae are, however, what we as clinicians must address on a daily basis. In addition, research evidence (Terr, 1988) demonstrates that psychic trauma is the most memorable of early experiences, if a memory of sorts can be substantiated in infancy. If Freud's (1920a) hypothesis regarding the repetition compulsion is correct, then trauma constitutes the type of infant experience most likely to be enacted later in life as well, through behavioral manifestations, symptoms, fantasies, transference manifestations, and the like. Thus, with trauma we have the best opportunity to see the living out of early experience in the adult character.

We begin our brief review, then, with post-Freudian analytic writers who addressed childhood trauma, including those who focused on pregenital and infant trauma, in particular, and those who expanded the concept of trauma to include shock, strain, and cumulative trauma. We shall review the attempts of classical as well as object relations theorists to formulate the nature of trauma, its effects on the development of the personality, the role of object relations in the formation and consequences of trauma, and its long-term outcome.

THE NATURE OF PSYCHIC TRAUMA: SHOCK AND STRAIN

The nature of trauma is most often discussed in terms of two differing though interrelated types: "shock trauma" and long-term "strain" or "cumulative" trauma (Kris, 1956). Each provides a qualitatively different experience, producing its own effects (symptoms and other distortions of the personality), and involves somewhat different issues in terms of the infant's or child's relationship to significant objects. The development of theoretical issues surrounding these experiences also comes from divergent traditions in psychoanalytic theory.

Shock trauma usually stems from one or a series of blows that so overwhelm the child that his coping and defensive capacities cannot operate effectively. An internal situation of helplessness is created. For purposes of this discussion, the blows are defined as external—a product of real experience, not fantasy. The child may have many fantasies about the experience, however, and fantasy itself may contain reactions to and imprints of trauma (Kris, 1956). Such traumas for the infant may involve surgeries or painful medical procedures, serious illnesses, accidents, assaults, traumatic birth procedures and experiences, the unexpected death of a parent, or the like. Though the trauma usually does not derive from the quality of the parent–child interaction, the parent–child relationship may have at least some, and perhaps a significant, impact on either mitigating or exacerbating the overall effects of the trauma. Single- or multiple-shock traumas are often conceptualized in psychoanalytic theory within the framework of Freud's (Breuer and Freud, 1893–1895) energic model, that is, a force that overwhelms the stimulus barrier, stimulation of such a magnitude that it cannot be coped with or discharged adequately by the organism.

Cumulative or strain trauma offers a kind of experience qualitatively different from shock trauma and is not considered "traumatic" in the way one customarily thinks of the traumatic impact of a surgery, accident, or assault. Strain trauma refers to the effects of a long-term situation involving the "accumulation of frustrating tension" (Kris, 1956, p. 73). Most generally, the parental object is the source of the trauma itself. Strain traumas usually involve excessive "impingements" (Winnicott, 1958) by inadequate parental care, projections of the mother's[1] pathology into the child (Khan 1964a, b; Reiner, 1993a, b), or both. An interaction that was initially experienced as a shock trauma may evolve into an ongoing strain trauma as it becomes a "way of life" within the family, e.g., ongoing sexual abuse by a parent. Distortions in the development of the child's personality (e.g., a false self-structure, pseudomaturity) occur as the child attempts to cope with the needs, inadequacies, and projections of the parent.

The focus on strain or cumulative trauma began to emerge in the psychoanalytic literature with the influence of the object relations

---

[1]The word "mother" is used throughout the book to describe the child's actual mother as well as any person who takes a mothering or parenting role, for example, the father or other caretakers (see Harwood, 1986, 1993, regarding the role of extended caretakers in the life of the child).

theorists. Thus, Winnicott (1958), Balint (1969), and Khan (1964a, b), for example, all saw the ongoing parent–child interaction as central, so that trauma began to be viewed as a qualitative, interactional experience rather than as a quantitative, energic one. Thus, a quantity of energy or stimulation too great for the organism to discharge (Breuer and Freud, 1893–1895) was not the focus. Rather, the capacity of the mother to cope with the infant's or child's projections and to modify them, and the extent to which the mother projects her own pathology into the infant, became central.

Shock and strain traumas exist as separate entities, but there may be complex interactions between them and they are often mixed (Kris Study Group, 1974). Shock can occur within the context of ongoing strain in the parent–child relationship. Strain trauma may foster the development of rigid defenses and leave the child without adequate internal and external resources to deal with the consequences of shock. The mother's (or parents') sturdy relationship with the infant or child prior to the shock, and their capacity to support the child through its effect, can minimize traumatic results. On the other hand, the parents' excessive anxieties and terror may further traumatize the child and burden his already beleaguered coping mechanisms. The severity of the trauma may also affect the child's perception of the parent and the quality of the ongoing parent–child relationship. For example,

> children . . . cannot realistically assess responsibility for injury or trauma. The parent may be blamed for the child's discomfort and pain, and illness itself may be unconsciously misinterpreted by the child as an attack by a persecutory or punitive object. The parent may also be blamed for being unable to comfort the child sufficiently or for not omnipotently making the pain go away and restoring the child to health [Blum, 1987, p. 615].

A young infant's lack of adequate self–other boundaries heightens the possibility that intense physical pain can be experienced as coming from the mother as well as from the self. In the projective–introjective process of the mother–baby relationship, severe trauma to the mother may be experienced by the infant as though it were happening to him (Greenacre, 1967).

A complex set of factors—including the severity, nature, and duration of the trauma; the age and developmental level of the child; prior experience; fantasy and object relations—influence the meaning of the trauma for the child and how the child makes sense of his or her experience. Let us look at some of the analytic writers who have approached these issues.

Phyllis Greenacre: Pregenital Traumas of Overstimulation

The classical analyst who contributed most to the psychoanalytic understanding of infant and early childhood trauma was Phyllis Greenacre. Her writings, through a body of work in the 1940s through the 1970s, heightened awareness of the role of early experience in later development, and particularly the importance of reconstructing specific real experience in the analytic process. Greenacre (1949) considered that trauma may be experienced differently depending on the strength of the child's reality ties and his particular stage of ego, libido, and superego development. She believed that the earlier a severe trauma occurs, the greater the somatic components and imprints (Greenacre, 1952; see also Lipin, 1955, and clinical example #5 in chapter 9). She also saw excessive stimulation as resulting in a "primitive erotization" (p. 414) and very premature genitalization. Thus, the stimulation brought about by intense and repetitive trauma can result in a precocious, but at the same time very vulnerable, development (see also Khan, 1964a, b).

Greenacre's (1952) examples of severe stimulation in infancy included forced feeding, giving enemas early in life, and early or very severe toilet training. (One needs to consider here not just the physical impact of the stimulating act but the nature of the parental pathologies and unconscious projections involved.) Children who suffered "overstimulation traumas" were those children who had been made to perform exceptional gymnastic feats when only two or three years of age, before the neuromuscular apparatus was sufficiently prepared. Others were raised in positive surroundings but were stimulated by acrobatic handling early in infancy, that is, tossing, teasing, excessive tickling, and so on. Still others in this excessive-stimulation group were children who had experienced the birth of a sibling within the first 12 to 15 months of life. Greenacre saw these children as having been "robbed of their infancy" and subjected to "continuous torments of bodily jealousy before speech and locomotion have been securely established" (p. 414). Interestingly, she saw this factor as contributing to the intensification of bisexual identification since the exposure may involve siblings of the opposite sex. From her adult reconstructions, she concluded that constant exposure to sexual differences may be traumatic, even for a baby of eight to ten months of age. Greenacre

(1952) noted what other theorists have also reported (Murphy, 1958; Terr, 1988), namely, that "vision in general and visual incorporation in particular are very important [in contributing to trauma] in the period of about six to eighteen months" (p. 414).

Greenacre (1967) addressed the profound impact of earliest trauma: "Severe trauma tends to leave an organized imprint on the young child and, absorbing and modifying the underlying fantasy, it may induce a greater need for repetition, usually in some acted-out form, than is the case with the fantasy alone" (p. 139; see also Kris, 1956). Greenacre saw the degree of imprinting as greater during the first 18 months, when external events are taken in by the child in an intensely sensory (often visual) way. Such events cannot be cognitively understood in a prior context at such a young age. A trauma after two years of age must be evaluated within the context of the first 18 months of life. The trauma will obviously have a more pervasive effect if the infant–mother relationship was disturbed during the first 18 months. Greenacre considered harm to the sense of reality and to the sense of identity as a possible consequence as well as prolonged primary narcissism and damage to the early ego.

Greenacre also emphasized the role of preexisting fantasy as well as preexisting object relations, in determining the influence of trauma. She suggested that the imprint would be more intense and fixation would be more significant if the trauma coincided with preexisting fantasy, for example, the effect of an illness or death of a parent when there was prior great hostility toward that parent (see also Blum, 1986).

Despite Greenacre's emphasis on the importance of early trauma and the necessity of reconstructing early experience in adult analysis, she expressed a note of caution regarding the reality of material involving traumatic events occurring as early as the second year of life. She suggested that these experiences may be projected backwards from later events. Despite this caution, however, she gave as her clinical examples several cases in which patients reproduced in their analyses behaviors having to do with the application of physical restraints in early childhood (see also Anthi, 1983). These people had no conscious memory of such experiences, although the events were later verified.

In one instance sensations had to do with orthopedic appliances and in another with bandaging because of severe infantile eczema. In both cases the restraints had gained later emotional significance in punishment fantasies associated with masturbation. But what was *reproduced* rather clearly had to do with the very early actual experience which was revived in its specific form [Greenacre, 1967, pp. 139–140, italics added].

I believe that Greenacre's examples show us that the body does not fantasize. The body does not "project backwards"; it gives us a true account of our traumatic pasts.

Greenacre saw a number of consequences resulting from trauma imposed on a faulty early ego. These included confusion of actual experience with fantasy, encouragement of omnipotence and magical thinking, and difficulties in developing a strong body image and self-image, in addition to the development of fetishes and other serious character disturbances in adulthood.

William Murphy: Trauma and Sensory Perception

William Murphy (1958) raised important issues related to the role of sensory perception in trauma and particularly its importance in infancy. He explored its role in repetitive reenactments of traumatic events. He focused on "sensory perception patterns," which emerge as actual traumatic memories recalled in the analytic hour (see also Niederland, 1965). He suggested that sensory and affective perceptions are focal points around which many traumatic experiences may be telescoped and condensed.

For example, in one fascinating case, Murphy presented a young man in whom visual sensory stimuli were prominent. The patient felt he saw differently with each eye. From the left eye, colors seemed brighter and objects appeared larger. When depressed, the patient seemed to look at the world through his right eye, where objects appeared smaller and the field of vision narrower. With his left eye, he had a vivid fantasy life surrounding his mother. His fantasies involved clothing, cooking, jewelry, and other aspects of feminine identification. This fantasy life from his left eye was used as a defense to help him deny the traumatic loss of his mother in the past. The patient's mother had gone abroad for six months at the time of his third or fourth birthday, and she did this six times before he reached puberty. She was also hospitalized for agitation and depression for a period of seven to eight months when he was seven or eight years old.

Murphy suggested that these defensive patterns of sensory perception may be an integral part of ego development and may first appear around the time of birth. They may play an important role in determining what is considered traumatic for a person as well as a person's particular style of response to trauma. He noted the differences in babies' responses to the birth process: "It is no exaggeration to say the sensory components of the birth process are the first major trauma of life and directly connected with the appearance of the primordial body ego or ego nucleus" (p. 563).

Murphy pointed out also the possible role of intrauterine life on the character of the perceptual apparatus.

> Who would say that the sound of the steady beat of its own and the mother's heart in the ear of the child before birth is of no influence on the pattern of and response to hearing after birth? . . . The major trauma of birth thus shapes but is also shaped by the daily trauma of the infant's earliest impressions and experiences [p. 564].

Margarethe Ribble: The Mother's Containing Function

Child analyst Margarethe Ribble (1941) foreshadowed the role of object relations in trauma formation. She saw the tendency toward "functional disorganization" as the most consistent characteristic of an infant during the first three months of life. She stressed the need for "a long and uninterrupted period of consistent and skillful 'psychological mothering by one individual" (p. 459). In her discussion, she alluded to the psychological function of the mother in containing and modifying the projections of the baby, thus providing the infant with a "psychological protective shield." Such a concept was later developed in the writings of Winnicott (1958), Bion (1962), and Khan (1964a, b).

Masud Khan: Cumulative Trauma

Building on Winnicott's (1958) emphasis on the early infant–mother relationship, Masud Khan (1964a, b) formulated a theory of "cumulative trauma." Here, the mother is seen as the organizer of a protective shield, as an "auxiliary ego" (Khan, 1964a, p. 46) for the helpless infant and dependent child. The shield is aimed at protecting the child from the difficulties in the mother–child relationship itself. Freud (1920) originally described the protective shield as residing in the infant. With the development of Khan's concept, the notion of a "protective shield" shifts from the infant to its mother. Cumulative trauma emerges when there are "breaches" in the mother's shield. Various impingements result, disrupting the baby's functioning.

In Khan's (1964b) definition, the traumas are not identifiable as such when they happen. Rather, they achieve the value of a trauma only "cumulatively and in retrospect" (p. 47; see also Hoffer's, 1952, concept of "silent trauma").

> It is only when the failures of the mother as protective shield are significantly frequent and have the rhythm of a pattern, and lead to impingements on the infant's psyche-soma integration, impingements that he has no means of eliminating, that they end up a nucleus of pathogenic reactions. . . . None of the failure in or impingement from the mother's role as protective shield is singly traumatic in any identifiable sense for the infant-child at this period. Hence, the difficulty in diagnosing or correcting such failure in the mother's role as protective shield at the time. Cumulative trauma, therefore, builds up silently and invisibly throughout childhood, right up to adolescence, and leaves its mark on all crucial stages of psychosocial development which becomes clinically observable later on in ego pathology and schizoid type of character formation [p. 273].

The mother's protective shield has the capacity to defend the infant against the mother's personal needs and conflicts, her own "unconscious loves and hates" (p. 48). She must allow herself to be a receptacle for the projections of unpleasurable experiences of the baby. She must provide care in such a manner that the baby can gradually distinguish inner from outer reality. And she must help the baby to develop the capacity to tolerate discomfort and lack of attention.

Khan's concept is extremely important in the development of analytic trauma theory because it points to maternal projections as a source of trauma, that is, the mother's unconscious is passed to the child (see also Reiner, 1993a, b). Khan also highlights the importance of the mother's capacity to absorb and modify the intense unconscious pains and projections of the baby. Bion (1962) later elucidated a similar understanding in his concept of "maternal reverie." (Clinical example #3 in chapter 9 is illustrative of the painful process involved in "strain traumas" resulting from projections of the mother's hatreds.)

Michael Balint: The Traumatogenic Object

Michael Balint (1969) dispensed with the quantitative energic aspects of classical trauma theory altogether and contributed to the object relations point of view of trauma. He emphasized the close and intimate relationship between the traumatized child and the individual who inflicts trauma. He characterized these trauma inflicters as "traumatogenic objects" (p. 431), seen as primarily the child's oedipal objects and displacements for them.

He described trauma in an older child as having a three-phase structure. In the first phase, the child, who is dependent on the adult, is largely trusting; the adult may be trusting and at times frustrating. In the second phase, the adult does something unexpected to the child. The interaction may be exciting, frightening, or painful and may be a single occurrence or a continuous one. There may be excesses of affection or cruelty that overstimulate the child. The child may be ignored, leading to rejected and disappointed feelings. In the third phase, when the child attempts to recontact the adult, there is often an unanticipated and complete refusal to acknowledge the trauma. The adult may behave as if he or she were oblivious to the prior stimulation or rejection or may act as if nothing at all happened.

For the earliest infant–mother interaction, Balint postulated a "primary object relationship" (p. 433) in which the infant's communications must be acknowledged and understood by the mother. It is in this phase, when no language exists, that there is the greatest danger of misunderstanding and the parent may react inadequately to the infant's needs. The parent's reactions may simply be wrong, and, unfortunately, the infant cannot defend himself against any misunderstanding. These unresolved "traumatogenic conditions" between the infant and the mother, carried on throughout the person's life, can lead to the creation of what Balint (1968) described as "the basic fault" within the personality. In a fashion similar to that of a person with a borderline/narcissistic disturbance, the adult with a basic fault feels that

> there is a fault within him, a fault that must be put right . . . the cause of this fault is that someone has either failed the patient or defaulted on him . . . a great anxiety usually surrounds this area, usually expressed as a desperate demand that this time the analyst should not—in fact must not—fail him [p. 21].

Though he theorized about the subtleties of mother–infant misattunements, Balint did not provide clinical examples of the formation of the basic fault reconstructed from mother–child interactions in infancy. The issues in his case examples appeared to be set at later points in development (latency forward). It is not clear whether he assumed the phenomenon would be understood by the reader and required no illustrations or whether he perhaps saw the fault as actually emerging in latency. The fault demonstrated in latency could also be a reenactment of what occurred in infancy. Balint did not state this, however.

Max Forman: Traumatogenic Transferences

Max Forman (1984) proposed that fixation derived from overt traumatic experiences is the most significant contributor of pathology in the character neurosis:

> It is this tendency to fixation due to overt traumatic experiences that I am asserting is the major cause of pathology in the character neurosis. It is not *a* source of pathology, as Greenacre points out, but I contend it is *the* source of pathology. The unconscious fantasies would not be so powerful or so pathogenically repressed were it not for overt traumatic experiences [p. 325].

Forman saw traumatic transferences as those which derive from traumatic experiences in childhood with parental objects. This includes a variety of experiences such as lack of responsiveness to the child, overt neglect, temporary separations or illnesses, and the like. Forman's emphasis on the child's experiences with the failures of the parental objects is complementary to Khan's (1964a, b) concept of cumulative trauma, Balint's (1969) concept of traumatogenic object, and Kohut's (1971) notion that empathic failures of the parent are sources of pathology.

Sándor Ferenczi and W.R.D. Fairbairn on Child Abuse

Let us consider for a moment two early writers, Sándor Ferenczi and W. Ronald Fairbairn, who addressed child abuse. We do so in order to touch on the alterations in the child's internal world that come about as a result of destructive parental actions and projections. Both writers emphasized the need for the child to protect the parental object in the matter of abuse and the consequent internal ramifications. Said Ferenczi (1932):

> Traumatogenesis being *known;* the doubt, whether reality or fantasy, remains or can return (even though everything points at reality). Fantasy theory is an escape of *realization* (amongst resisting analysts too). They rather accept their (and human beings') mind (memory) as unreliable than believe that such

things with *those* kinds of persons can *really* have happened. (Self-sacrifice of one's own mind's *integrity* in order to save the parents!) [p. 268].

Fairbairn (1952) believed that the victims of sexual assault resist the revival of traumatic memory primarily because the memory "represents a record of a relationship with a bad object" (p. 63). He saw a relationship with a bad object as both intolerable and shameful—shameful because the child identifies with his bad objects. "If the child's objects present themselves to him as bad, he himself feels bad; and indeed it may be stated with equal truth that, if a child feels bad, it implies that he has bad objects" (p. 64).

Fairbairn modified Freud's original repressed memories/impulses theory of trauma: "I now venture to formulate the view that *what are primarily repressed are neither intolerably guilty impulses nor intolerably unpleasant memories, but intolerably bad internalized objects*" (pp. 62–63). He went on:

The internalization of bad objects represents an attempt on the part of the child to make the objects in his environment "good," by taking upon himself the burden of their apparent "badness" and thus to make his environment more tolerable. This defensive attempt to establish outer security is purchased at the price of inner security, since it leaves the ego at the mercy of internal persecutors; and it is as a defense against such inner insecurity that the repression of internalized bad objects arises [pp. 164–165].

Ferenczi's and Fairbairn's conceptualizations demonstrate an understanding of the distortion that occurs in the internal world of the child. We see here a "compromise of the mind," which comes about so that the child may accommodate the needs of the parent and remain in contact with the parent, a relationship on which the child's very life depends (see clinical examples #3 and #7, chapter 9; see also Reiner 1993a, b). Thus, in Ferenczi's example, the child considers his own mind unreliable, and in Fairbairn's example, what is bad is made good and the child sacrifices himself, making himself bad to spare the parent.

Bernard Bail and Annie Reiner: Strain Trauma and the Development of the Body Ego

Annie Reiner, in two recent unpublished manuscripts (1993a, b), writes about and extends a theory of mind and analytic work developed over the past 40 years by psychoanalyst Bernard Bail. Bail and Reiner use principles of quantum physics as a framework for describing the infant's capacity to develop a mind and a unified sense of self. They take up the profound level of disturbance that develops in the unconscious of a baby when the parent is not attuned to the baby's needs and feelings and particularly when parental projections occupy the mental space that belongs to the baby. Reiner (1993b) writes:

> The infant who is understood by his parents will identify with them and gain from them what he can while still retaining his own individuality. If he is not seen or understood by his parents, his own identity will be subsumed within the identification . . . [In effect] his Mind is obliterated and his Self lost [p. 197].

Bail and Reiner (Reiner, 1993b) discuss the problems that evolve when the parents' minds are themselves deeply split and they are immersed in the loyalties to and the living out of their own disturbed pasts. Here, the parents cannot truly love the child in a unified way. In fact, in their attachment to the love and hate from their pasts, the parents cannot see the infant for himself in the present. The infant simply does not exist for them. "The child will sense himself to be caught in this mental time warp, suspended outside of real life, because he has no one to recognize him in the present reality into which he was born" (p. 83).

As a consequence, the child's emotional life becomes confused. In order to survive in the family to which he is born, he must "give up his mind," so to speak. He becomes, instead, identified with the parent and with the parent's pathology. His mind, his natural self, does not evolve. Faced with significant pathological parental projections, he may, in fact, have to "leave his mind" from the very first moments of life. His mind *must* become that of his parents. In this way, the infant can stay alive physically, meeting the parents' unconscious needs and the culture of the family into which it was born (Reiner, 1993a). We could say of this process that a strange irony occurs: a "psychological death" at the very first moments of physical life (see clinical example #3, chapter 9, for an illustration of this process revealed in a patient's dream).

Many are the consequences of this state of affairs. The infant does not have a unified, whole self from which to live. He may have to turn to a preoccupation with a bodily self to make up for the lack of mental contact with the parent. The fact that an infant's ego is first a "body ego" (Freud, 1923, p. 26) may in fact be a result of a lack of adequate mental contact of the mother to her infant (Reiner, 1993b). If, for example, Freud's hysterical patients truly did "make up" their seductions, we could speculate that the development of such fantasies of overstimulation were themselves the sequelae of a maternal deprivation of sorts. The infant-self of the patient was never truly held in a containing way by the mind of the mother. Thus, the baby turned to heightened sexual fantasies to fill in what should have been an ongoing mental and emotional contact with the mother at a very deep level.

Reiner (1993b) concludes:

[The] parents' inability to understand the child's mind leaves him mentally abandoned and so he loses touch with the more essential truth of his being. . . . It is this disappointed and dejected infant who must be reached if the truth is ever to be tolerated and his dejection overcome [p. 209].

CONSEQUENCES OF PSYCHIC TRAUMA

We have touched on the distortion of the mind and internal world of the child, the creation of a basic fault, the creation of perversions and other character disorders, premature genitalization and precocious development, possible damage to the sense of reality and sense of identity, and a need for repetition and acting out. What other effects of earliest trauma have been earmarked in the literature?

Masud Khan: Premature and Selective Ego Development

Masud Khan (1964b) proposed three significant effects of cumulative trauma on ego functions and ego integration: First is precocious ego development. Here, certain functions of the personality are prematurely developed and employed in a defensive manner to cope with impingements from the mother-child interaction. Khan felt that many of the perversions derived from the core of this issue. Second is an inadequate development and differentiation of the self. Instead of a unified ego structure developing, many dissociations emerge within the personality. Thus, for example, the child retains a primitive dependence on the mother and at the same time becomes precociously independent. Genuine object love does not develop. Third is intensive involvement in both an internal fantasy world and external reality. Disturbances in relation to the bodily self develop, and the need for stimulation is chronic. Love relationships are intense and intrusive. There is often a masturbatory type of pathology in the child that turns out to be the child's way of coping with the parents' traumatic impingements, which overburden the child's ego functioning.

Khan's concepts of premature and precocious development parallel those of Greenacre (1952) and Winnicott's (1958) notion of the development of the "false self."

Lenore Terr; Lee Gislason, and Justin Call:
Visualized Memories and Trauma-Specific Fears

One of the most important contributors to the subject of infant and childhood trauma, as noted in chapter 1, is Lenore Terr. She originally investigated the Chowchilla kidnapping incident (Terr, 1979, 1983b) involving 25 children ages five through fourteen who were kidnapped and terrorized. Her subsequent study of various aspects of the effects and memories of infant and childhood trauma (Terr, 1983a, b, 1985, 1988, 1991) culminated in her book *Too Scared to Cry* (Terr, 1990). Terr concentrated primarily on shock traumas, the terrifying events that occur in early childhood. She also documented experiences of ongoing sexual abuse and other strain traumas. She noted (Terr, 1991) four characteristics in particular that distinguish shock traumas of children and that last well into adulthood: 1) "Visualized or otherwise repeatedly perceived memories" (p. 13). These involve the ability to resee or to refeel the terrible event or series of events even when the event was not originally experienced as visual. For young children, the events may be played out or drawn. 2) "Repetitive behaviors" (p. 13). These are play and behavioral reenactments of both single shock and longstanding terrors. She said of these "behavioral memories": "They may recur so frequently as to become distinct personality traits. They may eventually gather into the personality disorders of adulthood, or they may recur so physiologically as to represent what seems to be a physical disease" (p. 13; see also Lipin, 1955). 3) "Trauma-specific fears" (p. 13). Here she distinguished neurotically phobic children from traumatized children. For example, a neurotically phobic child will fear the category of "animal," but a youngster bitten by an animal will fear the exact animal that bit him. (e.g, a Doberman pinscher). Neurotic children may have fears or anxieties about sex. Sexually traumatized children will fear the exact sexual act inflicted upon them, (e.g., oral copulation).[2] 4) "Changed attitudes about people, life, and the future" (p. 13). Traumatized children see the future as very limited, e.g., "I live one day at a time" (p. 13), and feel very mistrustful. They feel that future traumas are inevitable and "recognize the profound vulnerability in all human beings, especially themselves" (p. 14).

According to Terr, traumatized children, particularly those who have experienced a single-shock trauma, create "omens," or reasons to explain their suffering. They do this to master the feeling of lack of control that a shock trauma brings. Misidentifications, visual hallucinations, and peculiar time distortions are concomitants of sudden shock. Terr attributed the distortions, visual hallucinations, and illusions seen in sudden shock traumas to "massive releases of neurotransmitters in the brain at the time of the terror" (p. 15).

Lee Gislason and Justin Call (1982) found results similar to Terr's in relation to the effects of early trauma. They evaluated dog bites in infancy and the effects of this particular trauma on personality development. Children who had been bitten at 20, 26, and 36 months of age were evaluated. They were found to be fearful of dogs after the bite and were generally preoccupied with thoughts about biting. They clung to their mothers and evidenced damage to their self-esteem, nightmares, and fantasies involving revenge. The children appeared to exhibit constriction in their thought processes and in their fantasy life. They also had difficulty experiencing pleasure. The authors believed that these consequences might have long-term detrimental effects on future ego and character development.

Fred Pine and Theo. Dorpat and Michael Miller:
Enactments and Enactive Memories

Theo. L. Dorpat and Michael Miller (1992) see enactments or "enactive memories" (analogous to Terr's "behavioral memories") as indicators of trauma. They define enactive memories as "the need (rather than the wish or fantasy) to repeat involuntarily in emotions, actions, and

---

[2]Katan's (1973) clinical material on adult pathology in young women raped in early childhood suggested a similar result. For example, she described one patient whose adult symptom was an inability to tolerate being next to a man, particularly if he was standing behind her, indicating that she had been anally raped as a young child.)

dreams the salient aspects of traumatic experiences" (p. 87). Dorpat and Miller review a striking example of enactment in behaviors in a case offered by Fred Pine (1985). This patient was a bright and charming eight-year-old who was reported by school personnel to engage repeatedly in unprovoked aggressive behavior that seriously interfered with her peer relationships. The specific behavior involved her repeatedly charging aggressively through a group of classmates, knocking them over. This patient had been hit by a truck and was severely injured at 18 months of age. She had no conscious memory of the accident but was aware that her parents had not thought she would survive.

Each therapy session began with a behavioral enactment of the accident. For example, "she would suddenly drop to the floor, as if dead, or beep like the horn of a truck" (p. 87). Her school behavior became clear to Pine; she had identified with the truck and the group of classmates stood for herself in her repeated "group mowdown" behavior. After a period of treatment in which she talked through her associations to the accident, these enactments stopped. She developed, however, an interest in moving vehicles, biking, and skating— continuing to turn passive into active but now in a more sublimated fashion. (See more on the subject of behavioral memories and reenactments in chapter 4.)

Phyllis Greenacre and Harold Blum: Primary Identification and Identification with the Aggressor

Phyllis Greenacre (1952) and Harold Blum (1987) have emphasized the role of identification as a consequence of severe trauma. Greenacre (1952) in particular emphasized the "prolongation and greater intensity of the tendency to primary identification" (p. 414). She gave a detailed example of such a process in a patient whose younger sibling was born when she was 27 months old:

> This child was badly damaged at birth, suffering injury producing severe head mutilation (which was found to cause bilateral deafness). My patient had accompanied her mother to the distant city where this baby was born and had stayed in a hotel with a nurse while the mother was in the hospital. On the trip home, my patient developed a severe mastoiditis which required hospitalization and much traumatic dressing of the wound. The whole area became erotized, and the subsequent depressed scar was treated by the little girl in

autoerotic fashion. Whether the injury of the baby had any effect on the . . . infection by any process of identification could not be definitely told later, although that the occurrence of this infection and its treatment caused a secondary identification of both mother and infant in which there was a strong somatic pull was clear in the content of the analysis. It was most strikingly reproduced when the patient's mother became ill with a gynaecological condition requiring an operation, thus stimulating the early birth situation. The patient left the analysis to go to the mother who was at some distance away, . . . retracing the journey of her early childhood. Her return was delayed because, it was reported, she had contracted chicken-pox. . . . it developed, however, that she had not actually developed chicken-pox but an . . . eruption with small blebs, limited . . . to the old mastoid area, and clearly associated with the reactivated memory [pp. 414–415; see also Lipin, 1955, regarding physical illness as early traumatic memories].

Blum (1987) suggests that traumatic experiences lead to later identifications that have a major impact on the patient's entire life. He notes that traumatized persons experience multiple identifications: with the victim, the rescuer, the comforter. "Traumas may be experienced in terms of aggression, transgression, punishment, masochistic gratification, or the validation of death wishes, violent fantasies, etc." (p. 614).

Whether due to accident, illness or surgery, whether the result of natural or man-made disaster, whether sought or provoked, the traumatic situation itself usually mobilizes aggression and sadomasochistic fantasy. The individual identifies with the aggression and anger of the attacking object. But the mobilization of the person's own internal aggression and punitive tendencies is also very important [p. 615].

Blum notes that in situations of helplessness, identification with the aggressor can help to relieve anxiety, restoring a sense of power and mastery to a beleaguered ego. This is particularly noted in situations where adults who were themselves abused as children become child abusers.

Blum presents a clinical example of a reconstruction of early trauma in an analytic patient that exemplified these complex identifications:

She was hypersensitive to noise and was very angry at herself for being a party to loud altercations. She vacillated between shouting accusations and imprecations, being immersed in depressive silence and avoidance, and having feelings of remorse and mature concern for her family. . . . When she was four or five years old, she had suffered from recurrent pharyngitis and mastoiditis, requiring several hospitalizations. The hospitalizations included anesthesia and surgery for tonsillectomy and for mastoidectomies. The surgery had been preceded by several excruciatingly painful myringotomies (lancing of her eardrums). She had many feelings about her head and about disturbances in her head; these were related to her fears of going crazy and of penetration and impregnation through the ear. . . . Her illness was unconsciously regarded as retaliation and punishment for her shortcomings and transgressions.

The unconscious equation of illness and surgeries as punishment for masturbation and other wrongdoings is noted throughout the literature (see, e.g., Greenacre, 1952; Murphy, 1958).

Blum continues:

Her mother was frantic about her child's frightening recurrent illnesses, with their fever, pain, confusional states, and threats of complications of meningitis and encephalitis. The patient had fantasies of crushing her husband's skull, and then cradling the crushed victim in her arms like the Virgin holding the limp, crucified Christ in the Pietà. . . . Heterosexual rape fantasies were related to the repeated otolaryngological procedures and to the fact that her parents and the medical staff would forcibly hold her while she was being examined. At times the mother would plead for the child's cooperation and try to allay her fears and pacify her; at other times she would scream at the child and tell her that she was unfair to the doctors and ungrateful for their patience and therapeutic efforts. . . .

The trauma of the illness, the surgery, the intense parental anxiety and ambivalence, and the probable simultaneous traumatization of the parents, were all condensed in the violent, abusive rape fantasy. . . . In the transference, she would complain about my having her head in a vise. She often felt that my interpretations were piercing and painful and that my voice was too harsh, too loud, too abrasive [pp. 621–623].

Blum concludes his detailed description of the case by stating:

Trauma tends to arrest development at the time of the traumatic experience. Fixation to the trauma may have a persistent pathogenic influence on subsequent development. . . . As the trauma is repeated in the transference, the analyst is bound to be experienced by the patient as hurter and helper, as omnipotent protector and deliberate attacker [pp. 625–626].

Henry Krystal: Anhedonia

Another important consequence of severe childhood trauma, anhedonia, is described by Henry Krystal (1978): "What we observed in the *direct* after-effects of severe childhood trauma in adults is a lifelong *dread* of the return of the traumatic state and an *expectation* of it" (p. 98). Krystal noted that the traumatized person is often afraid of his own feelings and loses the capacity for affect tolerance. A "lifelong anhedonia" (p. 98) follows.

Discussing infant trauma, Krystal states that a baby can terminate a traumatic state by falling asleep; this is his safety valve. Krystal points out, however, the difference in the internal experience of a baby who goes to sleep in an exhausted and despairing state as compared with one who goes to sleep contentedly. Krystal believes that memory traces of early traumatic events remain in the infantile psyche and contribute to later anhedonia. He sees anhedonia as "the most reliable 'tag' of serious posttraumatic states" (p. 99). He hypothesizes that the regulatory functions of the pleasure and distress centers in the brain are modified by early trauma in ways that we do not now comprehend.

Krystal makes an important point in differentiating adult from childhood psychic trauma. He notes that, in the adult psyche, an observing ego and a capacity to develop trauma signals exist that can mobilize a person's defenses and allow him or her to work to obtain help. For children, and particularly infants, the intense feelings themselves become the trauma. In the adult, the intense affects do not constitute the trauma. Krystal suggests that the infantile form of trauma involving overwhelming affects contributes to preoedipal conflicts and lends them their "nightmarish intensity of fears" (p. 109). When the child reaches an age at which he begins to identify with the parents, including their way of handling feelings, and has developed some affect tolerance himself, there is a gradual transition from this infantile to a more adult form of trauma. Krystal observes that the severity and duration of the trauma are important for the young child: "A child may initially be able to respond to a trauma with affect-blocking and cognitive constriction, but if the traumatic situation continues, there may be a regression, with a massive response of primitive affect precursors" (p. 110).

Clifford Yorke: Post-Traumatic Neurotic-Like State

A striking consequence of trauma, quite relevant to our concerns here, is the development of the "post-traumatic neurotic-like state." Clifford Yorke (1986), in elucidating different categories of trauma, described this particular constellation in which the trauma becomes so significant that all later developmental events, conflicts, and experiences are drawn into it: "Future events are drawn back and absorbed into the single trauma long after it has occurred" (p. 234). Trauma now becomes an "organizer of experience," so to speak (see also Atwood and Stolorow, 1992). Yorke's example also illustrates the powerful tendency toward identification and identification with the aggressor in these types of cases (see also Miller, 1951 and Pearson, 1941, for discussions of similar phenomena in latency-age children undergoing painful surgeries).

Yorke writes:

> He [the patient] re-lived in the transference a fantasy that his head was inside his mother's bottom and was being constricted by it. . . . expressed a number of fantasies in which I was attacked about the head—first by unknown persons, then by himself. In these attacks the brain and the skull were seriously damaged [pp. 227–228].

When the analyst commented on these fantasies, the patient recalled that he had had a mastoidectomy at four years of age, after a period of a great deal of pain. The hospital stay was very traumatic. His family was not allowed to visit.

> The sadomasochistic transference expressed the reexperience of the frightening operation in which the he was either the victim or the vengeful attacker. I was repeatedly equated with the surgeon who drove knives into his body and mutilated his victim's skull, or who put damaging or dangerous words into his ears. The fantasy that he was a victim of a violent homosexual intercourse, experienced in terms of the chisel and the skull, soon came into awareness and became the subject of protracted working through. . . .
>
> Before long, it became clear that the reexperience of the operation was in no way limited to content of this kind. It had become the overdetermined center of all manner of conflict and anxiety. Almost everything that concerned or disturbed him appeared to have some reference to this one dramatic episode. The anesthesia under which the operation was conducted (in fantasy or reality) played a central role. Episodes of drowsiness

occurred in the analytic session; feelings of suffocation appeared with unfailing regularity; fantasies of being overwhelmed by smells, of being smothered and reduced to oblivion, brought repeated distress as the associated affects became more available [p. 228].

Phallic and anal material, as well as oedipal material, were drawn into this trauma.

At one time or another, every part instinct or its derivatives achieved some form of expression in the context of the trauma as he remembered it, or perhaps more correctly, fantasized it. Thus, the thoughts of being peacefully put to sleep were linked with the notion of satiation at the breast and resulting contented oblivion. But even this brought to mind fantasies of anesthetic intubation.

Exhibitionism and scoptophilia . . . were repeatedly presented in terms of the hospital experience. Getting undressed was linked in his mind with the fantasy of being stripped naked by the nurse. . . . Impulses to urinate and fears of wetting the couch were almost inextricably linked with fears of scolding for failing to ask for a bed pan. . . . Physical experiences . . . appeared in body sensations, in feelings of impaired consciousness, of unsteadiness, and of transient pain . . . all with rare exception were traced to fantasies and reexperiences of the hospital trauma, especially the operation itself [pp. 229–231].

Yorke writes that the hospital experience could be registered as a trauma that

appears to have attracted to itself almost like a magnet, nearly all the major conflicts . . . which preceded it, as well as many conflicts which must have followed. . . . the hospital experience functioned as an "organizer" . . . which structures the patient's disturbances and anxieties and lends them the shape they assume when they reemerge in analysis [p. 232].

He notes that the analytic task consisted of a gradual isolation of the trauma from what went before and all that followed.

Yorke differentiates this "post-traumatic neurotic-like state" from a screen trauma, where one trauma serves as a screen memory for another trauma, as described by Glover (1929). Yorke states, "What we are dealing with in my adult patient, however, is something more; *future* events are drawn *back* and absorbed into the single trauma long after it occurred" (p. 234).

Joseph Weiss and Harold Sampson: Pathogenic Beliefs

Joseph Weiss and Harold Sampson (1986) have put forth a theory that pathogenic beliefs are an integral part of psychopathology. Pathogenic beliefs are grim, constricted "ideas of reality" constructed out of attempts to adapt to acute trauma and intense frustration. They differ from unconscious fantasy in that, unlike fantasy, there are no wish-fulfilling elements involved. We could consider them the mental equivalents of traumatic "play" in infants (Terr, 1990).

> A pathogenic belief contains at least four components: 1) the attitudes, impulses, or goals with which it is concerned; that is the attitudes, impulses or goals it assumes are dangerous; 2) the kinds of dangers it foretells; 3) the kinds of remedies, such as repression or withdrawal, which it enjoins, and 4) the strength of conviction with which it is held. It is possible, by varying these four components, to derive the pathogenic beliefs underlying any kind of psychopathology [Weiss and Sampson, 1986, p. 325].

Weiss and Sampson give a clinical example of a two-and-a-half-year-old who was suddenly sent away for three months to stay with relatives because the child's younger sibling developed a contagious disease. The father did not give the child an explanation and, to avoid seeing the child's distress, left abruptly after dropping him off. The boy was in the midst of toilet training at that time and had been behaving in a provocative, mischievous, and rowdy manner. He unconsciously took the parental abandonment as punishment for his behavior. While staying with the relatives, he quickly became toilet trained and a very compliant, "model" child.

Thirty years later, he entered analysis. Initially, he was a "model patient" but then became "rowdy and mischievous" (p. 79), having numerous affairs, drinking, and giving boisterous parties. He feared that the analyst would reject him, thus punishing him for his actions. An understanding of the expectation of rejection brought more specific memories of his earlier experiences. His parents confirmed his memories about his behavior and its context in the early traumatic separation.

Joseph Sandler: Shock Transformed into Strain

All the authors just cited either implied or stated that traumatic experiences have significant, and at times profound, effects on the overall development and future personality organization of the child.

Joseph Sandler (1967), however, articulated another point of view. Evaluating the Hampstead Clinic records regarding childhood trauma, he explored how single-shock traumas actually play out as long-term strain traumas. Moreover, such long-term strain traumas, in his view, eventually become subordinated to and subsumed by advancing ego organization in many cases. He suggested that even with the death of a parent, a singular trauma does not occur. What happens instead is

> a series of adaptive responses of the ego, responses that change as the reality of the situation is brought home to the child and his needs and conflicts intensify. . . . an increasing state of *ego strain* [results]. Such strain can only be tolerated up to a certain point, and if the ego cannot adapt to it in time, so as to preserve its homeostatic equilibrium, a true *strain trauma* may result; the ego is disorganized, flooded, and overwhelmed. In the cases we are considering, however, the ego undertakes a series of maneuvers in order to accommodate itself in the state of strain, maneuvers that may . . . result in gross alterations in behavior or lead to the development of symptoms. . . .
>
> The child's response to a state of strain represents the development of a new organization that is progressively created in order to preserve the ego's feeling of safety and *to avoid the experience of being traumatically overwhelmed* [pp. 167–168].

Krystal (1987) presents a similar formulation. He states that catastrophic trauma involving a paralysis of all cognitive and self-preservative mental functions is rarely seen. What is usually seen is "near trauma," meaning that the threat is handled by defenses and symptom formation. Sandler, drawing a significant, and I believe, a controversial conclusion from a review of the Hampstead Clinic records, stated, "There is strong evidence that many children recover from truly traumatic experiences with little or no residual damage to their personalities" (p. 168). He cited parental support as an important factor.

SUMMARY

We could say that this chapter is about mental pain, the origins of mental pain in the infant. How does that pain come about, and what are its consequences in the personality? Freud's original model (Breuer and Freud, 1893–1895) suggested that mental pain came about through quantities of energy too great for the organism to handle. We have evidence that such a model may still be useful—especially with sudden and overwhelming shock traumas external to the mother–child relationship. But object relations theorists brought new thinking to these issues. They noted the importance of the two-person relationship: the mother and baby and what went on mentally between them. They focused on the projections and misattunements of the mother and the mother's ability to modify and soothe the intense mental states of the baby. They focused on how the baby copes day-to-day over a long period of time with maternal projections and incapacities.

Almost all the authors in this review noted the effects of trauma on the development of the baby's personality, effects that in some cases extended throughout a lifetime. These effects included discrete symptoms, fantasies and behaviors, and somatic reactions. With projections of parents' disturbances, these effects included a distortion in the development of the self and the internal world. The one unusual note was the finding of Sandler (1967) that "many children recover from truly traumatic experiences with little or no residual damage to their personalities" (p. 168). This finding most strikingly opposes Terr's (1988, 1990, 1991) research, which demonstrates that traumatic events often have lifelong effect and certainly that the memories of such events last that long. Where in Sandler's cases did the mental pain go? We do not entirely know the follow-up evidence on which Sandler based his point of view. It is at least conceivable that his patients underwent single external shock traumas in the context of an excellent mother–child or parent–child relationship that cushioned or modified the effects of the traumas in such a manner that later sequelae were minimized.

Such a finding was suggested in the Gislason and Call (1982) study of dog bites in children. For example, the child who was the most severely traumatized by the dog bites had an extremely close relationship with her mother. This mother had given her child a great deal of confidence before the trauma and provided a well-functioning "protective shield." Thus, this particular child had the fewest sequelae despite her most significant traumatization.

Ralph Gibson's (1965) study of infants who had congenital anomalies requiring surgery within the first four months of life suggested similar findings. He used projective tests and evaluated the mother's emotional stability. He noted that the reactions to and interpretations of the event by the parents, and the personalities of the parents, had considerable influence on the number and type of emotional difficulties the child experienced.

Lucie Jessner, Gaston Blom, and S. Waldfogel (1952), observing the reactions of 143 children undergoing tonsillectomy and adenoidectomy, noted that in most instances the outcome depended on the degree of anxiety experienced by the mother and communicated nonverbally to the child. A similar observation was noted in Anna Freud and Dorothy Burlingham's (1942) work with children in the bombing of London during World War II.

Much is at stake here in the quest for the answer to the question as to whether or not early trauma has enduring effects. If Sandler is correct—that many or most children survive specific traumas without significant sequelae—then we need not devote significant resources to this area of study. The results of Lenore Terr's work, however, along with some of the other examples in this book, and certainly my own clinical findings, indicate that such is not the case. In my own cases, difficult and at times profoundly disturbed parent–child relationships were evident. My patients as infants and children had no adequate "containers" for their mental pain, no "shelving" upon which to rest their suffering. Perhaps it is only in these cases that such effects are so global and consuming. Perhaps Sandler's patients who suffered no long-term effects from severe childhood traumas had mothers who could modify and absorb their pain. If such is the case, then it is a testimony to the power of object relations and lends real meaning to the fact that for the infant, the mother's "reverie" (Bion, 1962) becomes the world.

4
Psychoanalytic Reconstruction

I f the earliest experiences (or traumas) of life are recorded and retained in the mind in some form, how can we as analysts "reach" such data? This chapter examines how analysts since Freud have addressed the concept of reconstruction. We will explore the controversy regarding the feasibility of reconstruction, particularly reconstruction of earliest experience from adult analytic material. The discussion includes the various arguments against reconstruction (i.e., memory distortion, the lack of adequate mental structure, and the confusion between fantasy and reality). The resulting emphasis on the here-and-now transference interpretation and the narrative perspective is presented, along with arguments of writers supporting the importance of veridical reconstruction. We conclude with examples in the literature of attempts to reconstruct infant-feeding experiences during the neonatal period.

THE VALUE OF RECONSTRUCTION

The value of reconstruction in analytic work as outlined by Freud (1937) has been discussed by many writers over the years. For example, Blum (1978) suggested that "reconstruction leads to a unique way of understanding individual development and permits the integration of dissociated fragments of both life experience and the inner world" (p. 337). He saw reconstruction as strengthening the cohesive forces in the personality.

> Reconstruction assists in the analytic restoration of the continuity and cohesion of the personality. . . . In supplying and substituting for the missing memory, reconstruction becomes an integrative force . . . and a mode of reassembling fantasies, memories, and distorted historical fragments which will, within the analytic process, lead to a structural renovation and reorganization [Blum, 1980, pp. 39–41].

Eric Brenman (1980) viewed reconstructive work similarly. He addressed its place in securing one's identity and in knowing one's roots.

It is inherent in man to seek knowledge, to enquire and discover. It seems important for him to pursue enquiry about his origins, to find his roots; he needs roots and objects, he cannot function alone. To my mind, knowing his background provides him with a sense of continuity and meaning. Only if he feels he belongs can he achieve his own identity. Reconstruction is of value as a means of rediscovering roots, past objects and lost parts of the self [p. 53].

In more practical terms, Scott Wetzler (1985) has addressed the importance of reconstruction for improvement in judgment. George Klein (1966) noted the importance of accurate reconstruction for improving reality testing (also see Rosen's, 1955, case example). Edward Glover (1929), suggested that reconstruction strengthens the ego (cited in Wetzler, 1985). In terms of the preverbal period, Blum (1977) viewed analytic reconstruction as of real assistance in the "reordering of the infant's misperception of internal and external reality" (p. 778).

THE RECONSTRUCTION CONTROVERSY

Despite these claims as to its value and importance, the reconstruction of childhood experience from adult analytic material has been a much debated issue for many years. This is particularly the case for experiences in the preverbal phase of development but includes as well the reconstruction of later childhood and adolescent development. It may be useful for the reader in thinking about this issue to present here a summary of the arguments against veridical reconstruction. These arguments center on the problem of accurate memory, that is, can one accurately register, store, and recall specific discrete experiences and affects? The following arguments against veridical reconstruction due to memory distortion have been presented throughout the analytic literature since Freud's time:

1. Memory distortion based on one's *current perspectives, goals, needs, and wishes*. From this view, memory of the past is filtered through one's current needs and wishes, which may serve, as Freud

(1901) noted, purposes other than a veridical account of the past (see Kris, 1956; Schafer, 1978; Gill, 1982; Spence, 1982).

2. Memory distortion based on the *telescopic nature of memory*. The telescopic nature of memory was initially described by Anna Freud (1951). It involves a form of condensation in which a number of events, or a single event repeated many times, may be recalled as a single memory, for example, daily feeding experiences, nightly bedtime story-telling, and so forth. Stern's (1988) concept of "prototypic memory" is similar. In "prototypic memory," features in common or "invariant features" of repeated affective experiences form a pattern and it is this pattern that is remembered. Stern states that the composite memory helps the infant avoid "cluttering his mind" with specific memories of very similar happenings.

3. Memory distortion based on the *screening nature of memory*. As outlined in chapter 2, a screen memory (Freud, 1899) is a recollection, usually of an innocuous event or scene, that conceals a more affectively charged experience that is unconscious. An earlier traumatic experience, however, may actually screen a later trauma, and a later trauma may screen a very early one.

4. Memory distortion based on *defensive processes*. Kris (1956) noted the many defenses against accurate memory of traumatic events. He stated that one can not usually remember the sharp outline of a trauma because "the experience is overlaid with its aftermath, the guilt, terror and thrill elaborated in fantasy, and the defense against these fantasies" (p. 73). Defenses then alter accurate memory.

5. Memory distortion based on *varying ego states*. Niederland (1965), Rubinfine (1967), and the Kris Study Group (1971) pointed to the importance of reconstructing the particular ego state present at the time the trauma took place; for example, a half-sleep state offers a different state of consciousness than does a fully awake state (see Breuer and Freud's, 1893–1895, description of the hypnoid state). Rubinfine pointed out that memory and recall of a particular experience may be different depending on the state of consciousness in which it took place.

6. Memory distortion based on *preexisting schemas*. Similar to distortion based on one's current perspective, this concept, described by Bartlett (1932) and elaborated by Paul (1967), suggests that internal "schemas" of psychic organization of past reactions, experiences, and affects form a framework through which new perceptions are filtered. As noted in chapter 2, memories then are reconstructed on the basis of schemas rather than on a veridical recall of a specific "memory trace."

7. Memory distortion based on the *acquisition of new meaning through development*. Helen Schur (1966) elaborated this concept, originate by Freud (1901), in which advances in development bring new understandings to prior experiences. The concept of deferred action (Freud, 1896c) is an example of such a process. Here, an observation of the primal scene or a molestation in infancy becomes traumatic retroactively in puberty after one acquires the mental and physical maturity to understand the experience in a new way. Terr (1988) described the subsequent layering of meaning of very early trauma with significant developmental symbols as the child matures. Paul (1981) and Dowling (1985) also described the reworking of primitive sensorimotor experiences into more mature symbolic forms as development proceeds.

8. Memory distortion based on the *confusion* of *fantasy with reality* and memory distortion based on a *lack of adequate mental structure* to register and store unique experience. These last two arguments are particularly pertinent to the preverbal period of development and are discussed in this chapter. Infants are not believed to have the ability to differentiate fantasy from reality and thus to retain an adequate memory of a real event, nor are they believed to have a mental structure sufficiently developed to store discrete experience.

Michael McGuire (1971) outlined the often-cited complications of attempts to reconstruct early experience from adult analytic material. He stated that, because the unconscious operates in ways that distort perceptions, thoughts, and feelings, there exist at least five logically distinct pasts with which the analyst must deal:

1. *The real past.* The past as it in fact existed outside the patient.
2. *The experienced past.* The past as it was in fact experienced.
3. *The patient's present understanding of the experienced and real past.*
4. *The psychoanalyst's understanding of the real past.*
5. *The psychoanalyst's understanding of the experienced past* [p. 94].

McGuire did not consider that the unconscious can also tell us the most profound truths of our experience and our deepest reality notwithstanding manifest distortion. Thus, he concluded: "Indeed, as one reads a variety of case reports on the same patient, the only legitimate conclusion is that the real past exists as a kind of ill-defined shadow under which a psychoanalyst is continually at work" (p. 95).

THE NARRATIVE PERSPECTIVE

The problems with veridical reconstruction have led to two distinct trends in psychoanalytic theory and technique: the first emphasizes here-and now transference interpretations as opposed to reconstructive methods (Gill, 1982). The second focuses on the development of the "narrative perspective" in psychoanalytic work (Ricoeur, 1977; Spence, 1982).

Merton Gill (1982), the most significant proponent of the here-and-now transference approach, proposes that here-and-now transference interpretations should serve as the center of psychoanalytic work. These interpretations involve the "moment-to-moment taking into account of the real relationship between the patient and the analyst by interpreting how it appears to the patient" (p. 107). Gill expresses concern that, although reconstructive and extratransference interpretations can be of value, they lend themselves to a "flight from the immediacy of the transference" and "defensive intellectualization" (pp. 123–124). He makes an essential point when he urges that the real situation of the patient and analyst be taken up because the realistic situation of the patient and analyst determines the patient's responses.

> The very existence of the analytic situation provides the patient with innumerable cues which inevitably become his rationale for his transference responses. . . . An effort to deny the real impact of the analyst can only result in its remaining implicit so that it exerts its effects without being understood. [p. 86].

Gill's (1986) overall position is stated as follows:

> This account amounts to an increased emphasis on work with the transference in the here-and-now both in the interpretation of resistance to the awareness of transference and the interpretation of resistance to the resolution of transference. It de-emphasizes interpretations outside the transference, whether current or past, as well as genetic transference interpretations [p. 179].

Gill's shift of emphasis raises an important difficulty: how are we to reach obscure infantile trauma if our analytic methods center almost exclusively on the adult here-and-now? Blum (1986) has addressed the difficulties with this point of view most succinctly. He points to the dangers of using here-and-now interpretative methods exclusively when early trauma is involved.

The patient's past traumatic experience cannot be understood in depth in a here-and-now treatment which dispenses with genetic interpretation and reconstruction. Disguised derivatives of traumas in symptoms, transference, screen memories, nightmares, and so on, have to be analyzed to their genetic roots. A one-sided here-and-now or transference only position may unwittingly become a shared denial of prior trauma and a turning away from recognition of the childish character of neurosis and its transference repetition [p. 15].

Furthermore, I would ask whether reconstructive work lends itself to a "flight from the immediacy of the transference" and "defensive intellectualization." I believe that the reconstruction of earliest infant trauma and its living out in both the current personality *and* in the here-and-now transference reaches the patient in an emotionally powerful and meaningful way. The patient's feelings are touched, and the affect changes strikingly in the hour (see, for example, Rosen, 1956).

Concerns similar to those voiced by Blum in relation to here-and-now transference interpretations apply as well to the exclusive use of the narrative perspective. Michael Sherwood (1969) explained that from the narrative point of view, a person's history is not considered to involve a set of discrete "facts" that can then be reconstructed. Instead, the history is seen as forming a narrative "story," which is repeatedly rewritten over the course of a life. This rewriting is done to provide the person with a sense of inner consistency and inner coherence. (Interestingly, as noted earlier, one of the values cited for the use of reconstructive methods is precisely its ability to strengthen inner continuity and coherence.) From this perspective, then, "narrative truth" is considered much more important than "historical truth"; narrative truth is the center of psychoanalytic explanation. Such a position has been articulated by, in addition to Sherwood (1969), Ricoeur (1977), and Spence (1982), and supported by Novey (1968), McGuire (1971), and Schafer (1976).

Ricoeur (1977) described the historical origins of the narrative approach. Narrative truth, he stated, derived its foundation from the oral epic tradition of story-telling. In this tradition, one orders one's life episodes into the form of a story.

But what is to be remembered? It is not just to recall certain isolated events, but to become capable of forming meaningful sequences and ordered connections. In short, it is to be able to constitute one's existence in the form of a story where memory as such is only a fragment of the story. It is the narrative structure of such life stories that makes a case a case history [pp. 843–844].

Sherwood (1969) suggested that, to provide the patient with a sense of inner coherence and consistency, the narrative story must itself meet two criteria: adequacy and accuracy. Spence (1982) reviewed these two criteria and concluded that the criterion of accuracy is an ambiguous one when referring to psychoanalytic data and cannot really be maintained. He argued that what seems an historical psychoanalytic fact may really be just a plausible piece of history that helps to make an analytic story coherent. In the course of analytic work, what began as this "plausible construction" contributing to a coherent narrative, becomes upgraded, so to speak, to a "material truth." But such truth is actually unknown. Thus, from Spence's view, the accuracy criterion is not reliable in the domain of psychoanalytic work. The "adequacy" criterion is more important. The "adequacy" of a narrative story requires the qualities of "self-consistency, coherence, and comprehensiveness" (p. 180). It is this adequacy criterion that is considered to define "narrative truth." Spence (1982) explains further: "Gaps [in stories] must be filled; explanations must be supplied; puzzles must be clarified. What we are after, it seems, is a narrative account that provides a coherent picture of the events in question" (p. 180).

We might think of Spence's "adequacy criterion" as analogous to Freud's (1900) concept of secondary revision. In secondary revision, gaps are filled in to make a coherent whole of a dream story and to make explanation of the dream more intelligible. We could also discuss the analogy to dream interpretation in another way. The use of the narrative method from which early reconstructive work is excluded can be considered comparable to the use of the manifest content of a dream without obtaining associations to the elements of the dream. A picture would be formed, but its sources would not be understood. The picture without the associations (its sources) may be coherent and interesting, but it would not necessarily be accurate. Thus, one works in the analytic hour with a "loose fit" between past and present.

Inside the hour, we try to create continuity and coherence and make what sense we can from the emerging findings, not caring very much whether any particular memory or interpretation can be corroborated in any precise manner. We are comfortable with the rather loose fit between an early childhood event and its repetition in the transference. . . . To match early and late variations on the same pattern in any more precise a manner would seem ridiculous and out of place; it might easily interfere with the process of treatment [Spence, 1982, p. 24].

Wetzler (1985) summarized this narrative perspective:

There is no single ultimate account of the past [from this view]. Rather, there are multiple and shifting accounts with varying degrees of usefulness for varying purposes. . . . Does *this* narrative serve any useful clinical purpose for *this* patient at *this* time? [p. 195].

If one uses this "loose fit" technique exclusively, early traumatic experience as it manifests itself in the patient's current personality could very well get missed. Early traumas and their origins often present themselves in current behavior in obscure and subtle ways, for example, in nonverbal behavior (see Anthi, 1983) or a specific image or association in a dream (see clinical example #3, chapter 9). One would need to focus *in detail* on such elements to arrive at a specific reconstruction.

Can narrative and reconstructive approaches work together? I believe they can, but only in a particular way. After one has reconstructed the *actual experience*, or concurrent with such a reconstruction, one could, I believe, proceed with a narrative story in a meaningful way. A narrative anchored in the specific and real experience of the patient could then have genuine positive value. It could help to integrate the patient's inner world. It could "ground" the patient in his reality and an emotional understanding of his past as it now lives in the present. Only in this way, as I see it, can true inner coherence be achieved.

The focus on narrative and here-and-now transference interpretations may help to account for the paucity of reconstructive material of early trauma in the literature. Surprisingly and unfortunately, only a very small number of cases are to be found in all of the psychoanalytic literature relating to the specific and detailed reconstruction of early trauma from dream material and its living out in the adult character. Likewise, relatively few infant trauma reconstructions using transference manifestations, symptoms, and behavior can be found (see Pulver, 1987, for a concurring opinion). One factor to account for such a paucity may be that the mind of the infant has not been considered capable of storing and remembering such experiences. Another factor,

however, may be that narrative methods and here-and-now transference interpretations may not readily lend themselves to ascertaining
early trauma in its past and current manifestations.

Interestingly, though his writings on reconstruction and trauma
predate the narrative-truth controversy, Kris's position was consistent
with the narrative perspective. Kris (1956) proposed that one is limited
to the reconstruction of "general childhood patterns" as opposed to
specific experiences.

> The material of actual occurrences, of things as they happen,
> is constantly subjected to the selective scrutiny of memory
> under the guide of the inner constellation. What we here call
> selection is itself a complex process. Not only were the events
> loaded with meaning when they occurred; each later stage of
> conflict pattern may endow part of these events or their
> elaboration with added meaning. But these processes are
> repeated throughout many years of childhood and adolescence
> and finally integrated into the structure of the personality.
> They are molded, as it were, into patterns, and it is with these
> patterns rather than with the events that the analyst deals
> [pp. 76–77].

In that paper, Kris presented a very convincing argument against
the possibility of veridical reconstruction. It is pertinent to note,
however, that at one point in his argument he introduced a striking
example of a specific and verified reconstruction from infancy.

> I remember one instance in which the aggressive and teasing
> interplay between mother and child during early feeding was
> mainly reconstructed from the consistency and gradual
> sharpening of verbalizations in the transference situation—a
> reconstruction accidentally and spontaneously confirmed by
> an early observer, who had been in the house when the
> mother breast fed the patient [p. 72].

Kris did not reconcile this observation with his general point of
view regarding the inability to reconstruct discrete experience. He
acknowledged that retention of imprints of early trauma is possible
but went on to deny the possibility of really specifying these in any
consistent way. Such specification was seen as particularly difficult in
the case of long-term strain traumas, when memory undergoes
numerous transformations and elaborations. His most specific
statement regarding memories of traumatic events is that they may

become "nodal points" around which defensive efforts and affects coalesce.

> We are misled if we believe that we are, except in rare instances, able to find the "events" of the afternoon on the staircase when the seduction happened: we are dealing with the whole period in which the seduction played a role—and in some instances this period may be an extended one. The problem is further complicated by the fact that the further course of life seems to determine which experience may gain significance as a traumatic one [p. 73].

PREOEDIPAL RECONSTRUCTION: SEPARATION-INDIVIDUATION PHASE

The arguments against reconstruction are especially forceful in relation to preoedipal and preverbal experience. Ekstein and Rangell (1961) stated that reconstructive accounts going back to latency are more reliable and verifiable than are those which are preverbal, archaic, and primitive. In the latter case, "our reconstructive efforts frequently consist of rather indefinite speculations which perforce are often resorted to a greater and greater degree the farther back we go" (p. 686).

Reconstruction of particular "phases" of development (oral, anal, and so on) seemed to be considered a more acceptable focus for reconstruction than specific and unique experience. Reconstruction of the separation-individuation phase, for example, has been proposed, by a number of analysts (see, e.g., Kernberg, 1980; Davidoff-Hirsch, 1985). Davidoff-Hirsch, presenting two cases for reconstruction of the separation-individuation phase, noted that the darting-away modality in one of the patients and the clinging modality in the other represented aspects of these patients' separation-individuation problems.

Blum (1977, 1978) has been a strong proponent of preoedipal reconstruction, particularly from the separation-individuation phase of development. He includes specific traumas in some of his reconstructions. Thus, Blum (1977) wrote about the impact of the death of Freud's one-year-younger brother, Julius, on Freud and his relationship to his own one-year-old nephew when he (Freud) was between the ages of 18 and 24 months. Blum speculates that the loss of Julius when Freud himself was an infant, followed by his mother's mourning and subsequent pregnancy, were probably the source of Freud's later concerns with death and transience. Blum suggests that Freud's death instinct theory was linked to these early traumas.

PREVERBAL RECONSTRUCTION

The Lack of Mental Structure

The controversy regarding the feasibility of preoedipal reconstruction becomes even more significant when one attempts to reconstruct experience from the period commencing with the beginning of life *up to* the separation-individuation phase. It is here that the arguments regarding the lack of adequate mental structure to discern discrete experience and the confusion between fantasy and reality are most pronounced. Anna Freud (1969), Dowling (1985), Fajardo (1987), and others have suggested that the infant's undifferentiated mental structure is one of the issues precluding preverbal reconstruction. Some of the arguments are presented as follows.

> It is my contention that the infant must have achieved a developmental level in which consciousness has at its disposal hypercathexis or attentional energy which can be actively deployed before an experience can be "constructed," i.e., achieve thought connections and relationships, so it can produce derivatives. Only an apparatus that registers and organizes perceptual material from the inner and outer world can "construct" experience that can be tackled analytically and "reconstructed." . . . The primordial repressed elements cannot be "reconstructed" because the infant did not have the means to "construct" them at the time of their occurrence. For this reason they are not available for analytic exploration [Rubin-fine, 1981, pp. 387–390].

Jacob Arlow, as recently as 1991, presented the classical position:

> The problem of reconstructing traumatic events from the preverbal period, or to put it more correctly, the analysis of the persistent effects of experiences of the earliest months of life, becomes a problem of methodology. What constitutes adequate evidence for such reconstructions? What criteria for interpretation does one employ? Much of the difficulty resides in the fact that the child's capacity for symbolization, structuralization of memory, and fantasy formation, is limited,

compared to how these capacities develop after the second and third years of life. The concept advanced by certain object relations theorists is that specific sets of early interactions with objects come to have a dynamic thrust of their own, so that they are compulsively repeated in later life in situations in which they prove to be inappropriate.

To begin with, such formulations seem to deny the concomitant effect of drive derivatives. An object relationship without some drive investment is inconceivable. Furthermore, since new experiences are psychologically processed in relation to the memories of earlier experience, it seems impossible for the memory and the significance of early object relations not to undergo some transformation in the course of time [p. 557].

Confusion of Fantasy and Reality

As for confusion between fantasy and reality at the preverbal stage, the controversy looms, as it did for Freud, over how to distinguish between the two. Contemporary theorists have different postures regarding this issue. For example, Norman Reider (1953) took Freud's "middle ground" position.

It makes no difference whether a reconstruction has actual validity as an event, or whether it is a condensation of a set of circumstances within the condition of a particular time in the patient's life. . . . Most of the patient's symptoms could be shown to be derived out of *either* the truly actual past event (the reconstruction) or the childhood situation (as represented by the reconstruction). Either one or the other is true, or both. To argue the point further would be only specious and tendentious, since interpretations and reconstructions are at best but approximations [p. 404, italics added].

Oscar Sachs (1967) discussed the attitude that there is little difference between remembered traumatic events and fantasies. He stated that one cannot always be satisfied with considering these equivalent and that there are circumstances in which one must distinguish between them in reconstructive work (see Loewenstein, 1957, for a similar view). Jerome Neu (1973) stated that treating as a fantasy an event that actually happened can leave one's analysis incomplete. One often has the difficult task of distinguishing memory of reality from memory of fantasy, from fantasy of memory. Blum (1980) and Wetzler (1985) are both spokespersons for a clear distinction between fantasy and real experience. Wetzler states: "There are vast differences between the effects of a real trauma, a diverse spectrum of real experiences interacting with preexisting fantasies, and fantasies without any actual basis" (p. 194).

Christopher Bollas (1987) considers it very important to distinguish between the real and the fantasy mother. Bollas points out that both the real *and* the fantasied mother are internalized and that this internalization involves two separate systems of representation.

> Some of a patient's internal mental representations of a mother, for example, will more or less accurately register the true nature of this mother's personality reflected in her mothering of this child, while other mental representations will carry projective identifications of the infant's internal world [p. 6].

Bollas goes on to discuss the advantages of an analytic stance that keeps both these representations in mind:

> The historical and the fantastical, the actual and the imaginary, are engaged in a endless and inevitable dialectic. To give up the effort to speak about actual history (as opposed to the history of phantasy) is to absent oneself from the dialectic and inevitably, in my view, to diminish the richness and complexity of human life [p. 6].

In his thoroughgoing review of the controversies regarding reconstruction, Wetzler (1985) writes, "common sense alone suggests that actual events will have a different impact on the individual than a fantasied or plausible one" (p. 187). He states that interpretations that are specific and veridical have the most significant chance of being effective. He also indicates that the analyst and the patient should specify when a reconstruction refers to a genetic as opposed to a fantasied event and vice versa.

Criteria for Extrapolating Real Experience

Several writers, Greenacre (1956, 1981) being the most prominent, have expressed the view that it is extremely important to retrieve real traumatic experience. Concerned about the tendency to ignore the actual experience and concentrate only on the fantasy (Greenacre, 1981), she spoke of these fantasies in the following manner:

> Further, we know, but often forget, that specific "fantasies" which persist until adult life are rarely *only* "typical" fantasies common to all infantile development, but rather those typical ones which have been given a special strength, form, and pressure for repetition through having been confirmed by external events. . . . It should be realized that the unique *specific* (in contrast to the generic) elaborations of infantile memories are for the most part assembled from realities— either in small pieces, taken magpie-like from a number of different impinging related actual experiences and woven into fantasy; or determined largely from a single (or a very few) actual events of life. They represent in either case some combination of infantile wishes with reactions of other people in the outer world. If the reinforcement has been much influenced by a single disturbing experience, verifying the infantile fantasy and making it powerfully real, the organizing effect of such an event is very great and the fantasy behind it gains much force. This predisposes to later repetition and acting out [Greenacre, 1956, p. 440].

Greenacre specified a number of criteria for extrapolating real experience:

> There is always some bland representation of it [the trauma] or some vacuole of memory which is a warning, and which may be brought up incongruously again and again when certain fantasies or experiences of the infantile years are being considered. In addition, the repetitive appearance in dreams or free associations of some specific age or place, seemingly inappropriately but insistently associated with events belonging to another period; the special repetition and content of the dream within a dream; the frequent appearance of dreams which exactly reproduce reality events but seem at first barren of other associations; the occurrence of isolated and peculiar delusions or hallucinations in a setting of a generally sound sense of reality; the repetition through a series of dreams (or similarly through a series of symptomatic acts) of some unimportant but realistically embellishing detail; all these are indications of the reality of some experience which is being worked with in the unconscious [pp. 442–443].

She suggested that acting-out tendencies indicate specific traumatic experiences and that screen memories always contain elements of real events that are hidden and distorted (see also Kris Study Group, 1971).

Blum (1986) described other indications of repressed traumatic experience:

> The concomitant use of denial and isolation, the need to continue denial in extended situations in adult life, the significance of denial in fantasy, words, and deeds all point to a past traumatic reality which is being disavowed. . . . Nightmares and night terrors are gross indications of trauma. But more subtle indications of trauma appear in fantasy play, repetitive daydreams, dreams, screen memories, peculiar ego states or dystonic moods, and disguised, partial, often unnoticed reenactments which may be rationalized and often seem adaptive to reality [pp. 22–23].

Blum gave an example of a patient who wanted to open the window in his office because he felt the office was stuffy. The patient had experienced and survived smoke asphyxiation, which had killed some of his family.

Max Hayman (1957) noted that very intense trauma is difficult to work through within the mental realm (thought, dreams, fantasies); hence the reliance on acting out. He pointed out that repetitions of traumatic events persist into adulthood with very little change, whereas psychoneurotic elements undergo "rich and variegated development" (p. 20).

Ella Sharpe (1937) emphasized the importance of working with and finding the repressed actual infantile experience. One may have to approach repressed experience through a fantasy that is presented. Even an infantile omnipotent fantasy is based on an actual experience or situation that has never been subjected to mature reality-testing. She described fantasy and reality as "two facets of a total experience" (p. 151), neither of which can be neglected if the truth is to be fully understood.

> If an hour is mainly occupied by recovery of phantasy or elucidation of phantasy through a dream I should reserve in my mind the unsolved problem of where and how this phantasy is linked with actual repressed situations and how this is being re-staged in the transference setting [p. 151].

In her discussion with the Kris Study Group (1971) seminar on reconstruction, Greenacre stated that she saw actual traumatic experiences as generating considerably more guilt than unconscious fantasies do, and as functioning more significantly as "organizing experiences" (p. 114) for future development (see also Yorke, 1986; Atwood and Stolorow, 1992). Acting out in these cases is also more prevalent. Greenacre (1979) also noted the importance of nonverbal reactions as containing the derivatives of early trauma. She stated that patients who have undergone early disturbances show nonverbal reactions more significantly than others do (see Anthi, 1983). She saw these patients as often having "florid physical complaints" (p. 139) analogous to those of a hypochondriac. She speculated that "the body participates in the analytic situation to an unusual degree, essentially with a primordial cry to get back to an illusory comforting mother" (p. 139). Irritability and then rage follow from relieved acute distress. She proposed that these elements may appear in dreams. Greenacre's comments were made in the context of her discussion of the phenomenon of the imprinting of earliest experience in the general constitution, which was then thought not to be accessible to psychoanalytic work.

Joseph Lichtenberg (1983) also has described examples of physical or bodily residues of early experiences. These experiences are coded in what he terms the "perceptual-affective-action mode" and do not necessarily receive recoding into symbolic representation. Blum (1986) concludes that reconstruction of real experience can remain significant *without diminishing the importance of unconscious conflicts and fantasies.* Blum appears to be able to see *both* the impact of reality and the influence of unconscious fantasy without highlighting one to the detriment of other. He suggests that preexisting fantasies can be validated and reinforced by certain traumatic experiences; for example, a surgery or car accident may be experienced as a fantasied punishment for wrongdoing (see Blum's clinical example in chapter 2). He, like Greenacre (1981), pointed out that reconstruction does not mean a retrieval of external events only, but includes emotional and somatic components as well as the fantasy formation related to events. For example, in referring to a parental loss in childhood, Blum (1980) stated, "[One must reconstruct] the intrapsychic meaning of the experience, its ramifications and *sequelae*, its traumatic impact, and antecedent and subsequent influences which determine the effect of such a stressful, depleting loss" (pp. 41–42).

RECONSTRUCTION RELATED TO
THE NEONATAL PERIOD

Otto Isakower, Kurt Lewin, and René Spitz

We conclude this chapter with examples of some of the first attempts to reconstruct the earliest experiences of life—the infant at the breast. These examples come from the work of Otto Isakower, Kurt Lewin, and René Spitz, who attempted to reach and describe the neonatal experience as demonstrated in adult analytic material. They presented evidence of phenomena that they viewed as representations in adult behavior, sensations, or dreams of experiences involving the feeding infant. These phenomena are considered aspects of passive primal repression, "something [that] is 'remembered' which could never have been 'forgotten' because it was never at any time noticed—was never conscious" (Freud, 1915a, p. 149). These are the unrememberable "memories" of childhood that

> at times can be inferred through deductions based on alter-
> ations in ego states and certain characteristics or contents of
> these states; certain "screen" phenomena; certain symptoms,
> symptomatic behavior and character alterations; and the
> reproduction of early impressions by reliving them in the
> psychoanalytic situation. Paradoxically, some of these same
> "memories" could as aptly be titled *unforgettable* as *unremem-*
> *berable*, so profound is their effect [Frank, 1969, pp. 62–63].

Isakower (1938) described one such state of mind, usually represented at the time of falling asleep and often associated with sleep disturbances:

> Sensations very different from those of waking life are
> experienced in certain regions of the body and conveyed to
> the subject by more than one of his senses. The principal
> bodily regions concerned are the mouth, the skin and the
> hand. In many cases there are distinct sensations of floating,
> sinking and giddiness. . . . [There appears to be a] blurring of
> the distinction between quite different regions of the body,
> e.g., between the mouth and the skin, and also between what
> is internal and what is external. . . . We note too the amor-
> phous character of the impressions conveyed by the sense
> organs. The visual impression is that of something shadowy
> and indefinite generally felt to be "round," which comes

nearer and nearer, swells to a gigantic size and threatens to crush the subject. It then gradually becomes smaller and shrinks up to nothing. . . . The tactile sensation is of something crumbling, jagged, sandy or dry, and is experienced in the mouth, and at the same time on the skin of the whole body. Or else the subject feels enveloped by it or knows it is close at hand. Sometimes it feels as if there were a soft yielding mass in his mouth, but at the same time he knows it is outside of him. [It at times seems to be like] a lump of dough [pp. 332–333].

Isakower concluded that what is being described is

a revival of very early ego attitudes . . . mental images of sucking at the mother's breast and of falling asleep there when satisfied. The large object which approaches probably represents the breast with its promise of food. When satisfied, the infant loses interest in the breast, which appears smaller and smaller and finally vanishes away. . . . The infant's mouth is full of something, "but not of anything from outside"; his hand presses into it, as though into a lump of dough. The crumpled or sandy feelings in the mouth seem to point to sensations of dryness in the suckling's mouth, which are unpleasant and unfamiliar (for in the intrauterine state he probably never experienced anything of the sort) [pp. 341–342].

Lewin (1953) described a similar phenomenon in his concept of the dream screen, in which the blank dream represents the background of the earliest experience of the mother's breast. This period is represented in memory traces older than pictures and is probably composed of memory traces "more like pure emotion made up of deeper tactile, firm and dimly protopathic qualities that are in their way memory traces of early dim consciousness of the breast or of the half-sleep state" (p. 198). This he considered the level of integration evident in the blank dream. René Spitz (1955) provided an alternate view to those of Isakower and Lewin regarding reconstruction of the infant's breast-feeding experience. According to Spitz, the first visual perceptions progress over the course of the first three months of life, rather than occurring at birth (see chapter 5 for current research disputing this view). The first object the baby perceives is not the mother's breast, but the mother's face, the object at which the infant stares throughout the feeding. Spitz therefore felt that all the details described in the Isakower and Lewin examples were to be found in the human face: "the cracks, the wrinkles, the roses, the spots" (p. 218). He suggested that in actuality the breast and the face are fused in these combined, amorphous images. Spitz concluded that the level of regression involved in the Isakower, Lewin, and Spitz primal-cavity phenomenon goes back to a period earlier than that in which there are reliable visual mnemonic traces—perhaps somewhere between the first half and the end of the first year.

The data offered in the Isakower, Lewin, and Spitz phenomena provide some evidence that earliest memories can be recorded, retained, and possibly reconstructed. On the other hand, it is not clear if these are actually specific, discrete *memories* of experience or are composites (or general schemas) that create templates for a class of experiences associated with breast-feeding. In addition, the descriptions of the Isakower, Lewin, and Spitz phenomena are often considered evidence for a very vague and amorphous state of mind of the infant, a view of the infant that was quite prevalent in their era. Thus, for example, Isakower's (1938) comments that

> a considerable part of this experience consists of amorphous sensations in several sensory regions. This appears to bear out the much disputed notion that sense organs at this stage of development in general transmit nothing but chaotic impressions [p. 339].

Some of the work of retrieval of earliest discrete memories represented by Niederland (1965), Bernstein and Blacher (1967), Laibow (1986), Terr (1988), Perris, Myers, and Clifton (1990), and others cited in this volume, indicates that infants are capable of storing and retaining discrete memories of very distinct phenomena and experiences from earliest time. Isakower, Lewin, and Spitz, writing in the late 30s to mid-50s did not have these data available to them.

SUMMARY

The material reviewed in this chapter establishes that preoedipal and preverbal reconstructions are taken up regularly by some analysts, although a very strong debate continues about its feasibility as well as its preferability. Some consider such reconstructions not only feasible but actually essential to the "completeness" of an analysis, especially when early traumatic experience is involved. In the chapters to follow, we will review some of the evidence on which such reconstructions are founded, evidence for prenatal and neonatal mental life and infant memory. Recent research has at least the potential to clarify the issues involved and to change the image of an entire culture regarding the infant at the breast as capable of only the dimmest consciousness. Such evidence will, it is hoped, also widen the scope of our analytic theory and methods such that we seek ways truly to know the past and to see how it is absolutely alive in the immediate present.

5
Prenatal and Neonatal Mental Life

T hat the present is determined by the past (psychic determinism) is a concept at the very foundation of psychoanalysis. It implies that the past is somehow registered and stored in the mental (or somatic) apparatus. But how far "past" does "past" go? Does it go to the very beginning of life? Can it go as far back as prenatal life? When, in fact, does human mental life begin, and how early is a "memory" of that life possible? We do not have definitive answers to these questions, but we now have a compilation of both research data and psychoanalytic writings suggesting that "mental life" begins much earlier than we ever imaged.

This chapter focuses on both psychoanalytic and scientific theory and data relating to the beginning of human mental life. These data should provide a context for the examination of infant memory and the possibility for storage and later reconstruction of the earliest experiences of life.

The first section of this chapter deals with evidence from the *psychoanalytic* literature of prenatal and neonatal mental life, evidence that includes material gathered from dream analysis. The second section presents evidence from the *scientific* literature; it addresses evidence of prenatal mental capabilities (awareness, feeling, memory, learning, etc.) that may imply prenatal mental life. This section also addresses the most recent research findings on neonatal and infant capabilities. These findings demonstrate that an infant is a competent little being—capable of learning, remembering, relating, and integrating complex mental processes. Taken together, the psychoanalytic and the scientific research evidence demonstrate that fetuses, as well as neonatal infants, have the mental equipment to perceive, register, and store *in some form* earliest experience.

THE PSYCHOANALYTIC WRITINGS

Sándor Ferenczi

Psychoanalytic thinkers have, from the beginning, theorized that birth and prenatal experiences may have important influences on the development of the personality. Sándor Ferenczi (1913, 1933) was the first analyst after Freud to elaborate the prenatal experience. He saw fantasies underlying adult sexuality as involving a wish to return to the ideal conditions in the womb. He thus implied a memory for or imprints of intrauterine experience. Birth experiences, he thought, were "indelibly impressed upon the mind" (Ferenczi, 1933, p. 402).

Ferenczi saw the individual as occupied "from the moment of birth onwards by a continuous regressive trend towards reestablishment of the intrauterine situation" (p. 380). He saw this profound urge as evident in particular conditions or ego states represented by fantasy, adult sex life, and sleep (dreams). "The Oedipus wish is precisely the psychological expression of an extremely general biological tendency which lures the organism to a return to the state of rest enjoyed before birth" (p. 379), he wrote. His views were further articulated by Rank (1929), Fodor (1949, 1951), and Roheim (1952).

Ferenczi (1913) took for granted fetal mental life. Showing the origins of omnipotence in pre-natal experience, he wrote:

If, therefore, the human being possesses a mental life when in the womb, although only an unconscious one—and it would be foolish to believe that the mind begins to function at the moment of birth—he must get from his existence the impression that he is in fact omnipotent. For what is omnipotence? The feeling that one has all that one wants, and that one has nothing left to wish for. The foetus, however, could maintain this of itself, for it always has what is necessary for the satisfaction of its instincts, and so has nothing to wish for; it is without wants . . . the traces of intra-uterine psychical processes do not remain without influence on the shaping of the psychical material produced after birth. The behavior of the child immediately after birth speaks for this continuity of the mental processes [pp. 219–220].

Ferenczi, speaking to the issue of trauma to the mother during pregnancy, suggested that life in the womb may not always be all that one wants. Illnesses or injury to the mother or to the umbilical cord can rob the fetus of the important experience of omnipotence and require him to "effortfully work towards changing the outer world" (p. 219). Ferenczi did not describe sequelae to these kinds of experiences, nor did he take up how the mother's mental states may affect the fetus. Nor did he provide case examples illustrating his conclusions.

Otto Rank

Following Freud's (1926) statement that all anxiety originates in the anxiety at birth, Otto Rank (1929) was the first analyst to theorize about dream formation in relation to fetal and birth experiences. He saw wish-fulfilling dreams as attempts to reinstate the intrauterine condition and anxiety dreams as representations of the birth trauma. He saw the birth trauma as a source of neurosis, a view echoed by Ferenczi (1933), Fodor (1949, 1951), and others. Rank postulated that the birth trauma and attempts to overcome it are the primary motivators of human experience and action. He viewed analysis as "a belated accomplishment of the incomplete mastery of the birth trauma" (p. 5). In particular, he identified the analytic situation with the intrauterine state. He suggested that the primal repression of the birth trauma is not only *remembered* but, in fact, is the beginning and *source of memory* itself. He noted that, in rebirth fantasies and dreams seen at the conclusion of analysis, patients repeat the pregnancy and birth *biologically* not just psychologically or metaphorically (see also Winnicott, 1949a, b). Rank emphasized that this biological repetition is not a regression fantasy about being in the womb but rather an actual *reproduction* played out under the sway of the repetition compulsion.

Although Rank did not provide any detailed case examples of his theories, he did describe categories of typical dream experiences in the context of intrauterine life. For example, sensations of flying were seen by Rank as a reversal of the birth process and plunging into water as a reversal of the birth process involving coming out of water. Rank differentiated birth/womb "fantasies" from actual "unconscious reminiscences," which he saw as occurring in dreams of intrauterine posturing or in dreams detailing the specifics of the actual birth. He concluded, "We maintain then neither more nor less than *the reality of the 'womb fantasy'* as it is manifested in child life, in neurotic symptoms, and in the physiological state of sleep (dreams)" (p. 84).

J. Sadger

Perhaps the earliest writer to speculate on the specific details of the mental life of the fetus was J. Sadger of Vienna. Sadger (1941) suggested that neurotic symptoms often do not disappear until the actual embryonic period has been addressed (see also Fodor, 1949, 1951; Peerbolte, 1951, 1952). Sadger presented as evidence secondary-process associations and adult patients' seemingly "conscious memories" of preconception experiences as ova and spermatozoa. There are neither any indications of how these "memories" arose in the analytic hour, nor any representations of associations or transference material that would lead a reader to understand how such memories were arrived at by the patient. Even Sadger himself was uncomfortable with these memories. He did not know whether they had actually been experienced or were patient fantasies. His clinical experience, however, led him to propose that "there is certainly a memory, although an unconscious one, of embryonic days that persists throughout life and may continuously determine one's actions" (p. 333). He suggested that the embryo already feels whether or not its mother wants it and loves it, that the fetus can distinguish between love and hate (see Bion, 1979, for a similar conceptualization). Sadger saw feelings of guilt as arising from "awareness" that the conception had not been wanted by the parents. He cited, for example, one patient who stated:

> I forced myself through and I pressed with great pleasure into the ovum. . . . Even as semen, a sense of guilt clung to me because I left the testicle and procreated against my father's will. . . . This original fault then became the foundation for all other guilt [p. 339].

Sadger also asserted that a mother's reluctance to become pregnant may be at the root of a patient's severe depression, including suicidal thoughts. As one patient said, "I have already been in the world too long. I should have perished long ago" (p. 340).

Nandor Fodor

Far more convincing than Sadger's presentation was the detailed work of Nandor Fodor (1949, 1951), the psychoanalyst who most persistently sought evidence for the presence of fetal and birth memories in dreams. Fodor (1949) viewed life as a continuity that did not begin with birth but was "split up" by birth, resulting in a prenatal amnesia. He saw birth as representing a change from one life form to another.

Like Greenacre (1941), he considered the trauma of birth as creating a "predisposition to neurosis" (p. 31). If trauma accompanied birth, a person might begin life with a neurosis. He suggested that such complications as illness, painful medical procedures, and injury after birth could prevent the birth trauma from receding into the unconscious and result in a fragile, complaining child. "The greatest danger of injuries in early life is that they may mobilize and keep active the trauma of birth" (p. 34), he wrote (see also Winnicott, 1949a).

Fodor (1949) gave a striking example of the profound impact of early trauma on later adult character:

> An Italian woman came to me with nervous symptoms bordering on the psychotic that had tormented her for years. She felt as if the nerves all over her body were being tied into knots. At the same time she felt a sharp pain in her navel. She insisted over and over again that her nerves were being tied in knots. After considerable inquiry, a significant fact was elicited about her birth. She was delivered at home, and her grandmother tied the umbilical cord, making a very bad job of it. The bleeding was unchecked, and by the time this was discovered the child was half dead from loss of blood. Here was a possible clue for the knotting sensation and the pain in the umbilical region. I explained the connection, with the result that the pain stopped and the knotting sensation vanished [pp. 31–32].

Fodor's studies were primarily clinical investigations of patients' dreams. His books contain a breadth and depth of vignettes. These vignettes include patients' dreams, with day residue and detailed associations illustrating what he considered evidence of unconscious awareness of intrauterine and birth experiences. Each stage of labor and birth brings its own traumas which leave their traces. Fodor described the traumatic residues of sound, light, cold, and smell at the time of birth, as well as a series of symbols that he saw as evidence of intrauterine and birth phenomena.

> The elements of which birth dreams are constructed are simple and easy to recognize. Eggs, seeds, germs, fruits or things that grow or move underground represent the fetus. Gardens, parks, landscapes, islands, boats, trains, carriages, houses, rooms, cellars, lofts describe the uterus. Seas, lakes, rivers, waterfalls symbolize the amniotic fluid. Falling, compression, suffocation and burial alive and various forms of slow and painful death at the hands of humans, ghosts, animals, or machinery represent the ordeal of birth. Tunnels, caves, stoves,

archways, windows, doors describe the uterine passage. Riverbanks, rails and V-shaped structures refer to the mother's legs. Grass, bushes, forests, fur and hair allude to the pubic region [p. 137].

Fodor traced various symptoms in adult life to these experiences by way of dream material, for example, nightmares and fears of suffocation, claustrophobia, fears of falling, fears of drowning (water being equivalent to the amniotic fluid), and so forth. He saw later trauma, both sexual and nonsexual, as mobilizing the trauma of birth. For him, a key to understanding a dream as signifying the birth experience was the sense of fatality with which the person experiences his situation: the dreamer cannot escape except by waking up. There is no turning back (see also Winnicott, 1949a).

Fodor (1949) also took up the effects of prenatal physical disturbances of the mother on later behavior and fantasies of the child. He urged analysts to consider the possibility of a factual basis to fantasies that seem to be about a prenatal state:

The word "fantasy" implies the absence of reality. We have to use the word for want of criteria by which memories of the actual conditions within the womb imprinted on the organismic mind could be clearly recognized. We cannot approach the psyche of the unborn except through the study of postnatal dreams with a pre-natal setting. To distinguish between fact and fantasy is admittedly difficult. Yet fears and anxieties may point as clearly to an actual prenatal happening as ordinary nightmares in describing an infantile traumatic event. The real difficulty is in deciding whether the fear is retrojected from the higher levels of the mind to the prenatal foundations, or whether high level fear experiences have actually mobilized deeply buried, organismic memories . . . and, having associated with them regressively, succeeded in forming a constellation of great disturbing potentiality [p. 304].

Fodor, reminding us that a process of mental recording is not an exclusive attribute of the conscious mind, postulated an "unconscious memory": "The very function of our vegetative system is inconceivable without postulating unconscious memory. How could replacement of destroyed tissue take place without a memory in the organism for the original pattern?" (p. 194). Thus, he proposed an "organismic memory" or organismic impression "whose imprints may be just as real and vivid as the rings in the cross-section of a tree showing its physical growth" (p. 195). He hypothesized that organismic consciousness may be the bedrock of the unconscious mind. He concluded that no psychoanalytic integration of the personality could be completed without addressing the fetal levels of the mind "because it is at birth that the psychic foundation of our being is laid" (p. 329).

In discussing nightmares of suffocation due to oxygen deprivation at birth, Fodor (1949) recorded the following dream of a patient:

> I came home late and, contrary to my habit, failed to observe that the window of *my bedroom was not open. I went to bed and dreamed of being buried alive. I found myself in a coffin and was struggling to lift the lid. Not being able to achieve this, I succeeded in waking myself. I was in a cold sweat. Then I discovered that the window was closed. I understood the dream, got up, opened the window, and fell asleep in peace* [pp. 37–38].

Fodor presented his own dream representing fetal distress at his birth:

> *A ship is under the water and I am in its belly. The air is becoming poisoned. I must get out. There are only two possibilities—diving out of the boat on one or the other side, and coming up to the surface of the water. I feel anxious regarding the left side as the way to the surface is obstructed by machinery all the way up; the vault may be completely blocked. To be caught there would mean death by suffocation. Then I discover that it is quite easy to get out on the right side where there is no machinery, only water. The discovery of this route of escape is somewhat due to my friend, Wishner* [p. 39].

The water in the belly of a ship is the interior of the mother's body; poisoning of the air refers to a progressive lack of oxygen supply. Fodor's association to the two-way escape involved the oral and vaginal outlets. Wishner, he felt, suggested his wish to be born.

M. Lietaert Peerbolte

M. Lietaert Peerbolte (1951) elaborated upon Fodor's views. He presented clinical examples of his patients' dream material and his interpretations of this material along the lines of Fodor's themes regarding the sequelae of prenatal and birth trauma. He concluded that, when an analysis of childhood traumas did not cause the disappearance of neurotic symptoms, the trauma of birth or some prenatal trauma must be analyzed to bring recovery. Concurring with Ferenczi (1923) and Fodor (1949, 1951), he concluded that all postnatal development aims at one purpose: the restoration of prenatal happiness. "All organic libido, oral, anal, urethral and genital, seems directed toward the re-establishment of some part of this state. Even incestuous tendencies seem to be an effort to realize the prenatal situation" (p. 602).

Peerbolte was skeptical about traumas involving the unborn child's reaction to prenatal sexual intercourse being represented in dreams, but this skepticism disappeared when a patient reported the following dream:

> I am in a church, all is good. But then Christ enters. He has a wooden leg and I become extremely afraid of the rhythmical clashing sound of His foot in the floor [p. 596].

Fodor took the wooden leg to mean the penis in erection, with the patient associating Christ to the creator. He observed that the entire threatening scene could have been interpreted as a repressed Oedipus complex. It is placed, however, in a silent church—the intercourse disturbing prenatal silence.

> Of course it is possible that retrojection of post-natal ideas referring to the Oedipus complex inspired the symbol of the wooden leg, but the extreme anxiety and the disturbance of silence and security indicate a pre-natal experience in this case. Moreover, interpretations of this dream in this way caused the anxiety to disappear at once [p. 596].

Phyllis Greenacre

Phyllis Greenacre (1941, 1945) wrote about birth and pregenital experiences and their impact on development. In 1945, she expressed the view that the birth process influences the psychic and physical patterns of the child. She placed greater emphasis on the influence of the patterns of distribution of energy and intensity of drives than on development of neurosis, as was suggested by Ferenczi (1923), Rank (1929), and Fodor (1949, 1951).

Greenacre (1945) speculated, as did Winnicott (1949a), that the normal, uncomplicated birth, even with a certain degree of trauma, may be advantageous to the infant, in that the "rough workout" provides a good introduction to life, serving as a bridge between the intrauterine dependence and the extrauterine independence.

> [Birth] continues to be a period of organization and patterning of the somatic components of the anxiety response. . . . I conceive of a situation in which the antenatal, natal, and neonatal experiences have very slight or no true (differentiated) psychological content at the time of their occurrence, but do nonetheless leave some individual and unique somatic

memory traces which amalgamate with later experiences and may therefore increase later psychological pressures [pp. 7–8].

According to Greenacre, if there is a rudimentary consciousness in the fetus, the birth process provides a self-narcotizing or anesthetizing experience to the infant "something akin to pressure concussion" (p. 17). Further,

> one is confronted with the problem whether during birth the extreme sensory stimulation to the infant is such that it leaves some sort of central record, whether at the cortical, thalamic, or spinal level, or in combinations of these. These considerations cannot be dismissed lightly [p. 17].

Greenacre saw birth as an organizer of the pattern of anxiety, including both somatic and psychological elements. Somatic elements would include, for example, cardiorespiratory elements, and psychological elements would include the "anxious attitude" (p. 19) or one's degree of expectation that things will go wrong. She saw such patterning as composed of genetic and constitutional elements fused with the actual birth experience and modified by traumas of later years. She saw the general effect of the profusion of sensory stimulation at birth as organizing and converting the fetus's biological narcissism from the more relaxed stance in the womb to one of a more "propulsive" sort in neonatal life. Greenacre went on to detail the many traumas of early life and what she saw as possible sequelae.

As an example of an early postnatal "stamp" on the organization of behavior, Greenacre (1941) described a female patient with hysterical symptoms who continued in analysis with a persistent symptom of an irregular, jerky movement with her feet. The symptom would appear when she was driving a car. The patient would also wiggle the toes of one foot or the other when she was tense and felt people were looking at her. She had a history of rubbing her toes on the sheet to put herself to sleep in childhood. Greenacre thought this symptom might be related to extreme penis envy of her brothers (displacement downwards, foot and leg being equated with the penis). Greenacre ascertained, however, that the patient's foot rubbing to put herself to sleep had begun in "earliest infancy." Her mother told her that she had been a quiet baby who slept well except for foot-rubbing and some thumb-sucking.

Another example of early infantile trauma was an extremely disturbed young woman who continued to enact psychologically the imposition of physical restraints from infancy. This patient had been put in leg braces at 18 months because the mother (who appeared psychotic herself) thought the child's legs were slightly bowed. The child was also put in aluminum mitts to prevent both thumb-sucking and masturbation. The child hated the braces and banged them against her crib. She became an "unbelievably stubborn" child. At age 20, when Greenacre treated her, she was an ambulatory catatonic and very angry. She enacted her "restraints" metaphorically in every aspect of her life and her treatment. For example, because of her parents' shame about the need for treatment, the patient was not permitted to live away from the family home so that the fact that she was seeing a psychiatrist would not be discovered.

> She was instructed in minute detail how to avoid or evade detection should she meet anyone in or near my office. She should ring twice before entering as a signal that it was she and that the way should be cleared. She must walk upstairs rather than ride in the elevator in order to avoid the elevator operator. The psychiatrist must never telephone her for fear the identity might be revealed to the servants. If she telephoned the psychiatrist, she must never leave her name with the secretary. She must pay the fee in cash so the psychiatrist's name would not appear on checks seen by the bank. [Greenacre, 1944, p. 87].

Greenacre discussed the lifelong "emotional strait-jacket" in which this patient lived and, in which she put the treatment, with the result that she had become a "living marionette" (p. 87) unable to separate her "self" from her mother.

Greenacre (1941) concluded her discussions of birth and infancy by drawing attention to

> a group of patients who are coming to analysts with increasing frequency, asking and needing help. It is clear that the consideration of these cases takes us back to the need for more observation with infants, work which appears to me the source of the richest material for psychoanalysis [p. 81].

D. W. Winnicott

Donald Winnicott (1949a) wrote, "The analyst must be prepared to expect whatever type of material turns up, *including birth material*" (p. 177). He commented on the importance of birth play in many child analyses: "In such play the material might have been derived from what had been found out by the patient about birth through stories and direct information and observation. The feeling one gets is, however, that the child's body knows about being born" (p. 180).

Winnicott found evidence in dream material and other bodily experiences (i.e., gesturing, posturing, and psychosomatic states) that the experience of birth may have significance in one's emotional development and that memory traces of the experience can persist and give rise to difficulties in adult life. He outlined three categories of birth experience. The first is a normal and healthy birth experience that is positive and of value. It provides a "pattern of a natural way of life" (p. 180). Here "the birth experience becomes one of a series of factors favorable to development of confidence, a sense of sequence, stability, security, etc." (p. 180). In the second category are common, moderately traumatic birth experiences that become "mixed in with various subsequent traumatic environmental factors, strengthening these and being strengthened by them" (p. 181). The third category comprises extremely traumatic birth experiences. Winnicott believed that if the birth trauma is significant, every detail of impingement and reaction is "etched in the patient's memory" (p. 183) analogous to the way patients relive traumatic experiences of later life. He considered the trauma of birth as "the break in the continuity of the infant's going on being. When the break is significant, the details of the way in which the impingements are sensed, and also of the infant's reactions to them become in turn significant factors adverse to ego development" (p. 189).

Winnicott (1949b) gave an example of a patient who demonstrated birth trauma through nonverbal behavior during the analytic hour. The example involved incidents in which the patient threw herself off the couch in an hysterical way. Winnicott suggested that this patient had regressed to a prenatal stage during the course of her two-year analysis. He began to understand this particular phenomenon as an unconscious need to relive the birth process. He felt that every detail of the birth experience had been retained in unconscious memory and that "the details had been retained in the exact sequence of the original experience. A dozen or more times the birth process was relieved and each time the reaction to one of the major external features of the original birth process was singled out for re-experiencing" (p. 249). Winnicott enumerated the specific pieces of "acting-out":

> The breathing changes to be gone over in most elaborate detail. The constrictions passing down the body to be relieved and so remembered. The birth from the fantasy inside of the belly of the mother, who was a depressive, unrelaxed person. The changeover from not feeding to feeding from the breast, and then from the bottle. The same with the addition that the

patient had sucked her thumb in the womb and on coming out had to have the fist in relation to the breast or bottle. The severe experience of pressure on the head, and also the extreme of awfulness of the release of pressure on the head; during which phase, unless her head were held, she could not have endured the re-enactment. . . . The changeover from pressure all round (which belongs to the intrauterine state) to pressure from underneath (which belongs to the extra-uterine state). Pressure if not excessive means love. After birth, therefore, she was loved on the under side only, and unless turned round periodically became confused [pp. 249–250; see Paul, 1981, for a similar list].

Among features of the true birth memory is the helplessness that comes from the feeling of being in the grips of something external without knowledge of when it will end. This idea was also taken up by Fodor (1949) and Rank (1952). Winnicott (1949a) noted, in relation to the point that Greenacre had made, that traumatic experiences "seem to me to determine not so much the pattern of subsequent anxiety as to determine the pattern of subsequent persecution" (p. 189). He also proposed a link between birth trauma and psychosomatic disorders, notably certain kinds of headaches and breathing disturbances (see Fodor, 1949; Paul, 1981).

W. R. D. Fairbairn

W. R. D. Fairbairn (1952) saw the infant's complete identification with the mother as evidence of "the persistence in extrauterine life of the emotional attitude existing before birth" (p. 275). He developed his thesis that the identification process represents the infant's attempt to restore the original secure state "which was rudely disturbed by the experience of birth" (p. 275). He saw birth as a shocking experience that includes both pain and anxiety and serves as the basis of all later separation anxiety. Like Ferenczi (1923) and Fodor (1949), Fairbairn saw later trauma or conditions of extreme anxiety as reactivating the original shock experience. He saw the birth experience as perpetuated "at a deep mental level" (p. 276) and as a source of common nightmares about falling from heights and being trapped in an underground passage. Fairbairn did not concentrate on this area in his clinical work; thus, he did not provide any clinical examples.

Paula Heimann

Paula Heimann (1958) suggested that earliest experience leaves somatic memory traces in one's unconscious. Physical experiences are stored as somatic memories that are awakened in specific, related situations throughout life. She considered earliest experiences to be physical ones that are organized for the infant along the pleasure–pain principle.

> The capacity of the human organism to form somatic memories which at a later time become actual psychological problems appears as the counterpart of the capacity to convert a psychological problem into a physical condition—conversion hysteria. If this hypothesis is correct, the latter process would traverse a pathway formed in early life in the opposite direction [p. 147].

Heimann noted that when physical illness is the early experience, two types of somatic memories are stored: memories of the traumatic situation in which the ego is overwhelmed and memories of the experience of having "surmounted annihilation and gained and regained well-being." "In the latter," she wrote, "I see a profound source for trust in the self, in the capacity for achievement, which will manifest itself in a variety of ways in the further course of development" (p. 142).

Arnaldo Rascovsky

Arnaldo Rascovsky (1960) is one of a group of psychoanalysts in Buenos Aires who investigated and theorized about the psychic life of the fetus. This group concluded that dreams are the best material for reconstructing the experience of the fetus.

Rascovsky proposes endopsychic representations that precede and operate independently of postbirth object relations. He considered these representations to be the source of a rich fantasy life. He also postulates a "fetal position" that precedes Klein's paranoid/schizoid position and functions during sleep as well as in myth and legend. (English summary from Spanish courtesy of Dr. Erna Osterweil, 1990, pp. 21–22.)

Calvin Hall

Calvin Hall (1967) conducted systematic research into whether or not the content of some dreams could be conceived of as imprints of experiences sustained originally during the fetal period and birth. Using Fodor's (1949, 1951) symbols and categories, he expanded them as criteria for identifying such experiences in dreams.

Five hundred and ninety dreams from 79 students enrolled in a psychology class at a midwestern college were collected. The manifest content that indicated possible representations of the fetal environment and the birth process was scored. In 370 of the 590 dreams, Hall found one or more manifest content representations from the fetal environment, from the birth process, and of returning to the womb. Thirty-four dreams were considered classical expressions of fetal or birth experiences. The other were probable or possible. Hall pursued the question of fetal memories because he believed that, if such memories do occur in dreams, then fetal experiences may indeed form a part of the unconscious and play a part in shaping behavior throughout life.

The difficulty with this study is that it was conducted from the manifest content of a *collection* of dreams. No analysis of *individual* dreams and associations within a given treatment hour was conducted. Such an analysis would be necessary to achieve a more substantial understanding of the meaning of any given dream material. The data obtained only substantiated that birth *imagery* or symbolism as Fodor had described it—not actual birth *experience*—is evident in the manifest content of dreams.

Philippe M. Ployé

Philippe Ployé (1973) investigated the possibility that imprints of prenatal life may be seen in dream material. Suggesting that bad experiences may take place in the womb and may lead to recoverable imprints, he raised the following questions:

> (1) [Are] there grounds for believing that the more difficult moments of a pregnancy could leave in the mind imprints just as recognizable, and just as recoverable, as those left by the more undisturbed moments, and (2) could [there] be ways of establishing that what we believe to be a prenatal imprint is, in fact, a genuine imprint and not something else [p. 241].

Ployé also wondered if prenatal imprints of traumatic events could help to shape postnatal mental life. He proposed three main types of imprints that could be used to try to bring to light prenatal trauma, all of which would be derived from dream material: dreams that include "(1) imprints of threats to pregnancy during the first month or two of pregnancy, (2) imprints of toxemia of pregnancy, (3) imprints of threats to the pregnancy in the later stages" (p. 243).

Examples of possible dream material that would illuminate these
issues include

> children's dreams containing a theme of hanging directly onto
> a vertical slope with no rope attached, or a theme of being
> dislodged from a niche or crack in which the child was
> embedded. Inquiries could be made about the possibility of an
> early threatened miscarriage or attempted abortion during the
> first few weeks, when the embryo was either "embedded" or
> hanging directly on to the uterine face before the development
> of an umbilical cord. . . . Imprints of toxaemia of pregnancy.
> Here the main theme is that of poisoning. . . . particularly if
> the poison reached the dreamer by means of a pipe, tube, or
> hose, i.e., an umbilical cord symbol. Objects like an open
> parachute, an open umbrella or flying a kite might be used by
> the mind to communicate about a prenatal experience in
> which the placenta had played a vital role . . . [pp. 243–244].

Ployé raised the question as to the mechanism for perceiving such
early experiences in the womb and speculated that some information
about the womb might be communicated from the mother to the fetus.
He noted that the umbilical cord does not contain nerve tracks and
speculated that the electrical conductivity of the blood flowing through
the umbilical cord might be involved (a hypothesis previously
suggested by Mott, 1964, p. 364). If not, then the mechanism for
placental perception would have to be accounted for if we are to
understand how the experiences would be perceived sufficiently well
to describe them through symbols and dreams. Ployé believed that
these intrauterine experiences should be as evident in the transference
as any other type of experience open to interpretation.

Wilfred Bion

Wilfred Bion frequently considered the possibility of fetal mental life.
He suggested, "The fact that there is no demonstrable communication
between mother and fetus as clear as that between mother and baby
is not an adequate reason for asserting that there isn't one" (Bion,
1979, p. 137).

Bion (1977) considered ways in which postnatal mental life could
be evident in the fetus:

> Are we to consider that the fetus thinks, or feels, or sees, or
> hears? If so, how primitive can these thoughts, or feelings, or
> ideas be? . . . The embryologist can speak about "optic pits"

and "auditory pits." Is it possible for us, as psycho-analysts, to think that there may still be vestiges in the human being which would suggest a survival in the human mind, analogous to that in the human body, of evidence in the field of optics that once there were optic pits, or in the field of hearing that once there were auditory pits? Is there any part of the human mind that still betrays signs of an "embryological" intuition, either visual or auditory? [p. 44].

Bion (1979) speculated that the fetus

could try to rid itself both of the senses when they became sensitive to changes of pressure in the watery medium, and of the feelings, "emotions" of sub-thalamic intensity; it might be prey to experiences unmodified in the way we expect them to be by the "higher" centres. Then comes the "trauma of birth" [p. 126].

Bion suggested that the fetus may be directly affected by the mother's (parents') love and hate (see also Sadger, 1941). Thus Bion (1979) speculated that the fetus, even the germ plasma, may be affected by the relationship between the parents.

I see no reason to deny that the fetus—the germ plasm itself for that matter—could be affected by the loving relationship between the parents. Could not the blush on the bridal cheeks be communicated by a corresponding blush on the walls of the uterus, and vice versa? [p. 129].

At the same time, Bion suggested that in an unwanted pregnancy,

the waves of pressure communicated through the amniotic fluid would form a different pattern from those usual in a mother pregnant with a fetus she wanted from a man by whom she wanted it [pp. 136–137].

Finally, Bion commented on the significance of prenatal emotional life for his analytic work with adult patients.

It occurred to me that the fetus might hear noises, see sights, smell odors in a watery fluid such as the amniotic fluid and meconium. The significance of this did not become apparent at once, but I felt that past experiences with patients would have been less obscure if I had dared to imagine that the emotions displayed might be pre-natal. They were often expressed in a manner that differed from commonly accepted modes of expression [p. 125].

Unfortunately, Bion did not provide clinical examples of this different mode of expression.

Mauro Mancia

In line with Ployé's (1973) work, Mauro Mancia (1981) elaborated upon the idea of fetal mental life. Mancia reviewed the fetus's signs of maturation involving the development of motor, sensory, and integrative functions of the central nervous system. In regard to the integrative functions, Mancia pointed to REM sleep in fetuses as the center of mental activity. REM sleep in a fetus is similar to "active sleep" in a newborn. Mancia hypothesized that during active sleep, sensory integration takes place, which is similar to the sensory integration that occurs in adults. He noted that some parameters of REM sleep (such as duration, distribution, and amplitude of ponto genicuto-occipital waves and eye movements) can be transmitted genetically.

Mancia further proposed that REM sleep may also serve as the occasion for transmission of *psychological* elements of the mother to the fetus. He characterized this type of transmission as "internal representations" (p. 353) and suggested that these maternal psychological elements may be integrated with sensory types of fetal experiences (cardiac rhythms, noises heard in the uterus, etc.) to constitute a "protomental nucleus" (p. 353). Mancia considered this protomental nucleus as "permeable to representations that reach it from the [fetus's] internal world as well as to the sensory experiences that reach it from the external and maternal world" (p. 353). He saw the task of this protomental nucleus as that of "transforming . . . sensory information that reaches the foetus from external objects into experiences capable of creating internal objects in the form of representations" (p. 353).

Mancia (1981) utilized Bion's (1962) notions of preconception to articulate the fetal mental processes he was attempting to describe.

> The prenatal psychic activity, as it has been defined, discussed above is built by virtue of sensory experiences that reach [the fetus] from the world of external objects. This activity presents some analogies with what Bion calls preconceptions. It is in fact only if the foetus has been able to elaborate external stimuli, making internal representations of these that we can explain the newborn's preparation for meeting reality; first of all the maternal breast [p. 354].

Alessandra Piontelli

The most innovative recent experimental analytic research in the area of prenatal mental life is that of Alessandra Piontelli (1987, 1988, 1989). Her ultrasound studies of individual fetuses and twins have broken new ground for psychoanalytic observation and theory. Her studies, clearly demonstrating a continuum between pre- and postnatal life, lend confirming evidence to Freud's (1926) statement that "there is much more continuity between intra-uterine life and the earliest infancy than the impressive Caesura of the act of birth would have us believe" (p. 138).

Each of the fetuses that Piontelli observed had its own unique "style" of responding to its prenatal environment. That "style" continued all during the two years of postbirth infant observation. Early manifestations of character were evident right from the womb.

Donald Meltzer

Donald Meltzer (1988) suggests that the fetus has emotional as well as physical experiences in the womb. He postulates that both physical and emotional experiences in infancy are registered in the mind "like shakes in a piece of timber mark early periods of drought" (p. 25) and can be represented symbolically in dream thought.

Meltzer proposes, as did Ployé (1973), that the impact of (normal) birth may constitute an important emotional experience without necessarily being traumatic. He also suggests that the fetus may not have an ideal experience in the womb, for example, maternal stresses as well as maternal intercourse may be distressing for the fetus.

Michael Paul

Michael Paul (1981), in detailing the process of psychological birth, reconstructed prenatal and birth phenomena from eight patients with severe narcissistic disorders. In one of his clinical examples, he describes an alcoholic patient who experienced chronic anxiety and agitation. In her fourth year of analysis, she had a dream in which she was in an autopsy room witnessing a postmortem that turned into an embalming session. The patient woke up with the feeling of being overwhelmed with sensations of being flooded and engorged with embalming fluid. These feelings reactivated an earlier choking phobia. Paul took this dream to refer not just to the patient's drinking, but to her prenatal experiences. After receiving this interpretation, the patient questioned her mother, who confirmed prenatal difficulties: a toxemia of pregnancy had become very acute immediately prior to birth.

Paul outlines verbal and nonverbal behavior that he feels refers to the experience of psychological birth. These behaviors include:

1. The consulting room is felt to be markedly different from the external world. Disorientation and/or severe dizziness often accompany entering and/or leaving. . . . In phantasy, the consulting room is experienced as "inside the mother's body." Often . . . [the analyst is felt to be] incidental or *not* present.

2. These patients show evidence of long-standing, rather complete projective identification and show extreme sensitivities to the perception of heat and cold . . . a quality of deep psychic fusion [exists] with an internal phantasy of being-in-the-mother's body. . . . [They] behave as though they were hermetically sealed in a world never to be exposed to the air.
. . .

3. Interpretation of the stages of projective states leads very rapidly to changes in the perception of sound, temperature, visual acuity, visual clarity, and will produce disorientation and dizziness, often with severe temporary vertigo as the boundary between inside and outside is crossed in phantasy. . . . In my experience, the shift in perception of temperature and the sudden onset of dizziness are the most reliable indicators of a change in state of mind which related directly to the experience of birth.

4. Sudden onset of headache . . . [resembling] a band-like pressure . . . is an associated phenomenon noted in the context of this change in state of mind from inside to outside. . . .

5. A sensation of "pressure" usually felt about the head. This is a transitional phase from inside to outside and is often accompanied by terror—panic . . . there is associated a profound splitting of sense modalities, for example, hearing from vision which seems to uncouple the transitional process of movement in psychic space. . . . The respiratory phenomena include . . . a sudden gasping for air. . . . Breathing is often "held" fixed for long pauses during which all activity stops and the consulting room atmosphere "feels" dead. Profound tightening of the throat musculature and intense fear of choking may ensue in selected cases [pp. 556–558].

In these cases, Paul suggested, the analyst is experienced as a "placental object." The relationship is tenacious and adhesive. The patient feels that he will die if he is separated from the analyst. "He feels 'cut off,' 'ripped off,' as in umbilical cord and placenta and cannot tolerate independent existence without the presence of a nourishing object" (p. 561).

Paul discerned a hatred of the feeding situation in these patients. Six of his eight patients had early severe digestive difficulties surrounding the feeding situation. The analyst's interpretations are seen as forced feeding and listening to the analyst is accompanied by pressure. "This pressure has similarity to the patients' experience when mentally located in utero just prior to birth in fantasy. It is almost as if any intake would destroy their delusion of being in a state of uterine sanctuary" (p. 562).

Paul states that the fetus and infant must be capable of registering this type of experience in memory and then retrieving it in some symbolic form. He suggests that later developmental achievements, particularly language, bring symbolic meaning to these primitive experiences (see also Schur, 1966; Bernstein and Blacher, 1967; Dowling, 1985; Laibow, 1986).

> If, however, when the child gains communicative skills, the verbal forms which are linked to invariant deep structural patterns (Chomsky) are capable of containing the code locked in the soma, the succeeding development of complexity of language better enables the person to transcribe and translate a primitive language which requires the symbol for further transformation. The development of language would then bridge the gap between a primitive somatic experiential language and what we understand as symbolic fantasy. That verbal forms can be utilized for transcribing primitive body language after birth has already been amply demonstrated by Melanie Klein (1961) and extended by Hanna Segal (1956) in her description of the development of the symbolic equation. I mean to extend these important discoveries to include an even more primitive state in order to postulate the existence of a form of experience in utero which is registered by the fetus and which is capable of translation at a later time into a symbolic form [p. 562].

Although I did not find any of Paul's listed verbal and nonverbal behaviors in my own patients, I do feel that his understanding of the transformation from *somatic experience* to *mental form* through language transcription is most apt.

THE SCIENTIFIC LITERATURE

The capacity for mental life or mental awareness in the fetus and the infant bears directly on the central issues of this work. It points to the possibility of a mental recognition or registration and storage of early experience and therefore the capacity for its reconstruction in adult analysis.

Concurring with Anna Freud (1969), Barbara Fajardo (1987) has stated the prevailing view:

> The evidence is clear from developmental research that thinking then becomes creative in the sense that fantasies and integral images can develop and be remembered. Events, things, and people can now have sustained meaning for the child whereas earlier learning and meanings have had only a short term duration. With the simultaneous emergence (at around 18 months) of language, of evocative (recall) memory, internal imaging and fantasy, the child becomes a different being. Prior to that developmental point, assumptions of fantasy or of recall memories for specific people or events cannot pertain. Explanations for pathology or genetic reconstruction based on specific noncontinuous traumatic events in infancy are insupportable. However, once the child can recall and fantasize, it becomes more reasonable to believe that a specific person or event (especially if it has a continuing presence) may take on special meaning and be elaborated in fantasy with enduring impact on personality development [p. 235].

The notion implied by Fajardo, that the infant is an undifferentiated mass mainly operating on the pleasure–pain principle, has been seriously challenged in the past decade by innovative research into infant capabilities. The infant is discovered to be an incredibly responsive organism, "prewired" as such and capable of learning, relating, remembering, and integrating very complex material from various modalities. These research studies challenge the long-held view that complex mental processes develop over time with maturation. Said David Chamberlain (1987), who extensively reviewed the research data on the fetus and newborn:

> Pediatricians and child neurologists were wrong when they claimed that cerebral hemispheres do not function in the newborn, or that the baby had "no volitional system"; psychoanalysts were mistaken that babies were autistic, unable to differentiate themselves from others and motivated only by

animalistic "drives." Developmental psychologists were wrong about imitation being impossible, memory being nonfunctional and perception meaningless at birth. . . . A remarkable number of important abilities have been forced back to birth itself, surprising the investigators, ruining theories, and violating a venerable rule that complex processes take time to develop [pp. 30–31].

I will briefly highlight some of the more compelling research providing evidence of a physiological basis for mental life in the fetus and for the perceptual-motor-affective capabilities of the fetus, the newborn, and the early infant. Some of these data clearly allow the possibility for infants to store and remember early, discrete, structured, and specific experience well before Fajardo's and others' timetables would indicate.

PRENATAL MENTAL CAPACITIES

The research data summarized here is largely from the work of Thomas Verny and John Kelly (1981), Daniel Stern (1985), Ernst Freud (1989), Pirkko Graves (1989), and most particularly, from an exemplary review by David Chamberlain (1987).

The Brain and the Nervous System

"Brain life" is said to begin between 28 and 32 weeks of gestation (Purpura, 1975c). By this time, maturation of the key dendrites critical to the functioning of the cerebral cortex (the part of the brain most associated with human thought and awareness) has occurred (Purpura, 1975a, b). Development and differentiation of dendrites and the dendrite spine provide a major portion of the membrane surface for an integration of the synaptic inputs from a variety of sources. Vaughn (1975) discovered that primary as well as secondary cortical regions are capable of responding to peripheral stimulation in three major sensory spheres (vision, touch, and hearing) by 32 weeks' gestation. According to Purpura (1975a), at this age the brain's neuronal circuits are just as advanced as they are in a newborn.

It has been suggested that the brain of the newborn is inadequate because myelination is not complete. Prechtl (1981), however, seeing this approach as outmoded, suggested that "at birth, neural functioning (breathing, sleeping, waking, crying, and spatial orientation) are not just simple reflexes but are fully developed complex control systems" (p. 33). According to Prechtl, the structures involved mature early: "It is not at all meaningful to speak of the 'immature' nervous system of the neonate" (in Chamberlain, 1987, p. 33). For example, "message-carrying hormones are circulating throughout the body as early as 30 days after conception. . . . Vasopressin, the hormone associated with memory traces, [is in operation] by the 49th day [after conception]. The hypothalamus, which works closely with the endocrine gland in producing these substances, is fully differentiated by day 100" (Fedor-Freybergh, 1983, in Chamberlain, 1987, p. 33).

The Development of the Senses

Touch. All the senses are active in utero. Touch is the first sense to develop. "By 17 weeks the entire body except for the back and top of the head has become sensitive to touch" (Hill, Breckle, and Walfgrum, 1983, in Chamberlain, 1987, p. 34). Touch is fully active by 20 weeks (Humphrey, 1964). By the second month, the fetus will kick and jerk if poked. By the fourth month, it will make a facial expression (frowning, squinting, grimacing), and move quickly if its scalp is tickled. It will kick violently if cold water is ingested (Verny and Kelly, 1981). The fetus can touch the amniotic fluid and the umbilical cord as well as the walls of the uterus and placenta. Ernst Freud (1989) speculated:

> Can we then speak of "body memories" when we observe a premature baby pressing hands and feet against the wall of his incubator, or when a colleague tells us a dream about his hands, pressing against a concave rubber wall, accompanying his account by demonstrating the "feeling" in his fingers? . . . Does the fetus cathect his mother in terms of body memories? We might then ask, What is or is not worth remembering? Does the fetus bond to tangibles, to that which he may be "in touch" with, like himself (narcissism), the amniotic fluid, the umbilical cord, the uterine wall, or the placenta? [p. 474].

Taste. The fetus can taste; taste buds are operating by 13 to 15 weeks (Bradley and Stern, 1967). Mistretta and Bradley (1977) suggested that the gustatory system is exposed to chemicals in the amniotic fluid for approximately 28 weeks before birth. They concluded that "taste preferences at birth are probably due to experience with taste in the amniotic fluid" (in Chamberlain, 1987, p. 35).

Hearing. The structures for hearing are complete by 20 weeks. In fact "from the 24th week on, the fetus listens all the time" (Verny and

Kelly, 1981, p. 38). Clements (1977) found that four- to five-month-old fetuses quieted to the playing of Vivaldi and Mozart but kicked violently to Brahms, Beethoven, and Bach. Verny and Kelly (1981) believe that the unconscious memory of the maternal heartbeat in utero is one of the reasons that an infant may quiet by being held to someone's chest or put to sleep by the ticking of a clock.

Truby (1965) found that fetuses receive and store speech features transmitted from the mother:

> Fetuses were found to be "practicing" in the amniotic fluid those neuromuscular gestures which would lead (in air) to crying and vocalization. Truby hypothesized that *incoming* speech reception must necessarily precede outgoing speech production. In some instances, they found specific correspondence of the infant cry to intonations, rhythms, and other speech performance features of the mother (Truby, 1975). They also reported that newborns of mute mothers did not cry at all or cried very strangely, as if they had missed out on the speech lessons in utero [in Chamberlain, 1987, p. 37].

Ernst Freud (1989) wondered to what extent intrauterine sounds could be thought of as "forerunners of transitional objects. . . . or imaginary companions" (p. 473). DeCasper and Spence (1982) demonstrated that infants who heard a story repeated a number of times in utero showed through their sucking response after birth preference for that same story over a new story.

Vision. Fetuses are light sensitive from the 16th week. Brazelton (1978) demonstrated that in response to a direct light to the mother's abdomen, the fetus will startle and turn away. Since premature infants at 29 weeks open their eyes, it may be inferred that fetuses may be able to open and close their eyes at that age. (Dreyfus-Brisac, 1968).

"[Experimental] work with premature infants indicates that discriminative visual functions are present at 31–32 weeks gestation and by 34 weeks reach maturity comparable to the patterns found in that of full-term infants" (Dubowitz, et al., 1980, in Chamberlain, 1987, p. 57). Haith (1976) identified patterns of scanning in newborns, including scanning in the dark. In the dark "infants even open their eyes more widely, seem to have better control, move more smoothly, and make more small eye movements than they do in the light" (in Chamberlain, 1987, p. 57). This ability of newborns suggests that it is also established in utero (Osterweil, 1990).

Spontaneous Motor Patterns

Patterns of spontaneous motor activity begin developing early and serve adaptive functions such as changing fetal positions. These patterns are similar to movement patterns of neonates and young infants (Prechtl, 1985). (This is a feature of fetal life also noted by the ultrasound studies of Piontelli, 1988, 1989). Graves (1989) speculated that "a great deal of reflex activity may occur as part of normal fetal functioning," and that "this 'practicing' serves a facilitating function for postnatal reflex readiness necessary for neonatal survival" (p. 440). Graves also suggested that reflexes present in the fetus and the infant neonate serve as building blocks for later sensorimotor intelligence (p. 440). According to Corliss (1976), "Movements create sensations which have patterns. These patterns are actually imposed on the musculature, and then on the cortex itself, as imprints or memories which remain like a permanent 'motion picture' to influence our consciousness and future reactions" (in E. Freud, 1989, p. 474).

Fetal Ego Activity

Clearly, developing motor, sensory, and perceptual systems are capable of functioning before complete neuromaturation. Both Verny and Kelly (1981) and Graves (1989) suggested that ego activity as such really begins in the fetus. Graves suggested that the formulations of Heinz Hartmann (1950) regarding autonomous ego activities were related to motility, perception, and protective and regulatory mechanisms may have their origins in the fetus.

Learning and memory are evident in some studies of fetal life. Spelt (1948) taught the fetuses of women in their last two months of pregnancy to respond to a vibrotactile stimulus in a classical conditioning experiment in which fetuses learned to change position in response to a vibrator.

Perhaps the most interesting study of fetal learning, habitation, and anticipation comes from Lieberman (1963). Lieberman studied a group of pregnant women who were habituated smokers whom he denied cigarettes for 24 hours. Each woman was then offered a cigarette. Even before the cigarette had been lit, there was a significant acceleration in fetal heartbeat. Lieberman concluded that "the effect of the mother's emotional response was mediated through placental interchange, which induced the accelerated fetal heart rate" (in E. Freud, 1989, p. 476).

Chamberlain (1987) concluded:

There is mounting evidence for a theory of "cellular" memory which reaches back into the prenatal period. These memories are called cellular because they are usually behavioral rather than verbal memories and because specific parts of the body seem to hold and express these memory patterns [p. 62].

NEONATAL AND INFANT CAPABILITIES

Contemporary research

reveals a newborn who begins life with a high degree of organization and endogenous control, a complex repertoire, able to give precise attention, learn from experience, express a range of appropriate emotions, signal strongly, learn contingencies and accumulate experience in memory. . . . The key is integration, the ability to put it all together [Chamberlain, 1987, p 41].

Mother, Self-, and "Meaning" Recognition at Birth

As mentioned earlier, DeCasper and Spence (1982) demonstrated that infants who listened to a story repeated frequently in utero showed a preference, through their sucking response, for the same story over a new story introduced after birth. Mehler, Bertoncini, and Barriere (1978) demonstrated that the *meaning* of what is heard by the newborn is also registered and responded to by a sucking response. The Mehler group found that when mothers read passages of material backwards (nonsense), the babies stopped sucking, but the babies responded with active sucking responses when the stories were read correctly, particularly when their own mothers read the material. Similarly, DeCasper and Fifer (1980) demonstrated that neonates would suck at different speeds, choosing the speed at which their mother's voice was reading a story. The "infants quickly learned at which speed they could hear their mother's and sucked at that speed more often, indicating a preference" (in Chamberlain, 1987, p. 56). Martin (1981) found that "babies less than 35 hours old would . . . cry at the sound of other babies crying but would *stop* crying at recorded sounds of their *own* crying, indicating that they not only heard but *recognized* their own voices" (in Chamberlain, 1987, p. 38, italics added).

Cross-Modal Integrative Capacities at Birth

Research studies also demonstrate the newborn's amazing cross-modal integrative capacities. Neonates only two hours old could correctly look in the direction of a sound source, evidencing integration of auditory and visual systems (Wertheimer, 1961). Similarly, information gained from one sense modality could be immediately transferred to another. This was demonstrated by an experiment in which newborns identified by sight the type of pacifier (smooth or nubby) they had just sucked when blindfolded (Meltzoff and Borton, 1979). Stern (1985) holds that the infants could not perform such a task according to a Piagetian model.

> A Piagetian account would have required that they first form a schema of what the nipple felt like (a haptic schema) and a schema of what the nipple looked like (a visual schema); then these two schemas would have to have some traffic or interaction (reciprocal assimilation), so that a coordinated visual-haptic schema would result. Only then could the infants accomplish the task. Clearly, the infants did not in fact have to go through these steps of construction. They immediately "knew" that the one they now saw was the one they had just felt [p. 48].

The Papouseks (1987) suggested that the various cross-modal integrative studies indicate an integration of perception, learning and memory that includes "sensory awareness, information processing, the organization of adaptive, behavioral responses, cognition, affect, and memory—an integration basic to all interactions with the environment" (in Chamberlain, 1987, p. 42).

Meltzoff and Moore (1983) discovered that babies could imitate. Two-week-old infants were able to imitate a series of an adult's mouth and tongue gestures. Field et al. (1982) also confirmed the imitative capacities of newborns. They found that "infants 36 hours old were able to discriminate and imitate various affective expressions such as happiness, sadness and surprise" (in Chamberlain, 1987, p. 45).

Infant Dreaming

Dream researchers Roffwarg, Muzio, and Dement (1966) studied the sleep patterns of both full-term and premature newborns in an attempt to ascertain the origins of dreaming. These researchers demonstrated that the sleep patterns of newborns and prematures are identical to adult REM sleep. "In dreams the full world of experience can be reduplicated, involving substantial portions of the brain and nervous system" (in Chamberlain, 1987, p. 48). The more premature the infant, the more time spent in REM sleep. Thus, Roffwarg and his group (1966) proposed that

> dreaming sleep functions as a vital mental exercise necessary to the final development of the central nervous system. . . . since dream activity originates subcortically (in the pons) . . . dream onset can . . . occur early in gestation and . . . contain material from the baby's experiences to date [in Chamberlain, 1987, p. 48; this phenomenon is also suggested by Mancia, 1988].

Infant Learning

A host of studies has been done on newborn and infant learning. These include studies of habituation and classical learning and reinforcement-learning experiments. One of the most complex reinforcement-learning studies is that of Siqueland and Lipsett (1966). In 30 minutes on the first day after birth "newborns mastered a very complex and confusing set of contingencies related to the ipsilateral head turning reflex" (in Chamberlain, 1987, p. 44). Infants were taught through positive nutritive reinforcers to turn their heads one way to the sound of a bell and in another direction to the sound of a buzzer. The task would then be reversed. The infants had to discriminate between different sounds, left and right head turning, and new arrangements of reinforcements. Prior patterns had to be forgotten and new ones learned. When the reinforcers were put on opposite sides from the initial learned pattern, there was a gradual shift in behavior, and all the infants accomplished the new learning task within 30 minutes.

Sight and "Seeing" the Mother

Since acute trauma often involves what is taken in visually (Greenacre, 1952; Murphy, 1958; Terr, 1988), it may be useful to look at the visual and perceptual capabilities of newborns and infants in some detail. Dayton et al. (1964) found that newborns are well focused at a distance of about a foot. They show an ability to discriminate fine details. One-day-old infants show visual acuity of 20/150 (the limits of the test material) and "a following pattern" [following a set of moving stripes] (nystagmus) similar to that of adults exposed to the same material (in Chamberlain, 1987, p. 39). The Dayton research group also found that newborns have a well-developed "fixation reflex"—the ability to place and maintain the image of an object in the fovea. They concluded from a series of experiments that "ocular movement is purposeful and well coordinated instead of aimless and uncoordinated as previously thought" (p. 39).

Norcia and Tyler (1985) found that "visual acuity at one month of age is three to five factors higher than previously reported for pattern stimuli. By eight months grading resolution was adult-like" (in Chamberlain, 1987, p. 39). According to Peiper (1963), "newborns respond to color and discriminate hues . . . color perception is essentially the same for very young infants as it is for adults" (in Chamberlain, 1987, p. 39).

Robert Fantz (1963, 1965) conducted a number of experiments investigating infant perception and was able to isolate infant visual preferences that demonstrated discriminatory capacities. From birth on, infants could perceive and discriminate various forms in a manner similar to that of older infants. These experiments, indicating that newborns could perceive and discriminate circles and shapes, suggested to Fantz (1965) that "the traditional view that the visual world of infants is initially formless or chaotic [was incorrect]. . . . pattern vision [is proof that] the highest level in the visual system, the striate cortex [is] in service" (in Chamberlain, 1987, p. 57). Allik and Valsiner (1980) concluded that "a complete set of global visual abilities exists in the infant at or closely following birth" (in Chamberlain, 1987, p. 40).

Bower (1974, 1977) expanded Fantz's initial findings. He demonstrated depth perception in infants two weeks old; these infants could intrude their arms to stop the movement of an object moving toward them. One of Bowers's (1974) most fascinating experiments had to do with "multiple mothers." Babies were presented with images of their mothers and of strangers reflected in a mirror composed of numerous horizontal pieces that gave an impression of one object as "multiple" objects. Before the age of five months, the infants responded to their "multiple" mothers and ignored the strangers. After five months, the infants continued to ignore the strangers but now they cried at seeing multiples of their own mothers. This finding suggests—perhaps even in a psychoanalytic sense—that by five months of age, infants perceive their mothers as singular whole-object beings rather than as part-objects (see Mully, 1979, for a discussion of this process).

Investigating the capacity of infants to keep in mind what is out of sight (object permanence), a series of experiments by Baillargeon and De Vos (1991) demonstrated that infants as young as three and a half months could recognize that an object continued to exist when hidden. Infants this young could carry on rather sophisticated reasoning about these objects (i.e., taking into account their height, location, and trajectory). Piaget (1954) believed that such reasoning about objects apart from the self was limited until approximately 18 months and that, before this time, infants essentially knew of an object by virtue of their action on it. Baillargeon and De Vos (1991) concluded from their experiments that

> from very early on, infants conceive of occluded objects in the same general manner as adults, as inhabiting the same world and as conforming to the same patterns as visible objects. . . .
>
> Young infants are aware that objects (a) cannot exist at two successive points in time without having existed during the interval between them, (b) cannot appear at two separate points in space without having traveled the distance between them, and (c) cannot move through the space occupied by other objects. Furthermore, infants are able to use this knowledge to make (qualitative and perhaps quantitative) predictions about objects' displacements and interactions with other objects [pp. 1244–1245].

Thus, at an astoundingly early age infants can know about the existence of objects and anticipate their movements apart from their own perception of and action upon them.

With the results of these studies in mind, we can better understand the infant's keen attunement to the nuances of the mother's emotions. Trevarthen's (1980) films of infants and their mothers illustrated how "infants watch their mothers with intense focalisation of gaze and attentive expressions" (in Chamberlain, 1987, p. 58). Trevarthen (1980) also demonstrated that "as mothers saw and responded to their infants, the infants quickly reacted, changing gestures or vocalisations" (in Chamberlain, 1987, p. 58). Infants are also "exquisitely sensitive to changes in a mother's appearance" (Cassel and Sander, 1975, in Chamberlain, 1987, p. 58). In other experiments Brazelton (1978) had mothers fall silent for three minutes while feeding their newborns. The infants tried to influence the mothers to return to normal behavior by vocalizing, reaching out, looking, and so on. If unsuccessful, they withdrew. In an experiment in which a mother wore a mask during a single feeding, the infant took significantly less milk, seemed more anxious when put back in the crib, and then demonstrated disturbed REM and non-REM sleep (Cassel and Sander, 1975).

Most significant for our purposes is the demonstration of memory for these affective-perceptual experiences and their lasting consequences.

In an experiment with three-month-old infants, mothers were asked to look depressed. The babies cried in protest, looked away, and *days later* continued to appear to be wary of their mothers (Tronic, Ricks, and Cohn, 1982). These infants had clearly kept their "depressed mothers" in mind. Fagan (1976) demonstrated that 5- to 7-month-old infants remembered "for over a week a picture of a particular face seen only once and for less than a minute" (in Stern, 1985, p. 62). Stern said of Fagan's experiment, "This feat of long-term recognition memory required a representation of the unique form of a particular face" (p. 62). Stern concluded, "It is well established that infants by five to seven months have extraordinary long-term recognition memory for visual perception" (p. 92).

SUMMARY

It appears from the psychoanalytic literature that "from the beginning" some analysts intuited a fetal and neonatal mental life—even before research evidence supported such notions. Perhaps just working so intimately with the human mind and soul made such possibilities "obvious." Scientific research seems to have caught up with analytic experience. The evidence suggests that mental equipment and the potential for mental life exist from the earliest time of life. Birth experiences have been seen by some researchers as serving to organize patterns for later attitudes, character styles, and symptoms. Fetal ultrasound studies have demonstrated the central organizing role of prenatal "character" for postnatal life. Fetal REM sleep as a vehicle for registering internal representations of experience in the form of a "protomental nucleus" has been proposed, and scientific evidence for learning, memory, and a keen sensitivity to the meaning of the mother has been demonstrated from birth—all evidence suggesting a world of human experience we are just beginning to touch.

6

Infant Memory

W hat kind of memory could operate from the beginning of human life? Would there be a body memory made up of sensations (e.g., touch, smell, feel)? Could a true "mental process" be involved. Would there perhaps be different kinds of memories coming from the mind and the body? The notion that traumatic experiences of earliest life can be registered, stored, and later retrieved in dreams implies that there is in fact a memory system—unconscious, conscious, or both—operating from very early in life, much earlier than prior developmentalists understood or appreciated. Here we are going to extend our look into prenatal and neonatal mental capacities to examine the subject of infant memory in more detail. Psychoanalytic memory theory and anecdotal reports from the psychoanalytic literature are presented, along with evidence from recent key studies in neurobiology, child psychiatry, and experimental psychology. These latter studies provide evidence that infants can retain distinct memory of both affective and perceptual experience, and particularly of affectively charged or traumatic experience, from very early on.

MEMORY AND ITS VARIOUS FUNCTIONS

It may be useful to begin with some description of how memory theorists, primarily from the field of psychology, have detailed the various categories and types of memory functions. Psychologists and psychoanalysts who have written on the topic seem to agree that what we call "memory" is not a single entity but, in fact, involves a complex of systems, each with a different capacity and functioning under different rules, but together forming the entity of "memory" (Tulving, 1985, cited in Chamberlain, 1987). Chamberlain (1987) described some of these various systems:

> *Procedural memory*: refers to retention and recall of learned connections between stimulus and response. . . . [It] involves memory for muscle patterns and coordination. Such memories

have an automatic and unconscious quality. . . . [For example] infants learn to operate a crib mobile by making certain moves with feet, hands, or head ("motor memory"). When provided with the same set of features weeks later (cued recall), they remember how to move (Rovee-Collier, 1985). . . .

Semantic or verbal memory: deals with . . . internal states of meaning not perceptually present.; it is therefore a more conscious form of cognition. Babies two weeks old have been checked for word recognition (Ungerer, Brody and Zalazo, 1978). Mothers were asked to repeat certain unfamiliar words ten times in a row, six times a day for two weeks. After a delay of 42 hours at the end of training, researchers found clear signs of recognition as measured by eye activity, head-turning, and raised eyebrows. . . .

Episodic memory: . . . [involves] various forms of recall of specific episodes in the past. These autobiographical memories are like time-capsules which contain perceptions, affects, actions, and thoughts [pp. 60–61]. [The study of Perris, Myers, and Clifton (1990) in this chapter provides evidence of perceptual and affective episodic memory.]

Chamberlain includes *affect memory* as a form of episodic memory. This involves memory for feeling states and the emotional components of experience. The Nachman and Stern (1984) experiment presented later in this chapter exemplifies a study of infant affective memory. The experiment of Perris et al. (1990) also includes a significant affective component.

George Klein (1966), a psychoanalytic psychologist, wrote about memory functions from a psychoanalytic point of view. He categorized memory functions as follows: 1) *Registration*, which refers to "an after-effect or excitatory effect" (p. 380) of an encounter with a particular perception—auditory, visual, and the like. Klein noted that "not all input registers . . . and not all that register achieve the status of a trace or structured residue" (p. 381). 2) *Storage or retention*, which has to do with both short-term and long-term storage. Conditions required for short-term storage are not necessarily the same as those for long-term storage. 3) *Coding/categorization*, or location within schemata. Organization of new input within the existing schema of meaning is considered crucial to the continued utilization of stored experience. 4) *Retrieval/reconstruction*. Klein considered a retrieved memory to refer to "a condition of a former state of affairs that is acting in the present" (p. 381). Most pertinent to our work here is Klein's assertion that it is not necessary for a memory or stored event to be consciously recalled for it to influence current behavior. "Memories unaccompanied by recall may be experienced as reconstructions—i.e., aroused *beliefs* about past events. . . . We also *act out* our memories as well as experiencing them *qua* memories" (p. 382).

Ernst Lewy and David Rapaport (1944) elaborated on Freud's (1923) differentiation between a "perceptual image" and a "memory image" (p. 20). They noted that the "perceptual image" is the "trace of an original and simple sensory perception" (p. 146). It remains in its raw, sensory form with no particular meaning attached (see Breuer and Freud's, 1893–1895, concept of the "pathogenic memory structure"). A "memory image," on the other hand, represents a more complex unit containing "all the qualities a perception acquires when it becomes embodied in an individual psychic life—the spatial and temporal relations in which it participates, the strivings, affects and moods prevalent at the time it was being perceived" (Lewy and Rapaport, 1944, p. 146). This distinction between perceptual and memory image is important to the controversy over reconstruction of infant trauma.

Trace/Schema Concept of Memory

A central argument against the possibility of reconstruction of early experience is that, owing to the mind's organization of perception and memory, memory does not necessarily correspond exactly to reality, and that the raw data of perception are influenced by the existing memory schema (Spero, 1990; see also Rubinfine, 1967; Spence, 1982; Slap, 1987). The workings of a preexisting memory schema through which new experience and perceptions are filtered would distort the original experience, making it difficult to reconstruct a veridical account of the past. Some of this argument is based on the work of memory theorists, Frederick Bartlett (1932) and Irving Paul (1967).

Rubinfine (1967) offers a careful review of their work. Bartlett (1932) demonstrated that a trace theory of memory, in which the mind is composed of numerous veridical memory traces, cannot account for memory of complex material. He noted that such material requires structuring via "effort after meaning" (Rubinfine, 1967, p. 198). The individual fills in gaps to make sense of and find meaning in the material (perhaps similar to the idea of secondary revision upon waking from a dream). Memory, then, is greatly influenced by the individual's current interests, attitudes and feelings. To describe this phenomenon, Bartlett (1932) proposed the concept of "schema," which involves

> an internal psychic organization of past reactions, experiences (registrations of percepts) and affects, which function as a unified structure; or as Paul put it, as an "organ." In this frame of reference, memory is seen as the result of the interaction of percepts (registrations of percepts) with a preexisting structural organization, i.e., a schema to which coming percepts are recruited. . . . As Paul (1960) observed, "the psyche is made up of schemas about the world, rather than images or traces of the world" [p. 198].

Memory is thus reconstructed, rather than reproduced. George Klein (1966), as noted earlier, also considered categorization of a memory image within an existing schema as an essential process of memory functioning. Piaget formulated a similar schema concept, which was described by Peter Wolff (1960):

> The postulation of a schema as the mental process by which past experiences are stored and made the partial determinants of present behavior is significant because it implies that an inherent mental organization exists before the organism has experienced the external environment. The organism experiences the environment in terms of that existing organization, and all experiences of a certain kind which occur to the organism are molded in the already present schema which they in turn alter. . . . Consequently, experiences are not recorded as individual memory traces or engrams on a passive field, but are actively integrated into a constantly changing structure [p. 22].

Joseph Slap (1987) has argued that perception is also dependent on schemas that are affected by past experience, psychodynamics, affective states, and cognitive style. He cites Arlow's (1969) similar argument in relation to unconscious fantasy as the "underlying schema" which organizes incoming experience:

> There is a mutual and reciprocal effect of the pressure of unconscious fantasy formations and sensory stimuli, especially stimuli emanating from the external world. Unconscious fantasy activity provides the "mental set" in which sensory stimuli are perceived and integrated. External events, on the other hand, stimulate and organize the reemergence of

unconscious fantasies. . . . Derivatives of fantasies may influence ego functions, interfering, for example, with the neutral processes of registration, apperceiving and checking the raw data of perception. Under the pressure of these influences, the ego is oriented to scan the data of perception and to select discriminatively from the data of perception those elements that demonstrate some consonance or correspondence with the latent preformed fantasies [p. 8].

In addition to the objections to veridical memory raised by the foregoing theorists, Spence (1982) presents other objections based on the experimental work of Loftus and Loftus (1980), which suggested that original information stored in memory is erased or substituted by new memories. In reviewing the work of Loftus and Loftus, it is clear that their results are based on memory for information *not* personally significant to the subject (for example, recalling whether a book cover in a photo was blue or yellow), rather than on affectively meaningful events experienced by the individual.

Moshe Spero (1990), reviewing the experimental psychology data that counter Spence's arguments, cites the experimental work of Zaragoza and Koshmider (1989), which demonstrates that "misled subjects . . . tended *not* be 'fooled,' and were able to recall their original memory of the objects. The subjects produced errors . . . only when they had failed to commit the *original* event to memory" (Spero, 1990, p. 86). Graf and Schacter (1987) found that original material could be retained when subjects were able to form "meaning networks" for what was observed. In these cases, the introduction of confusing or misleading material postmemory did not substantially distort an accurate memory of the original data. This particular finding suggests that the process of registering and encoding new perceptions within the context of prior affective, perceptual, and memory schemas actually *assists*, rather than inhibits, the storage of discrete memories: "This research suggests it may be the very process of abstraction or the ability to develop mnemic schemas, which enables original memories to be stored discretely *and* eventually be retrieved" (Spero, 1990, p. 87).

If trauma forms an unconscious schema so early in life, than future experience and development would be filtered through the lens of such an "unconscious meaning network." To be noted, of course, is that such a proposition entails a leap from cognitive processes to unconscious processes. I believe that the clinical material from the literature and from my own clinical work demonstrates that such a leap may be warranted. For example, Yorke (1986) and Frank (1969) present case material illustrating the striking and pervasive effects of unconscious memory schema. If Graf and Schacter (1987) are correct, then the precise argument used to *negate* the possibility of veridical memory reconstruction becomes an important argument *supporting* such a possibility.

No Memories, No Reconstruction: The Lack of Mental Structure

In addition to the arguments based on the problems of storage of memory without distortion is the more basic question as to whether earliest experiences and perceptions can be stored and retained at all. Piaget (1945) took the position that no *evocative memory* of early childhood could exist. Evocative memory is defined as the ability to evoke a memory of a person or object unassisted by a specific cue associated with that person or object.

> There are no memories of early childhood for the excellent reason that at that stage there is no evocative mechanism capable of organizing them. Recognition memory in no way implies a capacity for evocation, which presupposes mental images, interiorized language, and the beginning of conceptual intelligence. The memory of the two- or three-year-old child is still a medley of made up stories, unorganized memory, and exact but chaotic reconstructions, organized memory developing only with the progress of intelligence as a whole [p. 187].

According to Piaget, it is only from 18 months of age that the child achieves internalized, stable representations of objects distinct from the self, that is, that the child can evoke a representation of an object notwithstanding lack of cue. Prior to 18 months, the infant operates by sensorimotor functioning. The sensorimotor period, divided into six developmental stages, comprises prerepresentational, presymbolic modes of mental organization. During this phase

> schemes or patterns of action are formed from reflex automatons; they are generalized and differentiated and joined with other schemes to build increasingly complex, precise, and well-attuned patterns of responses. . . . none of these attributes are available to internal manipulation by the infant—they are achieved solely in the pragmatic business of physical action [Dowling, 1985, p. 574].

Scott Dowling (1982b) suggests that the sensorimotor stage is that of *pre*primary process mentation. According to him, in Piagetian terms, primary-process mentation can begin only with the development of mobile imagery (the ability to move things about in thought) at 18 months. Making a case for his view that preprimary process mentation cannot be accessible to analytic work, Dowling (1985) states that his own analytic experience "suggests that preverbal experience appears, as would be expected, in sensorimotor forms, i.e., in actions, in conditions of altered sensations, and feelings, and in global attitudes and expectations" (p. 581). He finds examples of such sensorimotor mentation in the Isakower (1938) and Lewin (1946) phenomena, in some imageless and anxiety dreams, and in *pavor nocturnus*, as well as in some forms of acting out.

Sensorimotor forms of mental organization involve a "transitory, vague, diffuse, state of mind, a world of amorphous, static, or absent representation" (Dowling, 1982b, p. 301). Sensorimotor phenomena sometimes achieve representation in more mature forms, not as a "new" emergence of repressed representational memories but as a "more mature re-working of sensorimotor recollections" (Dowling, 1985, p. 581). Piaget and others have hypothesized that primitive processes are reworked into more mature forms with the emergence of the symbolic function, particularly with the advent of language (see Schur, 1966; Paul, 1981).

In contrast to Dowling's (1985) view, recent infant research and the case examples presented in this book suggest that these primitive processes are accessible to analytic work through specific somatic memories, nonverbal behavior, transference manifestations, and dreams. Certainly, the infant research alone suggests that the mind of the infant is capable of much more than "transitory, vague, diffuse, . . . amorphous, static . . . representations" (Dowling, 1982b, p. 301).

After compiling updated research on infant capabilities, Lichtenberg (1983) presents a view almost identical to that of Dowling. He suggests that the infant does not retain evocative memory, that is, an image of the mother when she is no longer perceived. Lichtenberg sees the first year of life as having a focus on the exchange between self and others. Lichtenberg, like Dowling, sees the infant as functioning through a "perceptual-affective-action mode" without the use of symbolic signification.

I believe that only that which has been encoded through the primary- and secondary-process modes of organization can be known through the analytic method of free association. Therefore, using the psychoanalytic method, we cannot expect to reconstruct events of the first 18 months. We can find out only how these events have been organized, first in the second half of the second year, and, later, through major transformations. Experiences in the first year may cast their shadow, but the recognition of discrete patterns of perceptual affective-action modes that have not received symbolic representation is "beyond interpretation" (Gedo, 1979) via the verbal communication of psychoanalysis. Such reconstructions must be inferred from observation of nonverbally communicated behavior, in the same way that researchers make inferences from observing the perceptual-affective-action modes of the infant. Empathic receptivity alone, rather than empathic receptivity and empathic understanding, is the analyst's primary means of apprehending a patient's earliest experiences. How often this may be necessary in the therapeutic endeavor is a subject for debate [Lichtenberg, 1983, p. 181].

The arguments presented by Lichtenberg and by Dowling are based on Piaget's formulation of cognitive processes in the infant and young child. Piaget's theories do not address unconscious forces, including unconscious representations, operating in the child's internal world (Hansen 1993, personal communication). For Piaget, *cognitively* there cannot be evocative memory before the construction of the symbolic function, the emergence of which he placed around 18 months of age. The existence of a cognitive capacity most likely indicates the existence of a corresponding unconscious representation in some form. But, the reverse may not be true. The lack of a cognitive capacity does not necessarily rule out the existence of some form of unconscious representation. As noted by Freud (1923), the conscious addresses only the surface of the mind. Lichtenberg and Dowling use Piaget's cognitive theory to delimit the capacity for analytic reconstruction of early unconscious processes. Recent research, including that of Perris et al. (1990) and Baillargeon and De Vos (1991), demonstrates that the cognitive capacities of infants are considerably more differentiated than Piaget indicated. Even if we adhere to Piaget's theory of cognitive organization, such limitations on the infant's conscious cognitive functioning do not automatically entail the absence of unconscious representations. Dowling and Lichtenberg are using (or perhaps misusing) Piaget's cognitive theory to address those capacities of the individual that organize the unconscious mind. Though their position seems eminently reasonable at first glance, recent research suggests that it may be open to significant emendation.

INFANT MEMORY RESEARCH

To shed light on the issues of infant memory functioning, let us examine several of the most recent research studies that relate to the infant's capability to store, "remember," and retrieve its experience. Among our investigations we shall look at, from neurobiology, LeDoux's (1989; LeDoux et al., 1989) studies of the amygdala as the center of early affective reception; from experimental psychology, the 1990 study of Perris et al. of infants' long-term retention of a single, unique experience; and from child psychiatry, the studies of Terr (1988, 1990) and Gislason and Call (1982) on infants' and young children's memory for trauma. In addition, several compelling pieces of anecdotal literature will be presented.

Neurobiology: Joseph LeDoux

From his extensive review of the literature (LeDoux, 1989) and his fear response extinction studies of fear-inducing visual stimuli with rats (LeDoux et al., 1989), Joseph LeDoux concluded that it is the amygdala, rather than hippocampus, that is the underlying affective learning system present in infancy. He found that the amygdala operates earlier than and separate from the hippocampus, the brain structure essential for processing cognitive data. He also found that the amygdala matures very early in life, well before the hippocampus. LeDoux noted that such an understanding helps to explain the findings of Zajonc (1980), who demonstrated through various experiments that affects can be processed before cognition. Zajonc's formulation is a direct challenge to the long-held view that emotional reactions *follow* one's cognitive grasp of a situation. Interestingly, Zajonc's finding might be considered analogous in the psychoanalytic realm to Bion's (1962) notion that thoughts occur before thinking. LeDoux's and Zajonc's conclusions point to a primary unconscious emotional processing system that develops very early in life and determines conscious emotional experience but operates independently of it.

LeDoux outlined the workings of the amygdala and its connections to both the cortical and to the thalamic systems, which enable emotional processing. The amygdala receives sensory input directly from the thalamus. It also receives input from the cortex. The thalamo-amygdala projections appear to be involved in the processing of simple sensory cues, whereas the cortico-amygdala projections are essential for processing more complex stimuli. It is these thalamo-amygdala circuits which LeDoux considers the key structures processing early affective data. These circuits are also involved in the control of emotional responses in infancy prior to the maturation of the neo-cortex. The thalamo-amygdala circuits, then, may be the structural "container," so to speak, for affective experiences and the place where affective "memory traces" are registered and stored prior to cognition in the infant.

LeDoux et al.'s (1989) fear-extinction experiments with rats are particularly important for their unexpected finding that emotional memories established in the absence of the visual cortex persist for unusually long periods of time—in fact, they are almost indelible. In laboratory experiments, the visual cortex of four groups of rats was located and lesioned by stereotaxic methods. Control rats were given a "sham" operation, but the visual cortex was not lesioned. After 20 days postrecovery, lesioned and sham-operated rats were placed in a conditioning chamber where they were subjected to aversive conditioning trials. The conditioned stimulus (cs) was a flashing lamp; the unconditioned stimulus (ucs) was a shock grid. Repression of drinking behavior was measured as evidence of the presence of a conditioned fear response. Visual fear was evident in both groups, indicating that in the absence of the visual cortex, fear responses were readily established for visual stimuli. Thus, visual fear conditioning was found to involve subcortical sensory pathways. Extinction of the conditioned visual fear response was greatly prolonged, if not prevented, by cortical ablation. LeDoux et al. (1989) reported:

> Lesions of visual cortex may prolong extinction by preventing the relay of visual inputs to areas such as the frontal cortex and/or hippocampus. Emotional memories established in the absence of sensory cortex, probably by way of thalamo-amygdala projections are, therefore, relatively indelible [p. 241].

LeDoux et al.'s findings suggest that the indelibility of subcortical emotional learning may help to substantiate the psychoanalytic hypothesis that emotional memories can be stored very early, in fact from the beginning of life. LeDoux stated (cited in Goleman, 1989), "precognitive emotion is based on neural bits and pieces of sensory information, which have not yet been sorted out and integrated into a recognizable object. It's a very raw form of sensory information" (p. 9B). LeDoux's description strikes one as analogous in the psychoanalytic realm to Bion's (1962) "beta" elements and Breuer and Freud's (1893–1895) "purest manifestation" in the "pathogenic memory structure." Freud's (1923) concept of the "perceptual image" would also be relevant. All three concepts attempt to reach the raw sensory data of experience. Because of their "indelibility," these early sensory/emotional memories of fears, resentments, and the like, would have the potential to be stored in dreams. They would also have the potential to affect behavior, thinking, feeling, and symptoms later in life. According to LeDoux, (in Goleman, 1989) these precognitive emotions can lead to enactments and other forms of unconscious manifestations throughout life rather than to conscious memories.

Child Psychiatry: Lenore Terr

The "indelibility" of affectively charged experience, and infants' capacity to retain memory of early "unique" experience, have been demonstrated respectively by the studies in child psychiatry of Terr (1988, 1990) and Gislason and Call (1982), and the experimental psychology work of Perris et al. (1990) as well as Nachman and Stern (1984).

Perhaps the most extensive research reported in the child psychiatry literature on the nature of early traumatic memory is that of Terr (1988, 1990). Her work with the Chowchilla school-age kidnap victims (Terr, 1979, 1983b) took place over the course of five years. She found that the children's "general ability to give complete remembrance of their traumas a year later, and then four and five years after the experience, was uncanny. A control group age-matched to the Chowchilla children also did not forget their worst experiences" (Terr, 1988, p. 96).

Following these initial studies, Terr (1988, 1990) investigated how infants and young children remember significant trauma. She studied the records of 32 children in which the trauma occurred when they were under five years of age. Terr had seen these children herself over a 12-year period. Twenty of the children had verifiable proof of their experiences, such as photos, police reports, eyewitness histories, confessions, or corroborating injuries. All the children played out, drew, or spoke about their earliest, most disturbing experiences. The age range of the children at the time of the trauma was six months to four years, with an average of 34 months. The average interval between the trauma and the memory assessment was four years, five months, with a range of five months to twelve years.

Terr found that there was no type of trauma that was best or worst remembered in words (verbal memory), although single, short events, regardless of type, were clearest. There was no correlation between the length of the interval from the traumatic event to the time of the evaluation and the child's ability to recall it verbally. There were no demographically important differentiating factors, such as intelligence, social class, or ethnic group, in relation to the completeness of their verbal memories; nor was there a difference in their ability to remember based on disruptiveness of the family background, willingness of the family to talk about the event, or whether an adult family member had been present during the event.

Two and a half to three years seemed consistently the age at which most children were able initially to register and later to retrieve a verbal memory of the trauma. Terr (1990) suggested that this age coincides with a significant spurt in left-brain development (where verbal skills reside in right-handed people). Terr noted that sudden, fast events—particularly unanticipated sudden terror—seem to be remembered most distinctly because a small child's defenses are completely overwhelmed by the trauma. Long-standing, repeated traumas, however, initiate defensive maneuvers such as "denial and splitting, self-anesthesia, and dissociation" (p. 183). These defenses interfere with verbal memory formation, storage, and retrieval.

> When the defenses are completely overrun by one sudden, unanticipated terror, brilliant, overly clear verbal memories are the result. On the other hand, when the defenses are set up in advance in order to deal with terrors the child knows to be coming, blurry, partial, or absent, verbal memories are retained. The child may even develop blanket amnesia for certain years in the past [p. 183].

Terr noted that, of the variety of verbal memory processes involved, an early spot (verbal) memory could stand for the whole experience (see Sharpe's, 1937, concept of synecdoche). A partial verbal memory could substitute for the whole, the substituted piece carrying the full meaning of the trauma. There was also "subtraction" from verbal memory; that is, a spot memory for the traumatic experience existed, but the affect was suppressed, particularly when guilt feelings were involved. Contemporary additions to and later elaborations on the verbal memory were also noted. These elaborations involved embellishments of the event with symbols appropriate to the child's current developmental stage, a process that would allow the event to sound fantasized while, in fact, the kernel of truth was quite evident. Embellishment, could take on symbols characteristic of oral, anal, and oedipal psychosexual stages. As traumatic memories "rest in storage, their meanings may be re-worked as the ongoing phases of childhood progress. . . . [There is an] accuracy of early verbal memories of trauma despite individual tendencies to add to or to delete from these memories over time" (Terr, 1988, pp. 102–103).

Also evident with time and maturation were "reappraisals through new cognitive advances" (p. 102), meaning the child used later conceptual knowledge to reformulate what had happened earlier. This process of reformulation based on later acquired knowledge has also been addressed by Schur, 1966; Paul, 1981; and Dowling, 1985.[1] There were also "condensations with memories of subsequent upsetting events" (p. 102), a process noted both by Freud (1901) and Kris (1956). Terr (1988) stated, in regard to the condensations: "Even so, the original traumatic material may be dissected out" (p. 102).

Most striking in Terr's study was the presence of "virtually universal behavioral memory . . . when little or no verbal memory exists" (p. 98). "Literal mirroring of traumatic events by behavioral memory [can be] established at any age, including infancy" (p. 103). Behavioral memories consisted of

> posttraumatic play; . . . personality changes related to frequent re-enactments or to long-standing grief and/or rage . . . and trauma-specific fears. . . . Play reenactments and fears strikingly mirrored what was in 16 of the 18 documentations. The children often played or reenacted parts, not the whole, of their experiences. Further, the play and reenactments included displacements to toys, friends, or family and often included feeble undoings and attempts at converting passive into active experiences [p. 98].

Terr speculates about the origins of these behavioral memories in a manner similar to the conceptualizations of Schur (1966), Paul (1981), Dowling (1985), and Laibow (1986), as well as to Freud's in his concepts of the "pathogenic memory structure" (Breuer and Freud,

---

[1]Dowling (1985) suggested that earliest sensorimotor experience can at times achieve representation in more mature verbal forms through a reworking of sensorimotor recollections. Schur (1966) specified that this process involves an integration of information of a higher order of abstraction acquired subsequent to the original perception.

1893–1895) and the "perceptual image" (1923): "Perhaps traumatic occurrences are first recorded as visualizations or—in young infants— as feeling sensations. These perceptual-behavioral registrations occur long before any remembrances can be recorded in words" (Terr, 1990, p. 182). These primitive "perceptual-behavioral" memories can occur from the "earliest moments of conscious life" (p. 182). Such memories are transformed into verbal memories around the ages of 28 to 36 months.

Terr (1988) puts forth an interesting hypothesis regarding these early behavioral memories, both for their continuity in time and their accuracy. She sees behavioral memory as operating by principles different from those governing verbal memory:

> Behavioral recall allows for repetition in action of multiple, variable, and long-lasting abuses, even where the verbal descriptions of these abuses seem forever lost to consciousness. Verbal recollections require conscious awareness, but behavioral memory does not [p. 103].

Terr came to another striking conclusion:

> Traumatic events create lasting visual images. . . . even when the trauma is first experienced as a nonvisual event, . . . the sighted person will retain his traumatic impression as a visual one. . . . Behavioral memory follows from visual memory, not from verbal memory. This accounts for the very early onset of behavioral memory. . . .
>
> When a child reenacts, he recreates and reinforces already "burned-in" visual impressions. . . . Associations to visual memories trigger behavioral repetitions and the behaviors, in turn, set off more behaviors and more pictures. Visual memory seems to last a lifetime. And the tendency to "remember" behaviorally persists right along with it. Traumatic visions from early in life seem to stimulate more action than words.
>
> When a trauma or a series of extreme stresses strikes well below the age of 28 to 36 months, the child "burns in" a visual memory of it, sometimes later becoming able as years go on to affix a few words to the picture. These words, late in arriving, can only describe *part* of the preexisting imagery. Parts tend to stand for the whole. To the professional, this verbal part memory may sound dream-like . . . or phony. . . .

These few words, however, represent true verbal remembrances of a fixed mental picture.

On the other hand, when trauma strikes after the age of 28 to 36 months, two memories, verbal and visual, may simultaneously be taken in, stored, and made ready for retrieval. The visual memory . . . remains true to the traumatic event that precipitated it. The verbal memory, however, may stray a bit from its origins through symbolic elaboration, cognitive reappraisal, and subtraction from content [p. 104].

Terr (1990) investigated the memories contained in the dreams of her traumatized children. She concluded that psychic trauma seems to lead to four types of posttraumatic dreams: "exact repetitions, modified repetitions, deeply disguised dreams, and terror dreams that cannot be remembered upon awakening" (p. 210; see Dowling, 1982a, for an example of the last). With time, exact repetition dreams become modified with new elaboration, although the original trauma remains at its center.

One child in Terr's sample, Tama, was a victim of a terrible forklift truck accident when she was two-and-a-half years old. Tama's teenage brother had offered her a forklift ride. He drove very fast, and when his sister screamed, he yelled, "Shut up, stupid." The brother subsequently lost control of the truck. Tama fell off; the truck fell over and her leg was crushed. After several operations, her leg was finally amputated when she was nine. Terr interviewed her when she was 15 and asked her to talk about her dreams. Tama reported having had repeated dreams since she was 34 months old that centered on a repetition of her brother's "shut up, stupid" comment. These dreams, according to Tama, had stopped spontaneously when she was six. At Terr's request, she then reported a current dream that she thought was unrelated:

> *My boyfriend proposes marriage. . . . We walk along a beach to an 18th-century house. Characters from the movie "The Shining" are there, waiting to axe me. I go over to the beach with my boyfriend. Giant crabs are there ready to attack* [Terr, 1990, p. 213].

No associations were given to the dream, but the imagery more generally suggests that the 18th-century house may represent something of the distant past, the boyfriend perhaps her brother when she was a baby; the Shining waiting to ax her, the amputation of her leg. Concerning the giant crabs, Terr pointed out, "What looks more like a forklift truck, after all, than an oversized, shiny, bright orange Alaska king crab?" (p. 214).

Of dreams connected to horrible traumas, Terr (1990) writes:

> Ordinary dreams are not equipped to dissipate traumatic anxiety, the anxiety of the external. . . . Dreams, the ordinary coping devices for warding off internal emotional conflict, do not "work" after massive horror, terror, and disgrace. . . . The dreams repeat and repeat. . . . The traumatized dreamer may be granted a month's rest or even a year's respite. But sooner or later the posttraumatic dream will come back. Traumatic anxiety apparently does not spontaneously dissipate during one's lifetime [p. 214].

Terr also discusses posttraumatic play and reenactments as forms of traumatic memory. She notes that "play" in these cases is grimly monotonous, entailing overspecific repetitions—no fantasy elaboration or fun is involved. The child continuously plays his traumatized self and cannot achieve enough distance from the trauma to achieve the relief that comes from normal fantasied play.

Terr presents another grim example. Two babies—a boy age 7 months and a girl age 15 months had been satanic-cult victims. The baby-sitter had written a confession to the infants' mothers, a document that Terr reviewed. Both infants had been squatted on, and urinated and defecated on, by the adults involved. The little boy's penis had been cut with a ritual knife; Terr saw the cut. Now the 15-month-old girl kept sitting on the 7-month-old boy's head at home at every opportunity possible. The boy played along without objection. Terr pointed out how unusual "shared play" is at such an early age—and how significant and absolutely literal was the compulsive repetition.

Terr concluded: "No child was too young to be traumatized. And no child was too young to show behavioral memories afterward" (p. 185). "Psychic trauma appears to leave an 'indelible mark' in a child's mind, no matter how young [the child]" (p. 182).

Child Psychiatry: Lee Gislason and Justin Call

In another study (Gislason and Call, 1982), infants who had been bitten by dogs were evaluated for the effects of this trauma on their personality development. The three children who had been bitten at 20, 26, and 36 months of age, respectively, each had 100 or more sutures. All the children were interviewed by the age of three. Each child in the study had a clear and accurate conscious memory of the bite, as seen through play and verbalization. "None of the children showed difficulty in presenting a detailed description of the dog bite incident" (p. 206). One child indicated her first memory was a dog bite. Another described the bite in detail. Another played out the experience with toys. The authors concluded:

> In the light of the belief that denial is the major defense of early childhood, an unexpected finding was that each child was able to communicate directly about the dog bite incident months later. . . . The children gave a repetitious, rigidly stereotypic account of the dog bite trauma in their play, suggesting a constriction of thought and fantasy. It was anticipated that much of the trauma would have been repressed, denied or worked through at the time of evaluation. This was not the case [p. 207].

Experimental Psychology:
Eve Perris, Nancy Myers, and Rachel Clifton

Experimental psychology has provided evidence of the infant's capacity to retain memories for specific experiences. The most important experimental study in this area was conducted by Perris, Myers, and Clifton (1990). They demonstrated evidence of memory for a single experience containing an affective, but not a traumatic, component, after a very long interval. Perris et al. described an experiment with 16 children two-and-a-half years of age and eight children one-and-a-half years of age, all of whom had participated when they were six-and-a-half months old in a study of auditory localization. The children had to reach, first in the light and then in the dark, for a sounding rattle. All 24 children had encountered the unique laboratory experiment only once at six-and-a-half months of age. One and a half or two and a half years later, the children were reintroduced to the same laboratory setting. A control group was also evaluated. Two experimental conditions were introduced: one was a brief reminder to some of the older children a half hour prior to the testing; the second was instructions to reach for the sounding rattle following the initial memory trials given to all the children. The children who had participated in the experiment as infants gave evidence of memory for that experience.

In virtually every comparison on trials in the dark, the experienced group performed differently than children in the control groups. . . . when first confronted with dark conditions, and given no verbal directions, the older children with infant experience in the situation clearly reached out toward the sound more than their inexperienced peers. . . . [the younger] children with infant experience showed marginally more reaching than those new to the task. . . . With or without instructions to reach, with or without the dark-sound context reminder, both younger and older children who had participated as infants were more successful in directing their reaches and obtaining the sounding object than those children without the early experience [p. 1804].

One component of the study was the somewhat disturbing experience of being plunged into the dark after reaching for the rattle in the light. The older children without infant experience in the dark procedure evidenced distress with this part of the experiment, and over a third of them terminated the trial before completion. This was more than four times the number of experienced older children who asked to stop because of their anxiety regarding the dark. The experienced children, then, tolerated the stressful aspect of the experiment significantly better than the inexperienced children did.

Perris et al.'s findings are extremely significant. In all prior experimental psychology literature, only one study had examined the duration of memory for events during the first year of life over delays greater than one month. In that experiment (Myers, Clifton and Clarkson, 1987), the infants had been introduced from *15 to 19 times* to the stimulus they were to remember a couple of years later. In the Perris et al. experiment—constructed in every other respect identically to the Myers et al. experiment—the infants were introduced to the stimuli and the setting *only once*, at six-and-a-half months of age.

Perris et al. (1990) concluded that

an early memory system . . . is functional in infancy . . . and can, at least by six months of age, mediate long-term memory [p. 1805].

Even if infant encoding processes were limited and the resultant memory traces fragile, forgetting was not complete. If the unique context of an unusual event is completely reinstated, then, and especially if a brief reminder of the event is introduced a short time beforehand, the memory system operational at 6 months and 2 years is powerful enough to facilitate performance of action sequences carried out during a single episode of infancy [p. 1806].

Amid original contextual cues, then, it appears that two years of physical, neurological and cognitive changes do not prohibit retrieval based on the infant memory processes. [p. 1805].

In relation to the emotional, affective component of the experience (the fact that experienced children could mediate emotionally stressful aspects of the experiment better than inexperienced children), Perris et al. stated:

Children with one early experience in reaching in the dark carry with them 2 years later not only a record of appropriate motor sequences but enough general emotional familiarity to mediate acceptance of a second experience aversive to the inexperienced peers. We conclude that the one unique experience at 6.5 months of age was sufficient to establish a memory of both action and *meaning* that become accessible upon reinstatement of the event in the third year of life [p. 1806, italics added].

Patricia Nachman and Daniel Stern

The evaluation of infant memory specifically for affective experience was demonstrated by the experimental study of Patricia Nachman and Daniel Stern (1984). They conducted an experiment designed to evaluate the capacity for evocative memory of affective experience (as noted earlier, evocative memory—the capacity to remember the object in its absence—is not considered possible until 18 months of age). Seventy-five infants, six and seven months old, were made to laugh at a particular hand puppet that appeared and disappeared in a peek-a-boo game. The babies were shown another puppet that elicited a neutral response. The infants were then shown the "laugh" and "neutral" puppets a week later. The sight of the puppet that made them smile initially elicited a smile response on the second showing; the sight of the puppet that had elicited a neutral response initially elicited no affective response the second week. The second smile was considered "cued recall" or evidence of "evocative memory" in that the sight of the puppet activated an affective response. The authors state that smiling after a period of one week suggests that "affects were a readily retrievable sources of memory after a long time delay"

(p. 99). They conclude: "Our finding suggests the presence of a memory storage system, including affects, that are recallable by cue very early in infancy, long before the emergence of a language or symbol-based semantic recall memory system" (p. 100).

ANECDOTAL REPORTS

A number of anecdotal reports in the literature demonstrate clinically the manifestations of the underlying assumptions of the foregoing experimental and psychiatric studies. A few of the most compelling descriptions are presented here.

Rima Laibow

This remarkable presentation involves the birth memories of an exceptionally gifted child reported to his mother (a physician) at 30 months of age. The baby was delivered by Caesarean section after a 42-week gestation.

> M's development was marked by unusually rapid neurologic, cognitive and language growth. He lifted his head, focused and followed with head and eyes on Day 1. He spoke recognizable words at 3 months, used nouns and sentences at five months.
>
> At age 2-1/2, while lounging in the bathtub one evening with both of his parents in the room, M began recalling his birth. He asked why were the lights so bright "when I was new?" and waited for a response. We did not understand the reference to being "new" and asked what he meant. He carefully explained that he had been "being born," and said that there were many things he did not understand. When encouraged to tell us what they were, he shared the following puzzles:
>
>> 1. He did not know why the light was circular and so intense where he was, but dim elsewhere.
>>
>> 2. He wanted to know why the bottom half of the faces of the people had been "missing" and a green patch had been there instead.
>>
>> 3. He wanted to understand why someone had felt his anus with their finger.

4. He was very puzzled by what was inserted into his nose that had produced a loud sound. When asked what sort of sound he had heard, he made a loud sucking noise.

5. He wanted to know where I was, since he knew he "had been inside" me before he was born.

6. He was troubled about why he was "put into a plastic box and taken somewhere."

7. He was not puzzled, but seemed upset, by the introduction of liquid into his eyes that made it impossible for him to see any longer [Laibow, 1986, pp. 78–79].

The parents explained the general surgical obstetrical procedure that he had undergone. M did not ask further questions. He volunteered, however, that he thought

the sudden opening in the wall of the uterus was "funny." He then laughed and said that suddenly there was a "fenster in the finster" which is Yiddish for a "window in the darkness." . . . He said he remembered that before he was born, there were many times when he felt cramped and squeezed painfully by the walls, and that certain loud, low frequency sounds sung by his mother were painful to him [p. 80].

Laibow noted that when she sang certain low notes, the fetus had responded actively. She took this to be the baby's positive response. "He also reported perceiving dimly a faint light through the wall of the uterus" (p. 80).

Laibow noted that her son was acquainted with specific information about vaginal and Caesarean birth. He had, however,

never seen a surgical unit, experienced its pattern of illumination, been party to the intimate details of postnatal handling of the infant nor been advised that silver nitrate solution is routinely used in the eyes of newborns. He had never seen surgical greens nor seen or heard a suctioning device used on the nostrils. Never, that is, except at the time of his birth [p. 80].

This child, who was fully verbal well in advance of his peers, demonstrated organized sensory awareness before and at birth and could retain these experiences at a preconscious and conscious level. "With his linguistic fluency, he was able to encode the experience in such a way that it matched his sensory phenomenology and could be communicated verbally to those around him" (p. 80).

Two additional brief reports of affective memorial capacities at birth support the possibility of the kind of awareness and memory so strikingly evident in Laibow's child. Mavis Gunther (1961) demonstrated affective memory at the very beginning of life, when infants experience breathing occlusions during breast-feeding. These infants were "breast shy" for the following several feedings, indicating "memorial capacities to register, recognize, and recall affective experience" (cited in Stern, 1985, p. 94). Equally significantly, A. W. Liley (1972) demonstrated that infants who had as few as ten heel punctures for blood samples in the first 72 hours after birth would cry for weeks and months afterwards if their feet were grasped (cited in Chamberlain, 1987).

Ann Bernstein and Richard Blacher

Another demonstration of the laying down of organized experience in precise, integrated memories at an extremely early age is cited by Ann Bernstein and Richard Blacher (1967). They suggest that their case example counters the view that young infants live in an "amorphous, undifferentiated state [in which] perceptions, sensations and experiences are fleeting and not integrated" (p. 156). They reported a two-year-old child's recollection of a traumatic medical episode that had occurred when she was three months of age. Like the Laibow case, this child was also extremely gifted. She consistently smiled at ten days of age. She spoke simple words at five months and had a vocabulary of 24 words by 17 months. The mother was a psychiatrist with an analytic background. The infant, Laura, was born with hydrocephalus of unknown origin but with no other difficulties. At three months, she was hospitalized and underwent X-rays and subdural taps. Her mother, Dr. Bernstein, reported:

> A pneumoencephalogram via the lumbar was performed, with spinal needle in place for 2 hours; during this time she screamed continuously. During the hospitalization, construction work was carried on in the hospital. There was much hammering in a nearby room and Laura seemed disturbed by this. . . . [Following the procedure on occasional nights], she would awaken screaming, in apparent terror, soaked with perspiration and rubbing her head. At three-month intervals, Laura was evaluated by the neurosurgeon in the office at the

hospital. On these occasions her head circumference was measured and a complete neurological exam was performed. . . . after the pneumoencephalogram, she began to scream whenever a man except her father approached.

At age twenty-seven months, Laura had an echoencephalogram in the outpatient department of the same hospital. This was a painless procedure. . . . It required the application of conductive fluid to the scalp and the placing of electrodes.

When Laura was twenty-eight months old a new neighbor moved next door. There were several days when much hammering was heard. . . . Laura seemed terrified and did not respond to explanation. . . . Again she woke up screaming from afternoon naps. She complained, "My dolly is not sleeping all night." When asked why, she responded: "Man is knocking—might knock her head off." To the query, "What man?" she answered, "In the hospital the man knocked my head off." Her mother then recalled the hammering that had taken place during . . . Laura's hospitalization. . . . She was asked, "What happened in the hospital?" She replied, pointing to her backside, "Man stuck me in the tushie and knocked my head off." She went on to explain that this meant it hurt her head.

She was then for the first time given the explanation that when she was a baby she had been in the hospital and had received an injection which had caused the headache. She was also told that at the time the hospital was being built and that there had been a great deal of hammering. Night terrors continued and during one she was heard to call out, "Don't hurt me! My daddy loves me." She was told, "You are a big girl now and no one is going to hurt you. The headache happened a long time ago when you were a baby." The night terrors ceased for a week and then recurred. When the explanation was repeated, Laura said, "But the man brushed my hair." At this point the echoencephalographic procedure was reviewed and Laura was told that this did not hurt her, nor would anything further be done to hurt her head. The night terrors again subsided. . . . Laura, at three and a half years, is still upset by noises, but holds her head instead of her ears as would most children [pp. 157–159].

The authors reviewed several possible explanations other than accurate memory capability but concluded that Laura's intellectual precocity, combined with a very severe trauma of which there were constant reminders—the regular check-ups in the hospital setting where there was a continuous focus on her head—allowed the memory to "stay alive" (see Fodor, 1949, in this regard). The stimulus of the neighbor's hammering allowed the terrifying memory to come into full focus, both for Laura and for her mother. The authors speculated that such early memory traces may be "more common than we assume, but are not noted and then lost in the process of further development" (p. 161). Because of the unique conditions in this case, such memories had an opportunity to be revealed.

This case may also be an excellent example of Schmideberg's (1950) observation: "I am inclined to think that much that is regarded as 'fantasy' contains such infantile memories, and many sadistic ideas and fears of torture and mutilation may be based on vague memories of illness and pain in infancy" (p. 472).

In both the Laibow and the Bernstein and Blacher cases the recall included information acquired in the interval between the original perception and its recall. Terr (1988) also wrote that growing cognitive capacities, particularly capacities for verbal representation, allow the child to affix precise descriptions to experiences that were registered and "known" in earliest infancy (see also Paul, 1981). The Laibow and Bernstein and Blacher examples are so interesting because the capacity for "verbal representation" was evident unusually early in their children. Thus, at 30 months and 27 months, respectively, these two gifted children were able to describe in verbal terms experiences "known" to them at the very beginning of life.

Helen Schur

Helen Schur (1966) gave further evidence for such a process. She described a 30-month-old boy who demonstrated a conscious memory for an experience that had occurred at 18 months of age. The child was able to describe the experience with vocabulary and information he had acquired in the 12-month interval between the original perception and the later description. Thus, at 18 months, he had been told that moving vehicles were called "cars." One year later, his parents were differentiating vehicles by their specific categories (car, bus, truck tractor, etc.), and the child's vocabulary had markedly improved. At 18 months, the boy and his father had visited a roadside stand with a tractor (which the father called a "car"). At 30 months, the boy and his father made a second visit, and the child asked, "Where is the red tractor?" The upper part of the tractor he had seen on the first visit was blue, but the lower part, situated at the baby's eye level, was, in fact, red. Schur felt that these observations supported Freud's (1901) hypothesis that "a recall of a memory trace of a visual perception carries with it information of a higher order of abstraction acquired subsequent to the original perception" (p. 477).

Melitta Schmideberg

Melitta Schmideberg (1950), consistent with the foregoing anecdotal reports involving infants' early structured memories, described a clinical situation in which a mother reported to her that her daughter of three used to play the role of mother while the child's father was directed to play the baby.

> She would feed, nurse, and wash him and wipe his eyes with cotton balls. One day, while doing this, she suddenly turned to her mother and said laughingly, "This is what you used to do to me when I was a baby." The mother, a sensible and trustworthy person, assured me that she had never cleaned the baby's eyes in this fashion after the age of seven months and that the child could not have seen it done to others. After some months the child ceased to play this game and forgot the matter [Schmideberg, 1950, p. 469].

As Schmideberg noted, this case suggests that quite conscious memories of infancy can be retained for a period of time, perhaps a few years. She also reported a case described to her by Glover in which "a patient had visualized green and red rails placed in a certain order and at a certain distance. They turned out to be the stripes of a dress his mother had worn when he was a baby" (p. 472).

Theodore Gaensbauer

In her critique of Lichtenberg's (1983) views on infant development, E. Virginia Demos (1985) discussed a paper by Theodore Gaensbauer (1982), "The Differentiation of Discrete Affects." Here, a study was conducted of a three-month-old girl, Jenny, whose father physically abused her. The parents lost custody of the child. Two months after her removal from the home, the infant was observed in a clinic setting. She differentiated males from females and displayed a fear reaction at the approach of a strange male. (The fear response is not considered established until approximately eight months of age developmentally.) The infant was also described as becoming depressed when separated from her nurturing mother and placed in a more distant foster-care situation. She expressed anger toward her mother during their reunions. Demos (1985) cited this example to demonstrate that "psychic experience can be meaningful and real" (p. 562) in infancy and may not just remain as a perceptual-action-affect experience without representation, as Lichtenberg suggested.

Gaensbauer (1985), in a separate critique of Lichtenberg's work, raised concerns similar to Demos's by questioning whether there could be some form of representation of external events evident in Lichtenberg's action-pattern memory, "some form of internal imaging corresponding to the various sensory modalities through which the experiences were perceived?" (p 520). In his very detailed observational study of this abused child, Gaensbauer (1982) stated that Jenny's case demonstrated that by three months, "affect states have a considerable psychological organization, involving perceptual discrimination, memory, affective learning, and the capacity for stimulus generalization" (p. 53). He suggested that these early affective states are linked to "action patterns" (à la Lichtenberg) and form memory schemas through which new experiences are interpreted.

Lichtenberg (1989) appears to have pondered Gaensbauer's and Demos's critique such that he included the example of Jenny in his book *Psychoanalysis and Motivation*. Here, he seems to have changed his views regarding the capacity for infant memory, particularly in the case of infant trauma. He states that he did not see Jenny's case as representing ordinary or general memorial capacities of the infant. However, he acknowledges that her case suggests that traumatic experiences may create different or special conditions for memory. He writes, "Even in early infancy, powerful affective experiences create special conditions in which memory encoding is more likely to occur" (p. 281).

SUMMARY

Recent and very significant research data in neurobiology, child psychiatry, and experimental psychology, as well as anecdotal reports, lend support to the possibility that the earliest affective and perceptual experiences/traumas can be stored in the unconscious, the conscious, or both and are capable of retrieval in infancy, early childhood, and even adulthood. Additionally, researchers have tentatively located a "place" (the thalamo-amygdala circuits) where such "memories" of affective experience may be stored and processed. What are we to make, then, of the opposing views regarding the possibility of early memory reconstruction—Terr (1988) on one hand, and Kris (1956), Dowling (1982a, b, 1985), and Spence (1982) on the other?

I think we could make of these opposing views the following: two *different* types of memories are being addressed. As discussed, Terr's (1988) "burned in" "behavioral memory" is one type of memory. It can be considered analogous to Freud's (1923) "perceptual image." Terr's "verbal memory" is a second type of memory. It can be considered analogous to Freud's (1923) "memory image." A "verbal memory" or "memory image" becomes modified, distorted, and overlaid with current experience and developmental issues over time. It does not lend itself easily to veridical reconstruction. Authors such as Spence (1982), Kris (1956), and Dowling (1982a, b, 1985), who purport the impossibility of reconstructing *specific* infant memories, or even broader childhood memories, because of developmental considerations, are referring to this *particular kind of memory*—Terr's "verbal memory" or Freud's "memory image." Those who say earliest specific memories can be reconstructed are referring to Terr's "behavioral memory" or Freud's "perceptual image."

This understanding would help to clarify the nature of the reconstruction controversy. Those who feel that reconstruction from earliest life is possible are referring to reconstruction from a *different type* of memory experience than are those who say reconstruction is impossible. *Both* types of memories exist in the mind. In fact, the narrative approach in psychoanalysis is particularly conducive to "memory image" or "verbal memory" data, whereas veridical reconstruction is more likely with "perceptual image" or "behavioral memory" data. The difficulties centered on "verbal memory" or "memory image" reconstruction would not, then, negate the possibility of "behavioral memory" or "perceptual image" reconstruction.

Such an understanding could have significant and perhaps even profound, implications for our theories as well as our work. Using reconstructive and narrative approaches in working with these two types of respective memories, we could reach the human experience of our patients at its very beginning while *at the same time* understanding the variations and developments that change such experience over time. Thus, we would be providing a narrative story of the patient's experience grounded in a veridical understanding of the past and how that past is still alive in the present. We would, in other words, encompass the universe of the mind and truly bring alive for our patients the meaning of their internal world.

7

Reconstruction of Infant Trauma
Cases from the Literature

W hat would traumas from infancy look like 20 or 30 years later? Would we see them in the way we walk or talk? Would they show in our mannerisms and idiosyncracies? Would they appear in our life's work or lack of a life's work? Would they be discovered in the way we love (or can't love) and in the way we hate? A few analytic writers have approached the issue and written about it. They have taken patient behavior, symptoms, transference manifestations, and dreams and "located" what they deemed to be the earliest trauma from the past. They have reconstructed the trauma and demonstrated to the patient how he is living it out in the present— even living it out right in the moment within the analytic hour.

Here we will look at cases from the literature in which analysts have made *very specific* reconstructions of earliest trauma and traced how these traumas were being lived out in the current personality as well as in the analytic transference. These reconstructions centered on evidence from (1) behavioral manifestations and symptoms, (2) nonverbal behavior within the analytic hour as well as within the analytic transference, and (3) patient dream material. All the writers presenting this clinical material demonstrated that infantile traumatic experience is encoded in the "being" of the person in some form, at times in the form of somatic memories. Each of the writers showed that these "encoded experiences" are analyzable through interpretive methods that are considered *standard* to traditional psychoanalytic techniques (i.e., dream analysis; transference interpretation; interpretations of behavior, verbal and nonverbal, within the hour). Twelve case reports, including one child case and one case followed longitudinally for over 30 years, are presented.

RECONSTRUCTION OF INFANT TRAUMA FROM BEHAVIORAL MANIFESTATIONS AND SYMPTOMS

Richard Robertiello

Richard Robertiello (1956) described a striking example of how an "accidental trauma" at weaning had created a significant effect on the personality. The patient was a 21-year-old man with a very caring and supportive mother. Despite his essentially healthy character structure, he evidenced a pattern of enormous sensitivity to rejection by women, occasional enuresis and depression, and definite suicidal thoughts and attempts. The problem centered on feelings of a life-and-death need for his girlfriend, which included extreme jealousy and rage at any evidence of rejection. There were also a number of dreams surrounding oral deprivation by, and anger at, women as well as repeated dreams and fantasies about swimming and being in the water. Unfortunately, Robertiello did not detail the dreams of this patient in his paper. He did, however, suggest that the swimming dreams represented an intrauterine regression due to oral deprivation. Robertiello also did not cite his evidence for a healthy character structure in the light of the patient's serious symptoms.

Robertiello happened to meet this patient's mother and found her to be very a kind, warm, sensitive, and loving mother. This characterization of the mother was also the recollection of the patient. Because of the discrepancy between the actual experience with the mother and the patient's symptoms, Robertiello suggested that the patient check with his mother regarding early trauma. He was informed that during the first weeks of life the mother's milk supply had been insufficient.

> He had nearly starved to death without the family or the doctor realizing it. During this period, he had yelled and screamed constantly and literally struggled for his life. . . . Upon unearthing these facts, the patient's enuresis practically ended, and he began to be less and less upset about rejections from his girlfriend. The enuresis had apparently been connected unconsciously with expression of hostility toward his mother [p. 503].

Robertiello concluded: "When the trauma occurs during the first few months and there is a threat of death due to desertion and starvation, the infant adopts certain patterns of reaction to the severe threat that may persist into his adult life and cause severe neurotic symptoms" (p. 503). He suggested that if such circumstances have an accidental cause, unrelated to the overall quality of the early mother–child relationship, then the trauma may act like a "traumatic war neurosis" and respond readily to psychoanalytic work.

Robertiello was addressing an issue that we have noted earlier: the differentiation between trauma related to ongoing pathological projections from the mother into the infant as opposed to trauma from external causes. Robertiello made a further differentiation. Trauma can take place within the context of the earliest mother–infant interaction and have significant consequences for the development of the personality. If this interaction does not, however, involve actual *pathological* maternal projections (i.e., maternal hatreds, rejection, and so forth), the consequences are amenable to therapeutic intervention. It is as if the analytic intervention, identifying and addressing the early trauma, separates the traumatic *experience* from the *person of the mother*, thus restoring the "good mother" to the patient. The patient can then proceed with development, as noted in Robertiello's case.

Melitta Schmideberg

Melitta Schmideberg (1950) gave a similar example of an accidental weaning trauma lived out in adult character. She described a patient who suffered from significant fears of starvation. He was completely occupied with concerns about becoming unemployed, penniless, unloved, and betrayed. He was equally anxious about the availability of the country's food supply. The patient longed for an enduring relationship, which he was unable to achieve. He was frequently depressed and lived in constant fear of imminent catastrophe. The patient's mother was able to connect some of the symptoms with the fact that her son had been abruptly weaned at the age of five months because of an illness that she had at the time. The baby cried ceaselessly for days. Interpretation of this material brought relief. Unfortunately, Schmideberg did not describe the ongoing mother–child relationship within which this "accidental" situation had occurred. She also did not state whether the interpretation led to a lessening of the patient's extensive symptoms and preoccupations.

Schmideberg also offered another reconstruction of an abrupt weaning trauma that she saw as manifesting in the patient's current symptoms and behavior. This female patient had much difficulty sustaining herself during the absence of her husband from home for several weeks. She could not eat, cried often, felt restless, and seemed particularly obsessed with the idea that she should not have others see how distressed she really was. According to her history, her mother had left for several days after weaning the patient. The patient did not appear to react significantly to this situation. In the patient's analytic material, however, it appeared that she had been strongly affected by this experience. Schmideberg interpreted the patient's distress over the husband's absence as a repetition of her weaning experience and her underlying reaction to it. This interpretation brought relief to the patient.

George Engel

George Engel and his colleagues (1985) conducted a detailed, 30-year longitudinal study of "Monica." Monica was born with congenital atresia of the esophagus. She regurgitated her first feedings, choked, and became cyanotic. An emergency esophageal fistula procedure was instituted on the third day of life. She and her family were observed in the hospital and at home from this point through the next 30 years on a regular basis.

For the first two years, Monica's feedings were conducted by having her lie flat on her back with a feeding tube inserted into her stomach. No physical holding of or contact with the baby was made during feedings at any time during the two years of fistula-feeding. Also, at no time did Monica participate in her own feeding. She was, in fact, often fed "while crying, fussing, playing, or sleeping" (p. 43). Pouring the formula for feeding took up a good deal of the attention such that the many persons feeding her during the two years varied considerably in how much they engaged with her during the feeding procedure. The esophageal fistula in the neck drained saliva on a continuous basis; the continuous presence of the tube protruding though the abdominal wall limited the way in which Monica could be held at times other than feeding. Monica's mother, needless to say, suffered great frustration, fear, and depression during much of this time, at one point seriously withdrawing from her child. In turn, Monica became very withdrawn and unresponsive and evidenced failure to thrive for a period of time. When she was two years old, Monica underwent a nine-month hospitalization, at the end of which a functioning esophagus was reconstructed and oral feeding began. Monica spent most of this nine-month period lying flat on her back or propped up in the crib. She was seldom held by the nursing staff.

Monica had no conscious recollections of her fistula-feeding experience other than what she was told by her mother at a later point in time. She was told that she had been fed by a tube through a hole in her stomach (she could identify the abdominal scar) and she still had pictures given to her by her mother of her hospital stay.

Engel and colleagues were subsequently able to observe Monica's feeding behavior of her own infants. The enduring somatic memory of Monica's unusual experience and its living out in the adult character was most remarkable. Monica married and had four children. She bottle-fed each of her infants in a manner similar to the way in which she had been fed, that is, resting on the lap with head supported on the forearm; lying on the lap with no support from arms or hands; or lying alone on a crib or sofa, supported on the side by a pillow with bottle propped. As a child, Monica had fed her dolls *in these exact* positions. As a teenager, she had fed her infant charges in the same positions. In addition, in her play and Rorschach responses as a child, she demonstrated evidence of unconscious residues (memories) of her early feeding behaviors and oral deprivation. For example, in her doll play, evidencing fear of getting wet from the feedings, she put the dolls down and stood at their side while feeding them (the position used by those who regulated the feeding tube during her feeding times). In a play session at 4 years, 8 months of age, she voiced very empathically, "Poor baby, you ain't got a mouth" (p. 75). In one episode at 8 years, 11 months, she noted that the doll was "leaking from the neck" (p. 75). At 10 years, 11 months, she noted, "Hey, I think some of it [the water] is coming through her neck. She didn't wet on me; she drooled on me" (p. 76). In her first Rorschach response at 5 years, 11 months, heads and mouths are missing: for example, Card IV; "That looks like a bird . . . it doesn't have any mouth . . . because they cut it off" (p. 75); Card V: "Like a girl, a half a girl. She has no head" (p. 75); at 7 years, Rorschach Card VI: "That looks like a cat: Whiskers, head, feet, and here's his open tum (tummy)" (p. 75).

Monica attempted to hold her first child on the first day of life but relinquished the position within a couple of minutes, saying that the weight of the baby fatigued her arms. She said of one baby, "When you hold her for a while, she feels like a ton of bricks" (p. 52). She had difficulty maintaining contact with the babies during feeding; she smoked or drank coffee, watched television, or talked to others while feeding. Once the babies were old enough to hold their own bottles, Monica seldom, if ever, held the bottles during their feedings. This despite the fact that as a child she had continuously observed her own mother feed her four younger siblings in a face-to-face, enfolded position and that her husband, mother, and sister all encouraged her to hold her own babies in an enfolded, face-to-face position. She persisted in this feeding mode despite her general character style of "going along with" what others told her and easily identifying with others. The researchers noted: "She repeated her own experience with her babies: body contact was minimal or nonexistent, and the face-to-face distance between mother and baby increased" (p. 46). Even when interacting with her children other than during feeding, Monica also did not hold her babies close to her. She did, however, engage herself more with the babies, maintaining eye contact.

Monica's children were observed in their doll play as they grew. They had experienced both the at-distance holding during feeding from Monica and the usual face-to-face holdings during feeding from their father, Dan. The three eldest daughters were observed on 19 occasions. The eldest daughter, Adele, at 19 months and then again at 26 months fed her doll exactly as her mother had fed her. When the children were older (from four through ten years of age) all four children play-fed their dolls enfolded, as they had been by their father—even when observing their mother holding a baby or doll in her usual across-the-lap position. During one observation, two of the children reported that, while feeding a month-old baby, their mother had cautioned them not to hold the baby's head "too high": she advised putting a pillow under the arm "just in case [your arm] gets tired." Both girls preferred the face-to-face, enfolded method: "It's more comfortable," said one of the girls (p. 85). The authors concluded that

> the demonstrated continuity between Monica's fistula-feeding experience in infancy and her subsequent doll-and baby-feeding behavior supports the notion that feeding experiences in infancy have enduring consequences for maternal behavior in humans. . . .
>
> But for Monica to have to conform with the expectations of others [to hold her babies during feeding] would have involved changing a body behavior that felt "natural" to her. We speculate that such body feelings of naturalness reflect processes embedded deeply in one's very being, the earliest body learning with which psychological development begins. . . . In this sense, Monica's infant-feeding behavior reflects her "natural" self, a genuinely enduring effect [pp. 85–87].

The authors speculate that feeding behavior may be so enduring because it (the symbiotic alimentary relationship between infant and mother) is a special kind of behavior—a biological process "fundamental for the survival not only of the infant, but, in the long run, of the species as well" (p. 86). We demonstrate in this work that a wider range of behavior and experience—which is not necessarily essential for the survival of mankind—creates enduring memories and effects and that such a capacity for enduring memory and effect is a part of the human repertoire.

Theodore Lipin

In line with Terr's (1991) comments that "behavioral memories may recur so physiologically as to represent what seems to be a physical disease" (p. 13), Theodore Lipin (1955) suggested that somatic memories may be a cause of somatic symptoms. He stated that the physical pain and bodily sensations may be actual *memories* expressed somatically rather than in mental form. "To recall in this primitive, preconceptual form of memory, is to re-experience the bodily sensations felt during the original event" (p. 336). Lipin briefly cited a case of a 33-year-old man who experienced the onset of severe back pain during analytic treatment.

> [This man] noted the onset of a constant, dull ache, radiating from the 12th thoracic vertebra to the left lower quadrant of the abdomen, and a similar ache along the anteromedial margin of the left lower rib cage. He could not remember ever having had similar symptoms.
>
> Associations during his analytic hours at this time were related to experiences when he was 3 years old. Gradually, memories of a severe injury to the spine and ribs were retrieved from his amnesia. As fragments of the episode were recovered, the pain lessened and disappeared, only to recur for hours or days in subsequent weeks and months whenever further ramifications of the experience came to light.
>
> Thorough physical examination was normal except for a slight scoliosis and a slight shortening of the right lower extremity. On x-ray films, extensive old fractures of the 12th thoracic vertebra and of the costochondral margins of the 9th, 10th, and 11th ribs were noted [p. 336].

What gradually emerged was a memory from three years of age of a severe injury to the spine and ribs. When this experience was reconstructed, the pain subsided and finally disappeared, recurring only at times when other manifestations of the experience came to light (see Fodor, 1949, and clinical example #5, chapter 9, for evidence of early physical trauma that continues to be lived out as physical symptoms in later life).

RECONSTRUCTION OF INFANT TRAUMA
FROM NONVERBAL BEHAVIOR
WITHIN THE ANALYTIC HOUR AND
WITHIN THE ANALYTIC TRANSFERENCE

Per Roar Anthi

Several analysts have written about the use of nonverbal behavior to address primitive experience (Deutsch, 1947; Braatoy, 1954; McLaughlin, 1989). However, the piece of research that is in tenor and interest most closely aligned with the intent of this work is that of Per Roar Anthi (1983), whose case report is presented in some detail in this section.

Anthi attempted to reconstruct very early experience through manifestations of nonverbal behavior in the analytic hour. Although he doubted that traumas that had occurred in the first six to twelve months of life could be reconstructed, he was interested in the reconstruction of preverbal trauma, how trauma affects the overall adult character, and how it may be manifested in the analytic transference.

Anthi gave a detailed presentation of a single case, that of a 46-year-old man who came to analysis because of marital difficulties, depression, and concern for the future. The patient was preoccupied with a need to be the very best at whatever he did. He was meticulous and would become furious if his wife or children messed up the house. Anthi noticed in the beginning of the treatment that the patient's associations were strained and that he spoke in an explicit and direct manner. His speech was rapid, forced, and loud. After about six months into the treatment, Anthi noted the following:

> Now and then, the patient would stretch his arms and make bending and stretching movements with his head. When I mentioned this to him, he passed it off as being just a habit. Gradually these movements increased in frequency and became more remarkable. I described and commented on this

nonverbal behavior and asked him to observe his sensations connected with these movements. He immediately touched his right neck muscle and said: "I feel some tightening here." I asked for his associations to this tightening, whereupon—more emotionally than usual—he told me that as an infant he had been given physiotherapy because of a defective right neck muscle. . . . Some months after his birth, he was operated on, and from the age of six months until he was three years old, he was given physiotherapy three times a week [pp. 37–38].

Anthi went on to describe his method of detailing particular nonverbal behaviors and eliciting associations to those behaviors.

He could remember nothing of the treatment [his physiotherapy] until one day, when he lay staring up to the ceiling, where the paint was peeling off. After a pause, I broke in and said: "You are staring up at the ceiling. . . . " He confirmed this and said he could imagine different patterns of pictures up there. One reminded him of a lion. Then, all of a sudden, he added that he remembered Mrs. Y (the physiotherapist) had shown him pictures of animals by holding them in different positions in front of him in such a way that he had to move his head into the right position. She had asked repeatedly, "Where is the lion now?" He vaguely began to remember how the physiotherapist and his mother, who assisted in the therapy sessions, used different tricks to get his head into the desired position. He remarked that he hardly had any other choice but to do as the adults ordered him. . . . he had to perform specific movements in the physiotherapy and to twist his head into the right direction. He had to do special exercises and be a good boy [pp. 38–39].

The patient recalled that he had been told that the physiotherapist was a tenacious woman, and he felt this must have impressed him deeply for the two and a half years they worked together. He then began to think of the analysis as drudgery. Anthi connected this to his experience of the drudgery of his physiotherapy. Similarly, the patient's feelings of being tired of the analysis were connected to his feelings of being tired of the physiotherapy.

Following this material, there was a change in his tone. He seemed to become more spontaneous and to have a greater variation of expression and freedom of movement. He recalled that during his military service he had been occupied with marching very correctly and very straight. He also seemed to need to speak in exactly the right manner and have his head in the right place. The patient noted his ongoing preoccupation with getting things into their right places, his body, his head, and his thoughts. He then remembered that children had laughed at him at school for his very erect posture. As this material was addressed and as Anthi worked through significant transference manifestations related to the early trauma, the patient began to feel that he was perceiving things differently. He began to feel an overwhelming need to turn his head in all directions. He began to feel more relaxed in the analysis.

Anthi posed the question as to which aspect of the cumulative traumatic experience of the birth trauma, surgery, and physiotherapy could be reproduced in the transference. He concluded that only the last phase of the physiotherapy would directly manifest itself. He suggested that before that time (when the patient was close to three years of age) the patient's psychic organization, object representations, and level of object relations would not have permitted earliest impressions to register in a manner that could have been reflected in later transference manifestations. Anthi did not address or present reconstruction from dream material other than a transference dream from a later period in development. It is at least possible that if he had used dream material more extensively, the experience of the birth trauma and early surgery might also have been retrieved.

Anthi pointed out that, in the transference, the patient saw him as a dominating and tricky person wishing to control and direct his behavior. This impression represented a combined and distorted image of the mother and physiotherapist in their attempts to correct his head movements. Anthi interpreted to him that the helplessness he had felt as a baby when lying on the table and being drilled was being experienced in the analysis. Anthi was now the one who was tricking and drilling him and forcing him to associate. This understanding was taken up again when the patient's wife left him. The patient imagined himself "tied down to rails waiting for the train to approach" (p. 43). Anthi suggested how bound and helpless he must feel when lying on the couch. He indicated that both in his marriage and in the analysis he felt himself caught in a power struggle with little control.

Anthi concluded that the early object relations involved in the attempts to have the patient get his head in the "correct position" had been introjected and became part of the patient's internalized object relations, self, and body image and contributed to the formation of his specific character structure. Object relations that had "been frozen" in the patient's character, attitude, and muscular armor could be "thawed" and released by a consistent analysis of the transference and the defenses. Anthi hypothesized that the central affective state was one of anxiety and helplessness accompanied by a fear of being manipulated and controlled by others. The patient would defend himself against such feelings by identification with the aggressor. He would become the active controlling person, exerting power over others in his object relations (see Blum, 1987). Particularly prominent issues centered on conflicts over power, control, and feelings of being exploited. The consistent analysis of both the anxieties and the defenses led to a tremendous freeing for this patient. He began to be able to express his feelings verbally and to write poetry, draw, and sculpt. He became more open and empathic, with a capacity for intimacy in his object relations. We see here very striking changes in this patient—a freeing of the personality and an opening up of his previously unknown creative capacities when early trauma and its many derivative manifestations were taken up.

Jonathan Cohen

Jonathan Cohen (1980) provided an excellent example and theoretical discussion of a somatic-behavioral memory of early trauma that evolved into a structured conscious memory as a result of the analytic process. He presented the case of a woman with marked obsessional symptoms and sexual development replete with humiliation and rage. This woman suffered early trauma at 16 months when she was given repeated enemas by her mother (see also clinical example #7, chapter 9). In the overall transference situation, this patient constantly anticipated being overwhelmed on the couch with associative thinking. She felt the analysis to be coercive and intrusive. An important goal of the treatment was to help her to see that *"her repetitive behavior and complaints about the destructiveness of analysis were as precise a statement as she could make of the psychic reality of her traumatic childhood situation"* (p. 423).

Cohen described how this early trauma was worked through behaviorally and in the transference and evolved into conscious memories. During the third year of treatment,

> a recurrent anxiety equivalent was to feel a dread of some-
> thing about to happen, accompanied by chilling and shivering.
> . . . She would feel the room turn suddenly cold, turn away
> from me and curl up, wishing for the end of the session. This
> seemed for many months the only way she could comfort

herself when in this state. Convinced that I would harshly disapprove, she would refrain from getting off the couch to fetch her coat. My interpretation that this must represent a reenactment of an enema scene, despite confirmatory associations, did not diminish the intensity of the reliving. . . . During one session, after we had lived through this experience numerous times together over the preceding months, she was suddenly able to question her perceptions, whereupon she dared to get up and fetch her coat. Returning to the couch feeling more comfortable, she was able to differentiate that it was not the room after all that was cold but her *insides,* and to recognize that this sensation must be in effect a somatic memory of much earlier experiences. . . . Following this session she felt less overwhelmed by this replica, as it began to be structured into various specific memories accompanied by discrete affects, such as of lying on the bathroom floor or being made to sit naked on the potty. There were hints that the primary experience of unpleasure may have been severe chilling following enemas quite early, before she learned the knack of retaining the fluid. It turned out not unexpectedly that her entire manner of entering the office, taking off her coat apprehensively and leaving it on a chair within view of the couch, was a fairly precise replica of a typical early childhood situation in which she would be undressed by mother and led, clothes outside the door, into the cold bathroom for an evacuation. . . .In terms of memory organization: traumatic experiences are reproduced initially in a primitive form, such as a somatic memory, presumably corresponding to their mode of registration. These are neither normal memories nor hysterical conversions, . . . but rather are the pathologic memory forms of otherwise unrecallable experiences. Through multiple repetition and elaboration under analytic influence such registrations are transformed into more nearly normal memory traces, a process of structuralization [pp. 422–423].

Cohen postulated that this "repetition compulsion functioning"— or "replica production" (see also Lipin, 1963) is characterized by "a somatic drive organization, characterized by the absence of normal memory traces and by diffuse affect" [Cohen, 1980, p. 425].

The nature of the experience being remembered and repeated in repetition compulsion functioning was so overwhelming and disorganizing to the child's regulatory capacities and developing sense of self, that it is not registered in recallable form, at the same time that it has created a powerful distorting effect on the child's personality [p. 425].

Cohen's genetic formulation might be complemented by the related hypothesis advanced by Dowling (1982a), who suggested that severe traumatic experiences can overwhelm the infant's growing ability for symbolic representation and thus can lead to regression to an earlier sensorimotor memorial form. Cohen felt that continuous repetition and elaboration within the analytic setting transforms primitive registrations into mentally more organized "successive editions." Eventually, more nearly normal memory traces emerge, thus representing a process of structuralization.

Alvin Frank

Alvin Frank (1969) presented a case involving a child whose passive, primally repressed earliest experience appeared to have become a dominant organizer for the patient's mental life following the trauma. Five-year-old Danny was described by his parents as very unhappy. Psychological testing revealed signs of mild retardation. Danny evidenced poor muscle coordination and severe constriction of movement. His mother had suffered a depression of a month's duration when the child was eight months old. The child subsequently evidenced sadness and poor coordination. In the course of the treatment, Danny began to live out a pervasive theme of being tied up.

> Since the age of four, he had been afraid of robbers that would come in his room at night and tie him up. One fantasy involved being in a boat, "pursued by hundreds of bigger people intent on subduing him and tying him up in retaliation for a theft." . . .
>
> Other fantasies involved having power and physical strength to break loose from bonds. Or, again repeatedly, a burglar climbed on him and pinned him down. His gun went off and shot the burglar, who then left to repeat the same act with his sister; the fantasy ended with the burglar capturing his sister and tying *her* up. Similarly, he was the world's greatest "wild horse catcher." He chased and pursued wild

horses and bulls, and then tied them up as they tried to escape. . . . Toward the end of the second year of analysis, the theme of being tied up began to be lived in the analysis, apparently in response to feelings about separation. . . . even accidental contact precipitated intense hatred: "You hurt me and won't let me go. I hate you, I can't stand it. I am leaving, I have got to get out of here, you are trying to tie me down." Fantasies began to be "lived in" in the analytic situation—so real that he completely ignored reality. When he sat, he felt himself completely immobilized and screamed that he was tied up and could not move. Alternately, he collected large bundles of string in order to surround completely his analyst's office with "ropes." He wove the bushes outside the analyst's first floor window so that they too enclosed the office and "tied up" the analyst [p. 67–68].

To understand this material, the analyst met with the parents to obtain more details of the early history, particularly the period surrounding the mother's depression. The mother recalled that her depression had been precipitated by the sudden accidental death of a very close relative. She had stayed at the relative's mother's home for the following month. During that time, she felt put upon by her infant's demands. She "strapped him into a baby chair and left him each day, and returned only to meet his physical needs, usually feeding him while he remained strapped in the chair" (p. 68). She felt extremely guilty about this and had forgotten this episode until the analyst described the patient's behavior to her.

The patient began to improve after he discussed this episode with his mother and worked it through in the treatment. Interestingly, Danny insisted on hearing about the experience directly from his mother rather than from the analyst. The patient's ability to identify reality and differentiate past from present improved greatly. Frank noted that the tying theme recurred in subsequent analysis of each psychosexual stage: "They were incorporated into the patient's perceptions, fantasies, and reactions in a manner characteristic of each stage" (p. 69). Eventually, the theme of tying stopped completely until it reappeared in a much less intense form during the termination process. One sees here in striking fashion the workings of earliest traumatic experience as an unconscious "template" or "schema" that becomes an organizing force for all later fantasy development (see also Yorke, 1986).

RECONSTRUCTION OF INFANT TRAUMA
FROM DREAM MATERIAL

Four striking cases in the literature of preverbal reconstruction through dreams, one of which involves reconstructions from the first half-year of life, provide evidence of specific structured, unconscious memories of traumas in infancy and early childhood.

Victor Rosen

Victor Rosen's (1955) presentation involved the reconstruction of a trauma that had occurred at age three and a half in a patient who suffered from symptoms of derealization. This case is regularly cited in the literature as a rare example of early trauma reconstruction.

> The patient was a twenty-seven year old professional man who was referred for treatment several weeks after the onset of his acute symptoms. These consisted of a feelings that the world around him and his "being" were "fragmenting". Everything seemed unreal. He struggled with feelings of depression and suicidal fantasies. . . . He was disturbed by bizarre bodily sensations. . . . These consisted of a more or less constant feeling of "fullness in the head" which was accompanied by confusion and despair. "My thoughts feel like cotton wool," . . . He also complained of a "twisting" sensation accompanied by a feeling of "choking." A third group of sensations centered about the lower chest and upper abdomen. The patient described these as "feelings of being transected through the diaphragm—it is as though my diaphragm were stretched unbearably tight and were separating my upper from my lower parts—the feelings get stuck in the middle and will not go up or down." . . .
>
> The illness had appeared suddenly following a broken engagement. . . . For a while he sought relief in a series of promiscuous sexual escapades with casual "pickups" and prostitutes. . . . he developed the . . . fantasy that the girl with whom he had just had intercourse would subsequently be found strangled in her room. The circumstantial evidence would all point to him as the murderer and he would be unable to provide a witness to verify his alibi. . . .

In the second year of therapy the patient began to recall incidents surrounding the discharge of a beloved nurse in his early childhood [between his fourth and fifth year]. . . . He referred to her as "the one witness in my behalf." There were recurrent references to recollections of "some horrifying experience which occurred while I was looking down the long dark hall of our home as a small boy." . . . The patient felt that "he had been a witness to something that changed my life" [pp. 211–214].

The patient was the product of a very conflicted marriage. The mother evidenced both rages and severe depressions and was seductive with her son. In the therapy, the patient continually experienced his analyst as unreal. What the analyst said to him never seemed to him to apply; the patient thought that Rosen had him confused with other patients: "I never know whether something belongs to me or to someone else" (p. 214). At times, he could not distinguish whether an idea which he had presented to the therapist was his own or whether the therapist had presented the idea to him. In the second year of treatment, he began to feel that money he received from work was "make believe," and he appeared to view his treatment in a similar manner. He eventually refused to pay the bill and therapy was terminated until the bill was paid. On his return, the patient reported the following experiences during the month's treatment interruption.

He had suddenly been seized with a wry neck. "It felt as if my head were being twisted from my body." He became quite depressed and had suicidal thoughts. At a party . . . he had done a "headstand" on a dare. While in this upside-down position he had the experience of a sudden clearing of his thoughts, "the world suddenly looked real for a moment." . . . He had been playing with the cords of venetian blinds, the day before he saw me, with the fantasy that they were "hangmen's ropes." He also fantasied that the therapist was giving him "permission" to recall something. He reported the following dream:

"There was a small chest like a trunk lying on the floor. I am trying to pick it up. I seem to have one end of it lifted from the floor. The left side of my body seems paralyzed and I wonder how I can lift the other side from the floor" [p. 215].

In association, the chest reminded the patient that the prior evening he had been looking in the medicine cabinet of his parents' home for some iodine for a cut. His father had never permitted iodine in the house when he was young. There had never been keys available to lock the bathroom door. With the associations and his current behavior, symptoms, and history, Rosen reconstructed the fact that the patient's mother must have made a suicide attempt that the patient had witnessed. Rosen pointed out that the chest/trunk was the chest of the mother. (See Sharpe, 1937, for a discussion of how the body as well as real traumatic experience may be symbolized directly in dreams). He also suggested that

> the neck symptoms, reference to the rope, the headstand and the earlier fantasy of the strangled girl, referred to an attempt by hanging. . . . [the patient] responded with a remarkable and violent flood of affect. He was racked with convulsive sobbing in a most dramatic scene lasting about ten minutes [p. 216].

This session was a "turning point in the treatment" (p. 216), producing a marked diminishment of the derealization symptoms and an increase in the patient's involvement in the treatment. The patient indicated that the interpretation had not restored a lost memory but appeared to have provided him with permission to talk about what he had somehow always known.

The patient discussed the matter with his father. Reluctantly, the father confirmed that the mother had made a number of suicide attempts when the patient was a young child. The one evidenced in the dream occurred when the patient was three years old. The nurse had heard noises in the bathroom and was able to prevent the mother from strangling in the attempt to hang herself. The patient went into the bathroom, but it is unclear exactly what he saw. This nurse, so important to the patient during his early years, was discharged a year later because her presence reminded the mother of the painful incident. Both the father and the nurse, describing the incident as a "bad dream" (p. 216), had treated the incident as something that the patient had imagined. Rosen suggested that the parents' denial of the reality of the experience had prevented the patient from employing the normal processes of repression and working through. The patient was constantly threatened by overwhelming feelings and thus regressed to identification with the suicidal mother. Unbearable affects were lived out as somatic sensations. Rosen inferred from this dramatic reconstruction and its consequences that the importance of distinguishing between reality and the fantasied event would be critical in the case of derealization symptoms.

There may be a lesson here for the analytic process. As it is important for a parent to acknowledge the child's reality (or at least not to deny it), so it is important for the analyst to acknowledge the reality of the patient. The analyst in this case took up the chest-patient configuration in the dream as representing the patient's *actual*, comatose, suicidal mother. Doing so helped the patient to "know" and thus to bear the pain of the reality of his experience. That the family members could not bear such a reality led to the patient's derealization symptoms and regressive identifications with the mother. This raises the interesting question of what happens in the analytic setting when the analyst treats the patient's real experience as if it were a fantasy or as if it did not matter whether it was fantasy or reality. Is such a stance tantamount to the analyst's denial of the patient's reality and might it not be experienced in the patient's *unconscious* as the analyst's unwillingness to know reality and to bear the pain of it? If the analyst cannot bear painful reality, then neither can the patient, and the analyst cannot help the patient to grow from the pain of his experience. Thus, the patient might continue in a state of "derealization" metaphorically if not in actuality.

William Niederland

William Niederland (1965) discussed the specific state of the ego in relation to its perceptual and sensory functioning at the time of a trauma and the effects of the ego's state on the recovery of repressed memories. He illustrated the role of auditory and visual perception (i.e., dreams as a form of thinking in pictures) in recovering the particular ego states evident at the time of the trauma, thus assisting in the reconstruction of earliest traumatic experience.

Niederland's case represents a reconstruction from a dream involving a trauma from the patient's first year of life. The patient was a schizophrenic, 19-year-old man who dressed in layer upon layer of clothes regardless of the weather. The source of this behavior in the patient's infancy became clear through the following dream in the third year of treatment.

> *I was near or at the North Pole in an arctic region. It was night and I was lying on an ice block or a refrigerator which was my bed or something. I was surrounded by ice and snow and it was totally dark. The night remained icy cold and dark for a long, long time as*

if it would never end. Finally the dawn came and some people were walking in and out of the room where I was lying on the refrigerator, which was also my bed [p. 567].

There were no associations to the dream. Niederland thought that the patient might be referring to an actual experience because the patient had emphasized the refrigerator by mentioning it twice and the refrigerator was described as the patient's bed (see Greenacre's, 1956, criteria for extrapolating real experience). He asked the patient if he had ever been frozen in a manner similar to the scene in the dream. The patient appeared at the next session in a state of high excitement. He had discussed the matter with his parents, and they expressed great astonishment. They told him that when he was less than a year old, they had "thawed him out of his urine, feces and vomitus" (Niederland, 1965, p. 568). The window of his room had mistakenly been left partially open on an extremely cold winter night. On the pediatrician's advice, the parents had ignored his cries. He developed pneumonia, had to be hospitalized, and remained very ill for a long time.

The dream was a turning point both in the treatment and in the patient's life. He recovered with what appears to have been a long-term favorable outcome (Niederland did not specify further details of the treatment). Niederland suggested that the revival of the real, traumatic experience through a dream was made possible by the slow change in the ego state following a long analytic treatment: "Imperceptibly the 'frozen' state of the ego had altered under the influence of the ongoing therapeutic process which made it accessible to a gradual 'thaw' long before the emergence of the dream" (p. 569). (See clinical examples #6 and #8, chapter 9, for similar revivals of trauma in dreams following a change of ego state.)

Frank (1969) remarked about this case of passive primal repression:

This patient could not forget his terrible childhood experience. As a matter of fact, without remembering it, he continued to "dress for the occasion." Not until a [verbal] memory was provided through Niederland's reconstruction could the patient realize that he was reacting to the past rather than the present. At this point he could leave the past and its awful consequences [p. 56].

Niederland noted that memories of a fragmentary type usually derive from childhood experiences and are taken in visually. He suggested that the process of analytic free association, involving fragmented and disconnected verbal productions, is well suited to the emergence of visual memories and experiences. The dream itself, and the process of acquiring free associations to each element of the dream in particular, may be especially suited to the task of retrieval of infantile experience.

Ella Sharpe

Ella Sharpe (1937) believed that dreams carry real childhood experiences and that they are very important vehicles for reconstructing earliest trauma. Perhaps her most poignant example was the following.

> I said goody-bye to G. and sent her away and then I turned to you to embrace you (i.e. the analyst) and said good-bye. But I was standing on stilts and my dilemma was that if I let go [of] my hand on the stilts to bend forward to kiss you it would mean my legs would give way and I should fall [p. 73].

From the associations (which Sharpe did not describe), she made the interpretation that the analyst stood for the patient as a child, and the patient in the dream represented her grandfather. The patient had been told, but had no memory, of an incident that occurred when she was two years of age. The grandfather was bending down to kiss the child when he collapsed from a seizure of which he died. Sharpe said that the dream gave the first clue to the repeated reenactments over the course of a long analysis that had not been understood and that involved anxieties related to the loss through death of a good real object.

Sidney Pulver

Sidney Pulver (1987) wrote that memories of unconscious early childhood experiences of a traumatic (as well as of a nontraumatic) kind may appear in the manifest content of a dream without significant distortion. He noted as well a conclusion drawn here: given the paucity of reported cases in the literature, such traumas are rarely detected and analyzed. Pulver pointed out that traumatic childhood experiences never serve as "indifferent" day residue of the dream and often function, as we have noted, as "organizers for constellations of . . . fantasies related to important emotional conflicts" (p. 111). Pulver reported the following case example:

A patient had been reading an article on the historical background of surgery before the advent of anesthesia and of some of the experiences of the patients undergoing such procedures. The night of the reading she dreamt the following:

> *She was lying on a bed in a sparsely furnished room. Two women who were with her began to leave, through what was either a door or an opening in the wall. . . . She half-awoke, and, in the hypno-pompic state which immediately followed, felt her head turned sharply to the left by an external, viselike grip. She then heard loud music and simultaneously experienced a loud buzzing noise which seemed to fill her head. The noise lasted only a short time, and she then awoke completely. During the entire hypnopompic experience she felt overwhelming anxiety and helplessness* [p. 113].

Neither the analyst nor the patient could make sense of this dream, although it was clear that the day residue was the reading of the anesthesia article. Pulver does not seem to have asked for specific associations nor to have questioned what the patient's experiences with anesthesia, surgery, or medical procedures were. Pulver knew from other contexts that as an infant (the patient thought before four months of age) the patient had undergone radiation treatments to her throat for thymus enlargement. Later in the analysis, the patient wondered if her early radiation treatments had had any enduring psychological effects. Pulver reports that he was noncommittal about this since he thought that the infant experience had occurred too early to be meaningful. The patient remained interested and contacted the physician who administered the treatments, from whom she learned the following:

> She had had six irradiation treatments . . . between ages six and fourteen months. During the procedure she was immobilized, wrapped in a sheet. Her father held her head turned firmly to the left while her mother, unable to stand her distress, waited in the adjoining room and played phonograph music loudly to drown out her cries. All the details of the manifest dream (the women leaving, her indistinct perception of the door, the positioning of her head by an external force, the buzzing noise of the X-ray machine, and the music) were confirmed by this description. It seems reasonable to infer that as an infant she experienced the same feelings of panic and helplessness she felt in the hypnopompic state immediately following the dream.

The recovery of this traumatic experience, while not pivotal, was of therapeutic value. . . . For as long as she could remember, the patient felt moderate anxiety accompanied by fantasies of pain and mutilation preceding visits to physicians. . . . On several occasions it increased to an overwhelming degree, and she felt immobile, helpless, and panicky. When this happened her fantasies of mutilation disappeared, and she had no thoughts of any kind except a frightening awareness that she had no idea of what she was anxious about. Since the recovery of the traumatic experience, this new type of anxiety has stopped, and her usual anxiety before visiting physicians has been much less intense [pp. 113–115].

Miriam Williams

Miriam Williams (1987) described her analysis of a 40-year-old man who had been sexually molested at the age of two. He came to analysis with a great deal of guilt, a pervasive sense of dirtiness, and a fear of seeking out friends because he felt "soiled" and had symptoms of depression and insomnia. The patient's parents had divorced when he was two years old. The mother left him right after the divorce to go on a trip of many months. The patient was cared for by an elderly aunt and uncle, a strict nurse, and male servant hired by the relatives. From the dream material, exact details of the seduction by a servant, including the servant's taking the boy to a dilapidated house, the fact that the event occurred a number of times, and that the patient had witnessed other people's sexual activities in the house, were reconstructed. This case is interesting in that this was the second analysis of this particular patient. The patient reported that his first analyst had reconstructed the molestation from several screen memories and repetitive dreams. The analyst took this up with the patient as a homosexual trauma and did not pursue the subject further. Williams, however, pursued the matter at great length through the patient's repetitive, at times violent, dreams. Williams reported the following dream fragments among several in her very detailed case study:

> He came to a building that is dilapidated and very dirty. He enters a room. There are several beds, all dirty and disheveled. The

bathroom door is open; the toilet is filthy and overflowing. Large pieces of feces, like big salami sausages, float on the top. . . .

The patient comes to some dirty and ugly buildings. [He stressed that the dirty buildings were perceived suddenly in the dream.] . . . He goes in and enters a bedroom with many beds. Some are occupied. The patient finds himself in bed, and a man joins him, lying against his back. The man does something to the patient's anus, producing great anxiety in him, both within the dream and as Mr. B recounted it [pp. 150-151]

Mr. B expressed surprise that I treated it [the molestation] as the most crucial experience in his early childhood. In this connection, the patient mentioned that relatives had told him how he had followed Joseph [the servant] around everywhere.

I explained in detail to the patient how crucial, in my perception, the relationship to Joseph had been after the break-up of his parents' marriage and during his mother's long absence and that, furthermore, I suspected Joseph had seduced and molested him, leading to serious consequences in the patient's life, as the message of the violent and endlessly repetitive dreams revealed. On many occasions I explained that these dreams have preserved experiences and impressions of an indelible nature. . . .

At first, my emphasis on the meaning of the seduction and early childhood experience was met with disbelief and abhorrence. The patient challenged me . . . about the verity of such assumptions. He wondered repeatedly why his first analyst had not given it the same significance. . . .

Only gradually and with considerable trepidation did the patient begin to perceive the dreams as a key to his deep disturbance. He came to understand the delicate psychic equilibrium that exists in the development of a two-year-old child and the profound impact of his seduction by Joseph. He accepted that conscious memories from that age may only be fragmentary at best, and that sexual events were almost never remembered later on. A further reconstruction added the meaning of the dilapidated houses in the dreams. It could be reconstructed with reasonable certainty that Joseph took the boy to his home or homes—in the dreams, to the dilapidated buildings—and seduced the child there, perhaps exposing his young charge to other people's sexual activities. When this material was so interpreted by me, the patient, who until then was quiet, said spontaneously as though in a trance, "I didn't go there once, but many times" [pp. 152–153].

This material was crucial to the involvement of the patient in the analysis. Williams stated in regard to reconstructing early traumatic experience that often the only material that comes from dreams is material for which there is seldom day residue. One assumes that the "endless continuity of dreams" acts as the day residue and the "stimulus for supplying material for the subsequent dreams as if they were running on a conveyor belt" (p. 146).

SUMMARY

The traumas reported in the foregoing case reports seem like little dramas or short stories that are encapsulated in the behaviors, symptoms, fantasies, transference manifestations, and dreams of these patients. It is as if all modes of human expression are used to demonstrate to the world where the pain once lay. The modes of expression are many: an obsession about the country's food supply; a manner of draping one's coat across a chair; a physical pain in one's back; the way one holds one's babies. In retrospect, it appears difficult not to miss it—if only one knew when and how and where to look. The analytic process, it appears, is very important as a catalyst for the recognition and metabolization of early trauma. The presence of another who is willing to consider the whole of a person's life and to understand it at its very depth seems to help the patient to "mentalize" the terrible pain—to bring it to a form in which it can be thought about, talked about, and mentally borne. Once it is borne, a turning point seems to occur in the treatment—symptoms are alleviated, and real life begins.

8
Psychoanalytic Dream Theory

P sychoanalysis as we know it began with Freud's (1900) discovery of dream analysis. Dreams were, and I believe still remain, "the royal road to knowledge of the unconscious activities of the mind" (p. 608). Many of Freud's specific theories regarding dream formation and dream interpretation required considerable revision, which they have undergone by contemporary dream researchers as well as by clinicians. Nevertheless, Freud's basic understanding of the power of the unconscious mind to affect feeling, motivation, and action is one of the pivotal human discoveries of the nineteenth century.

Here we will review very briefly Freud's dream theory. Then we will turn to more contemporary theorists for a brief overview of those who have addressed aspects of dream functioning specifically relevant to the subjects of this work and to the manner in which dreams are taken up in the clinical examples presented in the following chapter. Four frames of reference emerge (1) the dream as it represents the individual's current state of mind and internal object world; (2) the dream as it represents real experience, including earliest experience; (3) the dream as it represents traumatic experience; and (4) the dream as it has adaptive and problem-solving functions. We will also cite some of the work of experimental dream researchers as well as the tachistoscopic studies of Otto Pötzl (1917), whose study we include for its contribution to the hypothesis that prenatal and neonatal experience may be registered in dreams.

FREUD'S DREAM THEORY

Freud (1900) postulated that the primary function of dreams was to provide discharge or gratification for impulses or wishes—usually infantile in nature and unacceptable to the conscious mind—and to do so in such a way that the process did not disturb sleep. During sleep, a person regresses to early developmental forms of drive discharge, such as hallucinatory wish fulfillment. Freud believed that if the forbidden infantile wishes were evident in the content of the dream, the material would be so distressing it would wake up the dreamer. Therefore he postulated a censor that disguised the dream wish and therefore preserved sleep.

In line with the wish-fulfillment function of the dream, Freud proposed that primary-process thinking operates in dream mentation. An unconscious form of thinking, primary process is ruled by the pleasure principle. Thus, wants are immediately gratified without regard to reality; rules of logic and syntax do not apply; and stable categories of time, place, and person are nonexistent.

Freud proposed several components to the process by which unconscious thoughts and feelings are transformed into a dream. He called this process the "dream work." A "day residue" instigates the dream. The day residue is an experience, thought, feeling, or memory, usually of the preceding day, which may be trivial or emotionally significant (although a trivial element always stands for an emotionally significant one). The day residue makes contact with both current and past emotionally significant events and feelings, awakening an unconscious infantile wish. The wish is then transferred onto the day residue, which, particularly if it is benign, can escape the censor and take form in the dream.

The dream is represented by its manifest content, by a visual scene or series of scenes or impressions. The latent dream thoughts are thoughts that enter into and make up the dream and reflect the underlying motivations and conflicts of the manifest content. To unravel the latent meaning from the manifest content, one must use free association. One of Freud's essential technical discoveries was that one had to ascertain the associations to *each component* of the dream, rather than to the dream as a whole, in order to unravel its underlying meaning (which Freud took at the time to be the dream wish). It is the associations to each element in the dream, as well as the associations within the hour itself, that unravel the distortion and "crack the dream code." Many contemporary clinicians would no longer consider the central meaning of each dream to be an infantile wish. Freud's specification, however, of the need for detailed associations to each dream element (as well as associations from the hour as a whole) remains of great importance, especially when early trauma is involved. As Greenacre (1952), Murphy (1958), Niederland (1965), and Terr (1988) have pointed out, early trauma may be stored in visual form. Thus, these experiences may be most readily ascertained through associations to the visual elements of the manifest dream.

The picture arrived at in the manifest content is accomplished through several mechanisms of the dream work that, according to Freud, distort the latent dream thoughts. These mechanisms are part of primary-process thinking. One mechanism is *condensation*, a fusing together of two or more images and is responsible for the fact that the manifest dream has a smaller content than the latent dream thoughts. Thus, for example, if one were trying to say that one's spouse and one's father have very similar personalities, that idea might be expressed in the manifest content of the dream by a fused figure: the face of the spouse, say, with the hair and dress characteristic of the father.

[Another mechanism, *displacement*, is the transfer of one idea or image to another. With displacement, one can replace people, locations, objects, or feelings, substituting one for the other or parts for the whole.] Thus one of my patients who was severely traumatized by the death of her mother when the patient was a toddler expressed the consequences of this experience for her psyche by a picture of a living room wall with a gaping hole in it. Two workmen were trying to figure out how to repair the hole. The large, empty wound left in her from such an early loss was "displaced" onto the picture of the wall with the hole. She and I were displaced onto the two workmen attempting to figure out how to repair such an early loss.

Means of representation speaks to the fact that what is represented in a dream must appear in pictorial form. It has to be expressed in such a way as to be visualized. For example, to make a statement in pictorial form regarding something that happened a long time ago people may appear at a great distance and seem very tiny. Or the fact that something happened in childhood may be expressed by a little person sitting at a very large table.

Symbolization involves "a universal primal language representing an association between ideas" (Altman, 1969, p. 17). These ideas have in common what the infantile unconscious mind would consider similar (often forms, shapes, and sizes). In dreams, the referents for symbols are limited to "the basic and universal preoccupations of children: birth, death, the body and its functions, sexual organs, people, especially members of the family" (p. 17). Birth and pregnancy may be represented by immersion in water. A house with windows and doors may be the body orifices. Caves may be the womb, and so on. Finally, *secondary revision* involves the filling in of gaps following waking to make the dream appear more intelligible.

Freud (1900) saw the entire process of dream formation as an attempt to make contact with early infantile experience, needs, and wishes.

If we now bear in mind how great a part is played in the dream-thoughts by infantile experiences or by fantasies based upon them, how frequently portions of them re-emerge in the dream-content and how often the dream-wishes themselves are derived from them, we cannot dismiss the probability that in dreams too the transformation of thoughts into visual images may be in part the result of the attraction which memories couched in visual form and eager for revival, bring to bear upon thoughts cut off from consciousness and struggling to find expression. On this view, a dream might be described as a *substitute for an infantile scene modified by being transferred onto a recent experience*. The infantile scene is unable to bring about its own revival and has to be content with returning as a dream [p. 546].

Freud initially saw all dreams, including anxiety dreams and dreams with very unpleasant content, including punishment dreams, as representing wish fulfillment in terms of the latent dream thoughts. He staunchly maintained this view until he saw World War I veterans suffering from severe posttraumatic stress. The dreams these veterans were having could not have been a result of wish fulfillment and could not be conceptualized as regulated by the pleasure principle inasmuch as the dreams were detailed reenactments of traumas that the veterans had experienced in the war scene (see Lansky, 1991, for a different view). Freud (1920a) revised his theory, but only somewhat, stating that traumatic dreams represented attempts to master trauma in a retrospective manner. Freud postulated that mastery of trauma represented an earlier and more fundamental function of the mind than the wish-fulfillment function.

Freud's understanding of dreams was thought to be so complete at the time that clinicians and researchers were slow to revise his original views. In addition, the psychoanalytic community gradually moved away from a focus upon the unconscious as revealed in the dream to the study of the ego and the mechanisms of defense. Interestingly, analysts ranging from Sharpe (1937) to Sloane (1979) and Meltzer (1984) have protested this trend and offered various explanations, generally centered on defensive processes in the analyst, to account for it. Greenson (1970) noted that fewer analysts had their dreams systematically investigated in their own training analyses. The manifest content of dreams became prominent, and attempts to elicit detailed associations to the dream elements and to provide interpretations that included a synthesis of the whole dream diminished. Thus, dreams came to be considered no more important than any other type of communication in the analytic hour (see Altman, 1969, and Greenson, 1970, for a discussion of this point of view). In the 1950s the work of laboratory dream researchers sparked a renewed interest in dreams, but from the perspective of the physiology of dreaming. The results of their efforts directly challenged some of Freud's assumptions about the basis of dream formation.

DREAM LABORATORY RESEARCH

Eugene Aserinsky, Nathan Kleitman, and William Dement: REM Sleep

In their studies of electroencephalographic changes of sleeping subjects, Eugene Aserinsky and Nathan Kleitman (1953) and William Dement (1955) showed a connection between REM sleep activity and dreaming. Their studies demonstrated that REM sleep occurs regularly throughout the night. It produces a pattern of four or five dreams per night on a regular basis. Dreaming is a universal phenomenon, regardless of recall. Their results suggest that dreaming is essential to human functioning (see also Roffwarg et al., 1966). It has an integrative and adaptive significance that is more fundamental than that of infantile wish fulfillment or drive discharge. The function of dreaming as being to preserve sleep was challenged by these studies. A more accurate description would be that "sleep is the guardian of dreams" (Greenson, 1970, p. 521).

J. Allan Hobson and Robert McCarley: The Neurochemistry of the Dream State

J. Allan Hobson and Robert McCarley (cited in Begley, 1989) studied the neurochemical functioning of the brain in the sleep state. They hypothesized that dreams are generated in the brainstem. Two different neurons are involved in the function of sleep: one uses acetylcholine, which is active during REM sleep; the other uses norepinephrine and serotonin, available in non-REM states. When the latter are inactive, acetylcholine neurons generate a dream by sending electrical signals to the cortex. The cortex, the center of complex thought as well as of vision, makes use of the electrical signals to create a visual story. Memories from the past are used to create the story and appear as if they are happening in the present. Hobson

(1988) emphasizes that the brain is engaged in making meaning of experience. From his activation-synthesis view of brain functioning, he considers the brain to be "inexorably bent upon the quest for meaning" (p. 15): "the human brain-mind . . . does its best to attribute meaning to the internally generated signals. It is this synthetic effort that gives our dreams their impressive thematic coherence" (pp. 212–214). Dispensing with idea of a dream censor, Hobson argues that the brain-mind works metaphorically; thus dreams can be interpreted in this light. He suggests that since we dream in metaphors, human knowledge may be processed similarly (cited in Begley, 1989). That the dream works with remote experience, meaning, and metaphor is very significant. It suggests that dream analysis has the potential to reveal the unconscious meaning of one's earliest experience in metaphorical terms.

Hobson's clinical use of the far-reaching potentiality of the dream is limited, however. He makes use of the dream in its most transparent and unedited form. No distortion is considered important, and no distinction exists between manifest and latent content. He provides examples of the manifest content of dreams in which meaning is interpreted at the most superficial manifest level. For example, Hobson dreamed he saw Mozart play at a museum concert and was eager to tell his wife. Hobson interpreted this to mean that he would very much like to see Mozart play at the museum and would also enjoy his wife's getting credit for arranging such a feat. It appears that, although Hobson understands the functioning of the *brain* in sleep states, in his approach to dream *analysis*, he has underestimated the depth and complexity of the unconscious mind and its contributions to true human meaning. He does, however, allow that more profound unconscious understanding can be derived from dreams. He just does not feel it is necessary to pursue it. His approach to dream interpretation precludes the possibility of retrieving early experience to bring alive for the patient and the analyst an understanding of current personality.

CLINICAL CONTRIBUTIONS

Analysts and psychoanalytic psychologists have made many valuable contributions to the revision and expansion of Freud's dream theory. According to these authors, dreams can reveal much more than a forbidden wish, the mechanisms of dream formation providing only attempts to disguise. Dreams can illuminate one's internal world, ones's self-representations; they can portray real and traumatic experience and explicate the range of efforts made by a person to solve essential human dilemmas in facing life's vicissitudes.

In his theoretical work on dream formation, Richard Jones (1970) attempted to recast some of Freud's more restrictive theories. For example, Jones addressed Freud's wish-fulfillment hypothesis and his concept of the distorting function of the "dream work." Jones noted that REM sleep may be conducive to the stimulation of unconscious wishes. Thus, repressed wishes may be *incorporated* into dreams. REM-state research has made it clear that repressed wishes do not *initiate* dreams, however, as was Freud's view. Jones suggested that the "dream work" is really a transformative process rather than a process that only distorts for defensive purposes (i.e., for purposes of disguise). According to Jones, dreaming involves a *transformation* of both recent and past mental content into new forms. A disguise may be one form, but a revelation may be another. Niederland's (1965) case of a schizophrenic young man may be taken as an example of the latter possibility. The dream elements include the patient's lying on an ice block that serves as a bed at the North Pole. The ice block and the North Pole provide the most graphic *depiction*, not disguise, of this patient's actual frozen experience in infancy. They helped to reveal rather than distort his early trauma.

Dreams as Revelatory of the State of the Mind and the Internal World

According to a number of analysts, dreams also present graphic portrayals of one's state of mind, one's internal world. Dreams provide us with the most "condensed, vivid and complex specimens of the conflictual intrapsychic, intrasystemic, as well as the interpersonal experiences in any given individual" (Khan, 1976, p. 328). I believe that Fairbairn and Rycroft captured the essence of the dream most succinctly: Dreams are "dramatizations or 'shorts' (in the cinemato-graphic sense) of situations existing in inner reality" (Fairbairn, 1952, p. 99); the dream reveals in pictorial form "the total psychological state of affairs existing at the time the dream was dreamt" (Rycroft, 1979, p. 11). This current "total psychological state of affairs" includes the continued mental presence in adult life of earliest experience. Rycroft in particular emphasized that the dream requires some distortion in order to represent thoughts in pictorial form. It is the necessity to represent thought in visual imagery as opposed to the need for disguise, that he sees as accounting for the fact of distortion in dreams.

Mancia (1988) also saw the dream as furnishing a general "organization of the internal world with the function of representing . . . the internal objects" (p. 419). According to Mancia, dream work transforms emotional experience into knowledge, a view held by Bion (1962) and Meltzer (1984). Wrote Mancia:

> During the course of the process of analysis, dreams become a newspaper that has to tell the truth every night without fear, revealing moment by moment the state of our government— i.e., the state of our minds—represented by the internal world peopled with internal objects with their own values and relations and their own economics and politics [p. 422].

According to Bail (1993, personal communication), dream analysis, by bringing to the individual an understanding of the deepest layers of the unconscious mind, promotes the growth of the mind itself and of the personality.

Kohut and Atwood and Stolorow further developed the idea of the revelatory aspect of dreams. Kohut (1977) saw the "self-state dream" as portraying in its manifest content the dreamer's current psychological state, primarily "the dreamer's dread vis-à-vis some uncontrollable tension-increase or his dread of the dissolution of the self" (p. 109). Atwood and Stolorow (1984) see another purpose to the self-state dream:

> The dream symbols bring the state of the self into focal awareness with a feeling of conviction and reality that can only accompany sensory perceptions. The dream images . . . both encapsulate the danger to the self and reflect a concretizing effort at self-restoration [pp. 104–105].

They propose that concrete symbolization in dreams serves an extremely important purpose:

> The dream affirms and solidifies the nuclear organizing structures of the dreamer's subjective life. Dreams . . . are the *guardians of psychological structure*, and they fulfill this vital purpose by means of concrete symbolization [p. 103].

Dreams as They Represent Real Experience

Ella Sharpe (1937) emphasized the role of actual experience in dreams as opposed to just forbidden wishes.

> Dreams should be considered as an individual psychical product from a storehouse of specific experience, which

indeed the dreamer may in consciousness neither remember nor know that he knows. The material composing the latent content of a dream is derived from *experience* of some kind. All intuitive knowledge is experienced knowledge [pp. 14–15].

She included in her definition of "experience" occurrences that had happened in the past, and the affective states and body sensations accompanying these occurrences. She also saw dreams as representing the body ego from the earliest years. Leo Rangell (1987) agrees with her. For him also, dreams are a significant source of data for reconstructive work, especially because of the capacity of dreams to address the preverbal period, including early sensory memories. Similarly, Clifford Scott (1975) noted the important function of dreams in allowing the past to emerge, including memories from the infantile body. He stated of dreams in the latter stages of analysis: "Patients often seem to come close to finding in a dream a better understanding of the story of their lives than of anything they have ever understood before" (p. 325).

Stanley Palombo (1978) addressed the continuous role of actual experience in dream formation. He hypothesized that dreaming serves an important function for the memory cycle in which new experiential information is introduced into the permanent memory structure:

The most striking hypothesis of the memory-cycle model is that the critical step in the sequence—the step which matches representations of new experiences with the representations of closely related experiences of the past—takes place during dreaming [p. 13].

Dreams as They Represent Early Traumatic Experience

Ferenczi (1931) suggested that dreams involve mastery of traumatic memories as one of their primary functions. He noted that the state of sleep is conducive to the "the return of unmastered traumatic sensory impressions, which struggle for solution" (p. 240). His understanding of this function of the dream is particularly evident in the clinical examples presented in this book. Sharpe (1937) saw dreams as particularly useful in retrieving traumatic experiences in infancy. Thomas French (1970) noted that the original response to a traumatic memory becomes a pattern of reaction that can be stimulated by situations only somewhat similar. These patterns are resistant to modifications from later experience. They are repeated in dreams and become the focus of the dream's problem-solving efforts. Dreams are not merely wish fulfillment, but they describe present realities that are disturbing to us.

Angel Garma (1946) viewed traumatic situations as the instigators of dreams, a view quite different from Freud's idea that infantile wishes are dream generators. Traumatic situations include traumatic experiences from childhood. Garma's position was that trauma contributes to all dreams. "In the interpretation of dreams, an attempt should always be made to find the basic traumatic situation" (p. 137). Garma saw the dream wish as an attempt to overcome the "psychic displeasure" brought about by that which is traumatic to us.

Dreams following a trauma are significant because they include not only the reality of the traumatic experience, but also the important fantasies connected to it (De Saussure, 1982). Dreams, then, can help us to see in what particular ways the experience was traumatic for a person. Janice De Saussure touched here on how the dream has the potential to tell us the unconscious meaning of a trauma to a person. She also noted that a traumatic dream (i.e., a repetition of a terrifying event in a dream) can constitute a trauma in itself.

Dowling (1982a) discussed a type of prerepresentational childhood traumatic dream involving "image-less terror and diffuse feelings of loss and emptiness" (p. 165). The imageless-terror dream represents, in Dowling's view, experiences and feelings from *before* the mental structure became sufficiently developed to form a representational dream, that is, two years of age and younger. This type of dream makes use of preprimary-process mentation, largely in the form of sensorimotor organization and mental experience similar to the Lewin (1946) and Isakower (1938) phenomena.

Notwithstanding Dowling's assertion that the unconscious mind is not sufficiently structured prior to 18 months to form a representational dream, Milton Erickson (1941) reported two dreams with distinctly identifiable psychic and affective content from a child first at eight months of age and then at 13 months. This child clearly was replaying in her dreams a happy memory of an ongoing nighttime play sequence with her father. Each night, she would laugh during their game and move her head and legs in certain positions accompanying the laugh. When the father was absent one evening when she was eight months old, after many months of this pleasant ritual, the child was found dreaming, moving her head and limbs and merrily laughing in the identical manner to her usual game with father. This was repeated at 13 months.

Melvin Lansky (1991) addressed the role of shame and dissociation in the instigation of posttraumatic dreams. Lansky, considering current day residue in dealing with posttraumatic dreams, suggested that even posttraumatic dreams have meaning in terms of the current life of the person and are not just a "replay" of past trauma. The meaning may encompass intense feelings of shame that took place during the dream day (thus serving as the day residue) and that are then transformed into fear in the dream and linked to the posttraumatic situation. The posttraumatic situation can serve as a screen for many other traumas, including infantile ones. "The posttraumatic nightmare, however disturbing, screens out experiences of shame, often from a lifetime of traumata" (p. 487).

Dreams as They Represent Problem-Solving and Adaptive Functions

Several writers have described dreams as having adaptive and problem-solving functions.

A wish may, for example, be *one solution* to a problem with which a patient is struggling, but dreams can portray *a range* of both successful and unsuccessful unconscious efforts to deal with emotionally significant issues, going beyond efforts to disguise unacceptable impulses (Greenberg and Pearlman, 1975).

Frederick Weiss (1964) commented on the depth of human meaning evident in dreams:

> The most powerful motivations for dreams, however, are feelings of frustration and guilt—not the frustration of neurotic needs for power in "love" or the neurotic guilt associated with falling short of perfectionist standards. I am speaking here of feelings of existential frustration about unlived life and of existential guilt about unrealized potentials in ourselves. Repetitive dreams are not caused by the work of a fatalistic repetition compulsion. Instead, they repeatedly challenge the dreamer with the vital problems in his life until these are confronted and solved [p. 23].

Weiss noted the creative function of dreams. The dream is, he wrote, "a creative act in which the dreamer's striving, conflicts and attempts at solution are crystallized. The past enters the dream as a dynamic symbol of the present" (p. 25).

Thomas French and Erica Fromm (1964) proposed a problem-solving theory of dream motivation. They saw the central purpose of dreams as an attempt to find a solution to an interpersonal (rather than a strictly intrapsychic) problem. Earlier, similar problems emerge around the central problem. French and Fromm's methods are cognitively oriented in their focus on the adaptive and problem-solving nature of dreams to deal with past or present unresolved conflicts.

For Edward Tauber and Maurice Green (1959), "the dream appears to express man's way of organizing life experience and his inner reflection of himself" (pp. 170–171). They regarded the dream as a "metaphysical statement of a problem-solving issue, as an attempt to say something about one's way of life and about one's conception of one's self as a human being" (p. 171). They considered the impulse-discharge function of the dream as too limiting; the interpretation of dreams should always "aim to expand the meaning of the dreamer's life (p.177). . . . Can the core problem, the central focus or false solution of this man's existence, be identified?" (p. 179). A similar conclusion was drawn by Greenberg and Pearlman (1980), who concluded that dreams are dynamic because they are

> part of a struggle to make emotional sense of our experiences. . . . It seems to be a process in which the dreamer struggles to make sense of and thereby master his life experiences, while maintaining a continuing sense of himself in relation to the world. It begins with high levels of REM sleep at birth and persists throughout life. It shows evidence of both successes and of failure and is an accurate portrayal of life as the dreamer experiences it [pp. 94–95].

OTTO PÖTZL'S DREAM EXPERIMENTS

Although the laboratory research of Otto Pötzl (1917) is not germane to dream theory per se, the results of his experiments imply the possibility that infant experience in stored and retained in REM states. His studies demonstrated that experiential data may be integrated into memory storage without the requirement of a developed mental structure (e.g., conscious secondary-process thinking) for its processing.

Pötzl, beginning in 1917, conducted experiments demonstrating that visual stimuli presented tachistoscopically for a hundredth of a second underwent perceptual registration and transformation into a memory trace. Subjects in this experiment were shown tachistoscopic pictures and then asked to record their dreams the night of the experiment. Parts of the stimulus pictures that were *not* consciously perceived appeared in the manifest content of the subjects' dream material. Interestingly, parts of the pictures that were consciously perceived were *excluded* from the dreams. Pötzl's findings provided evidence that there is "unconscious cognition without awareness" (Fisher, 1960, p. 95). The memory images of the unconsciously registered elements in Pötzl's studies were either *photographic duplications* of part of the originally exposed stimulus picture or the stimulus picture *transformed* and distorted in a manner quite similar to the primary-process mechanisms of the dream work.

I believe that the findings of this early dream research are extremely important. If we have unconscious cognition and this cognition can be stored in our dreams, then we truly have a world of knowledge *derived from unconscious perceptions* that are preserved. Most important for our purposes is that Pötzl's results may apply to infants—even newborns, even fetuses; REM sleep begins in utero (Roffwarg et al., 1966). Recall Milton Erickson's (1941) report on the occurrence of a dream with definite psychic and affective content in a baby as young as eight months of age. If subliminal perceptions register in unconscious dream content, then perceptions from the first months and year of life, and perhaps even from the womb, could be registered in the mind in the subliminal manner found in Pötzl's work. Because this type of subliminal registration bypasses secondary-process thinking, the lack of a developed mental structure in the infant or fetus would not by necessity preclude registration and storage of experience in infant dreams. If the perceptions or experiences are of a traumatic kind, they may be *especially likely* to be registered and stored in dreams and then reappear through time in the course of adult analyses. It is this capacity for perceptual registration *outside of conscious awareness* that is the key to understanding how dreams can store human experience from the very beginning of life.

SUMMARY

Almost all the authors discussed here went beyond Freud's drive-discharge, wish-fulfillment function of the dream to take up dreams' much broader and deeper potentialities. Several writers view traumatic experience as the fundamental content of dream formation. Actual experience from infancy, including emotional and somatic components as well as external experience, were described by a number of the writers. The capacity of dreams to deal with human meaning and metaphor allows the process of dream analysis to bring both knowledge and growth of the mind to the individual. A significant purpose of dreams is to make emotional sense of one's experience, to allow one to grapple with the anxieties generated by what has not been solved (including earliest traumatic experience).

Perhaps most salient the central questions of this work are the tachistoscopic studies of Otto Pötzl (1971). His findings lend support to Mancia's (1981) hypothesis that data of a psychological nature may be transmitted to the fetus (and the infant) by way of REM sleep, forming internal representations and a "protomental nucleus." REM states (dreams) may, in fact, be one "place" (thalamo-amygdala circuits being another) where "memories" of earliest experiences, feelings, and needs are stored. Since the amygdala stores simple feeling states, such as fear, and the dream stores perceptions not in conscious awareness, infants and fetuses may actually *have* the mental structures available to "know" their experience in some primitive form and to retain it in their beings. Unconscious perceptions, for example, of the mother's mental state, may be processed directly in REM and in the amygdala. Hence, a baby's "exquisite attunement" to the state of its mother. The baby knows its emotional and perceptual world. It is the problem of the adult world to determine how to decipher it.

9
Reconstruction of Infant Trauma from Analytic Dream Material
Clinical Examples

T his book is based on the premise that birth and infant trauma can be reconstructed from dreams. Such material can be gathered by means other than dreams, for example, nonverbal behavior within the analytic hour (Anthi, 1983); symptoms and behavior (Robertiello, 1956); and transference manifestations (Cohen, 1980). I feel, however, that dream analysis offers a very rich opportunity to see the unfolding of the specific nuances and details of a patient's inner world, including his or her actual experiences, feelings, and fantasies. It is possible that through dream analysis we will be able to see the "story" of early traumatic experience and an expression of the meaning of such experience for the patient in metaphorical terms. Dream life, according to Meltzer (1984), is the generator of meaning. Thus, in studying dream life, we are studying the life of the mind.

The method used in the analysis of the dreams of the patients presented here involves some of Freud's (1900) rules of dream interpretation: ascertaining the day residue; following the patient's associations, both in the hour as a whole and to the specific elements of the dream; and attempting to unravel the latent dream-thoughts from the manifest content. The impetus for the dream, however, was not seen primarily as an infantile wish. In this respect, the interpretations followed the conclusions of more contemporary theorists who suggest that dreams may represent snapshots of the patient's endopsychic situation (Fairbairn, 1952; Rycroft, 1979) or a problem to be solved (French and Fromm, 1964; Greenberg and Pearlman, 1975). More specifically, one might say that the dream shows us the central unconscious anxiety or "state of affairs" to be addressed in any given analytic hour: it brings to us that which *must be known* at the current moment for the patient to "grow his mind" and to "move forward" in life (Bail, 1993, personal communication). Each interpretation, then, addressed the central unconscious conflict/anxiety/disturbing endopsychic situation as it could best be ascertained from the dream, its accompanying associations, and transference manifestations.

Certain assumptions about the unconscious underlie thinking about the material presented by my patients in their analytic hours. First, the unconscious stores everything from the beginning of life to the present. As Freud (1940) said, "The id contains everything that is inherited, that is present at birth, that is laid down in the constitution" (p. 145). The unconscious stores actual experience and memories as well as impulses and fantasies (Sharpe, 1937; Palombo, 1978); and actual experience can and should be distinguished from fantasy and wish (Bail, 1993, personal communication). The manifest content of a dream may be a *depiction* of an experience or psychological state rather than solely a disguise (Jones, 1970).

The method of dream analysis, the assumptions about the unconscious, and the particular way of understanding patient material have been put together in a method of relating to the unconscious derived from the work of Bernard Bail. This method of dream analysis is distinctive in that it focuses on the importance of gathering all possible associations to the dream and in the fine detail with which these associations are treated.

> There are no preconceived meanings or symbols, but each word, each dream element, each association is taken as new and fresh as if one knew nothing at all, as if one were a newborn baby. These disparate associations are then considered in relation to each other, and seem to reveal a coherent story that the patient's unconscious is trying to tell [Reiner, 1993, personal communication].

In all the examples presented, the traumas of birth and infancy were unearthed during the process of analyzing dreams. The material from the dream analysis was then linked to behavior, symptoms, character, and transference manifestations when possible and appropriate. What became evident in the hour was that experiences of the distant past remained powerfully alive in the immediate present.

The clinical material involves presentations of "moments in treatment" rather than the course of treatment itself. These moments include primarily only the actual dreams from which the infantile traumas were ascertained and only the specific information about the patient that was necessary for an understanding of the early trauma and the manner in which it was currently being lived out. Invariably a concern emerges in presenting one's clinical work: how do we insure the privacy and confidentiality of our patients and at the same time share enough of the process to bring new knowledge to the field and advance clinical skills? I hope the attempt here has provided a meaningful balance, although it is weighted on the side of patient confidentiality. Thus, all identifying information has been deleted to protect each person's identity. The case histories of these patients and the process of their treatments, including the process involved in the hours actually described, were much more involved than could be presented here.[1] In all the cases, many unconscious issues had to be analyzed to bring about substantial improvement. Such significant editing of the material as I have done brings to bear an impression of simplicity upon very complex material and an equally complex analytic process. It was, however, necessary for purposes of confidentiality as well as for considerations as to the length of this text.

Another point should be made. In bringing together here only a collection of cases in which traumatic birth or early infantile traumatic experiences were of significance, it can appear that all patient material is routinely analyzed in this fashion—that is, everything is taken back to birth. This is not the case. In fact, relatively few of my own cases over the course of the past 13 years have involved actual physical trauma at birth and interpretations to that effect. Some of the cases have been presented in this collection. Many more long-term strain traumas involving parental misattunements have presented themselves but are not reported here.

Example #1 (Ms. A) reconstructs an actual physical trauma at birth. Example #2 (Ms. B) reconstructs a physical trauma in the neonatal period. Example #3 (Ms. C) illustrates the emotional meaning of a long-term strain trauma beginning at birth. Example #4 (Ms. D) reconstructs a sexual molestation in infancy. Example #5 (Mr. E) reconstructs primarily an "environmental trauma" impinging on an infant at birth. Example #6 (Mr. F) illustrates the reconstruction of both the fact and the meaning of a very premature delivery. Example #7 (Mr. G) illustrates the combined effects of the trauma of a parental death at the time of the patient's birth and an overstimulation trauma in infancy. Example #8 (Mr. H) illustrates a patient's having "loosened the bonds" of his traumatic beginnings during the course of a 10-year analysis.

In one case (example #1, Ms. A), the patient was unaware of the birth trauma at the time of the dream and learned about it when she went to get confirmation of the dream interpretation from her mother.

---

[1]To preserve confidentiality, some associations to the dream elements in the eight case examples could not be presented in detail.

One patient (example #4, Ms. D) suspected (actually the patient's mother suspected) that she might have been sexually abused by her father as a child; however, the patient had no recollection of such an experience. In another case (example #7, Mr. G), the patient learned as an adult that he had been given repeated enemas by his disturbed grandmother but had no recollection of receiving the enemas. In another case (example #2, Ms. B), the process of analysis actually brought to mind a lifelong behavioral pattern that had not been mentioned previously, and the patient mentally connected this pattern to the early trauma for the first time. In the remaining cases, the patients knew of their traumas through information given them as children by their parents. In these cases, dream analysis elucidated the most significant emotional meanings of their traumas—how the traumas affected the patients' lifelong struggles to live in the world and be born psychologically.

Dream analysis illustrated how the transference was colored and shaped by the patients' traumatic beginnings. In addition, the material seemed to demonstrate how the analyst's actual understanding or initial *lack of understanding* of these experiences were perceived by the patient unconsciously. Elucidation of this for the patients seemed to be an especially important part of the analytic process. It allowed the patients to feel that the analyst was willing to continue to make contact with them even if such contact involved unfavorable or unflattering perceptions of the analyst.

In most of the cases, the dreams were precipitated by an actual event in the patient's life, usually the patient's birthday. In two of the cases (clinical examples #6, Mr. F, and #8, Mr. H), however, the dreams were precipitated by a "change in ego state" (Niederland, 1965). In other words, the patients had made a significant change in state of mind, and the dream seemed to provide a commentary on the profound meaning of that change.

CLINICAL EXAMPLES

Clinical Example #1: A Physical Trauma at Birth[2]

Ms. A was a 44-year-old female lawyer when she came to treatment with difficulties adjusting to a move to Los Angeles from Canada,

---

[2]I would like to extend appreciation to Dr. Lorraine Gorlick for her valuable consultation on the first two clinical presentations of this work.

where she had lived all of her life. She was the second of four children, with one older brother and a significantly younger sister and brother. From the descriptions of her interactions with her parents, one got the impression that they were distant, "stilted" people who did not seem to have a real feeling for how to relate to children. Ms. A had been divorced with one child following a marriage in her 20s. She was a warm, caring, and very intelligent woman whose troubled internal life clouded the many gifts she possessed.

In the initial weeks of treatment, and for a time before entering treatment, Ms. A had been fending off a significant depression by taking stimulants and mood-elevating drugs. These drugs were now beginning to have damaging physical consequences. Though intellectually gifted and quite capable in her field, she was unable to complete her legal briefs until the very last moment. This "last-minute pattern" led to complications in her work situation. New to the city, she began frequenting nightclubs in order to meet men with whom she could have a relationship. She would stay at the clubs until 2 or 3 o'clock in the morning, have a sexual encounter with someone she met, and then hope the man would call back to continue contact. She was mildly physically harmed on one occasion. Some of her money and possessions were stolen in another. In the countertransference, I had the feeling on hearing about these experiences of "holding my breath," so to speak, of waiting for a catastrophe. I never knew from session to session what would happen. Would she be seriously hurt in one of these encounters? Her employment was, at least metaphorically, equally precarious. Her failure to come through with assigned projects until the last moment nearly led to her being fired.

It seemed to be the "nearly" that was so important in my patient's internal life. She managed to come through, to save the situation at the last moment. No catastrophe actually happened—it just "nearly happened." I began to be occupied with this "nearly." What was it? Why was I always "holding my breath"?

Ms. A had not presented dreams in the initial weeks and months of treatment, and I was not initially focused on dream work as a significant aspect of the therapeutic process at this time. Thus, the interpretations I was making were without what I would now consider the benefit of a true perspective from the unconscious. One day, however, during the week of her birthday, and while discussing her near-firing at work and a nearly abusive experience with a man she had just met in a night club, she spontaneously reported the following dream.

I was at my home, and my mother dropped off a birthday gift for me at the door. I picked up the gift from the door and unwrapped it, and there were three decorative baskets. One was beige, a second was blue—a blue-gray, actually—and the third was also beige. They were decorated attractively with flowers in and around them, and were arranged in the specific order of the blue basket between the two beige baskets.

Her associations were as follows:

My birthday is approaching in several days. I think that is why I had the dream. I don't particularly look forward to my birthdays. They remind me of what I have not accomplished in life: a satisfying relationship, career, and freedom from the turmoil I experience just trying to go about living my life.

[Her mother drops off the gift at her apartment]: My mother would be giving gifts to us on our birthdays. She always did the right thing that way. She had unusual ideas about raising children, like toys were not necessary. Only educational items were important.

[The door of her apartment]: It is to the door of the apartment I live in now that she leaves the gift. The apartment also has some sense of the home I lived in when I was a young child: the first home I lived in. I cannot see details of the home in the dream—just the gift at the door: I have some decorative baskets in different colors. They're attractive but don't hold any special importance to me. None of them are beige or blue. The colors don't mean anything to me either. I have no particular reaction to or feelings about them. I don't particularly like them or dislike them. They are not "my colors," so I am not sure why my mother picked them. Blue is sometimes meant for a boy but I was not supposed to be a boy. There are four siblings. The second and third siblings are girls. I am the second of four, not really considered "the middle."

[Why were three baskets involved?]: Nothing of three comes to mind as important—nothing at all. What comes to mind about something in the middle or center between two things that are the same?) Nothing at all comes to mind about this. No sibling stood out as strikingly different from the others. I can't make anything of this configuration.

[The flower arrangement in and around the baskets]: They were an arrangement of flowers like you would send to someone as a birthday present or presents for some other special occasion. No particular kinds of flowers stand out. I just have an impression of flowers to indicate it's a birthday present.

I was left here with very few associations. Her mother had dropped off a birthday gift for her at the time of her birthday, but there with no associations to the unusual configuration of the gift. Her mother was proper and provided intellectual stimulation but not emotional contact for her child. The home in the dream combined that of her infancy and her current life. What could one make then of this dream? The most significant and clearest aspect of the dream was that it involved her birthday. Both the day residue to the dream and the actual gift in the dream centered on this event. I wondered, could the dream be presenting something to us of her birth, of, in fact, her actual *birth day*? I asked her if she knew of any of the circumstances or details of her birth. She said that she thought the delivery was on time, but she really knew nothing much about it. Her mother was a rather closed person. They had very few talks about anything personal. The patient's conscious knowledge, then, was not of help in deciphering this possibility.

I thought to myself that if the dream was about her birth, then understanding it had to come from the form of the gift and other associations to the dream itself as well as her general associations within the hour. From the dream, "three" had no meaning; something contrasting between or in the center of two similar things had no meaning. Perhaps, then, the arrangement of the gift represented a *sequence*: one thing or experience followed by a different or contrasting thing or experience, and then a third that was identical or very similar to the first. In the hour, I was again "holding my breath," waiting for a catastrophe as she was reporting that her delays in completing litigation work on a case involving sudden infant death syndrome had now led to probationary status with impending dismissal if things did not change. She also spoke of a brush with abusiveness from a man she had slept with the night before.

This material led me to think that perhaps a catastrophe or a "near catastrophe" was involved—analogous to a near "sudden infant death." I thought of babies at the time of birth. We know them by the response of their bodies. We do not yet know them by their minds or their feelings. Medical decisions are made on the basis of how their bodies respond. Perhaps some near catastrophe of the body had occurred at birth. Babies turn blue (or blue-gray) when they are in distress, particularly when they are deprived of oxygen (I recalled that I was literally holding my breath); otherwise, they have normal skin color, which, for a Caucasian infant, approximates beige. The baskets with flowers could represent fetus/womb imagery. This dream, then, might be imagery representing an actual, concrete experience involving severe distress or a near-catastrophe on the *birth day*.

I told the patient that one possible understanding of this dream—and it was just that, a possible understanding—surrounded her birth itself. The dream might be saying something to the effect that at her birth she was beige (having normal skin color) but had turned blue at least for a bit of time, and then returned to beige—meaning that there had been some problem, perhaps one that had led to near-death at the time of her birth. The patient recalled nothing at the time but seemed interested. In the brief time left in the hour, we continued discussing her current reality and its possible meanings.

Ms. A contacted her mother at some point following this session. Her mother informed her that she had had difficulties with her pregnancies, that there had been two miscarriages prior to Ms. A's birth. There had been an incompetent cervix. During the pregnancy with my patient, a procedure to attempt to hold the cervix together was performed. The doctor delivered the baby early by Caesarean section. An obstetric specialist was called in. No other details were provided.

If some precarious beginning had actually occurred (and, again, what had happened was not exactly clear), then could we consider Ms. A's continuous near-catastrophic behaviors in the light of this? I wondered, could she have been acting out her "life-and-death" birth in this way? Certainly, her mother's two prior miscarriages and the doctor's concern about delivering Ms. A early indicated that considerable anxiety would have existed in the mother as well as in the doctor. There must have been some concern throughout that the baby just wasn't going to make it. She had not been born in the usual way and had, in fact, been lifted or pulled out before she was ready.

Ms. A was consistently late on projects because she wanted to do things in her own time, not on the schedule of others. I said to her that perhaps she could not accomplish major life events in the usual and gradual way and still feel that the progress belonged to her. She was always in a "blue state," so to speak, moving into an "beige state" only at the very last second and with enormous amounts of therapeutic and other interventions. We do not know if there had, in fact, been a "blue state" (oxygen deprivation) but there certainly seemed to have been a feeling state of impending or threatened danger to life before or during the time of the delivery. The home in the dream was a combination of the home of her infancy and her current residence. We could say that some precarious experience happened at her birth (in her infancy), and was still being lived out metaphorically in her contemporary life (her present home).

The transference implications seem quite important here. I told Ms. A that if I was not understanding the profound nature of her early experience, then I was just like the incompetent cervix: the container that could not hold her properly and that therefore could not help her to get born in the usual way. This applied to the analysis as well. Each of her external near-catastrophes—her near job loss, her drug use, her near physical jeopardy in the nightclub situations—had the potential to lead to a "death" of the analysis such that she would not be able to continue to give birth to a real self on her own timetable.

On further reflection, it also seemed to me significant that in the dream her mother had dropped off the birthday gift and then went away. No mother remained present. I think this was the case with Ms. A's actual mother. She provided my patient with physical life, but not with a psychological birth. She did not remain an "in contact" mother who helped my patient to grow and develop emotionally. As a consequence, my patient suffered a great deal in her life. Things educational, not toys, were important. Thus, no mothering contact was made with the infant self on a level that was meaningful to the baby.

I believe that at this point in the treatment I was also this "drop off" mother. Perhaps without understanding my patient's precarious infancy, I was giving an "intellectual" understanding (things educational) to her but was not making genuine emotional contact (the children's toys) in a meaningful way that could help her to be fully present in life as well as in her analysis. My interpretations may have also felt to her as if I were trying to lift or pull her out in some way before she was ready. This could be experienced as a "brush with abusiveness," similar to her experience with her prior night's sleeping partner. In whatever way, the treatment seemed to be a "nearly" experience: neither fully life nor fully death.

Following an analysis of this particular material, Ms. A's "life and death" acting out began to decrease. She stopped going to the nightclubs and having encounters with abusive men rather immediately. She also stopped taking mood-elevating drugs and I lost the feeling that her actual physical well-being was in jeopardy. Much more gradually, she began to get her work assignments completed in a timely fashion. Further interpretations addressed, among other factors, her rage at parental failures to "know her" and to bring to her what she needed mentally in a timely way. I addressed this on a rather continuous basis when she seemed to be moving into a "blue state" so to speak. I also took up the possibility that at such times I might not be in contact with her. She never again, however, returned to the near-death enactments that were occurring regularly prior to the interpretation of her birth situation, its living out in her life and in the transference. I stopped holding my breath. The treatment that followed involved a deepening of the understanding of the emotional impoverishment she had experienced from her mother and of her father's complete inability to "see her" as a person. Over time she made significant advances in her career and also developed more sustained relationships with men.

There appear to be several possible explanations for the difficulties of her actual birth experience. If oxygen deprivation did occur, then the most likely possibility was a prolapse of the umbilical cord caused by one of the baby's limbs pressing on the cord or the cord compressed between the limb of the fetus and the uterine wall. Temporary fetal distress ensues, leading to a reduction of the oxygen supply. Thus the blue color. We speculate here because what actually happened is not known. A significant shift occurred in the patient's acting out however. Such a response would suggest that, in fact, something of the actual situation had been addressed in the interpretation. Since my understanding of this situation in the transference seemed meaningful, I think that the mother's merely dropping off the gift may have been precisely the reason that the birth situation was still so alive for this patient. The center of the problem was the failure to hold. My patient's manner of relating in the world might have been quite different had her mother presented her with the gift of life, however precariously, and then stayed with her emotionally to develop it. Perhaps under these conditions, the birth situation would indeed have been registered in her unconscious as only what it was: a temporary insufficiency having no lasting effect. We would not have seen the derivatives of it in so many of her later behaviors or in the transference. With no human object emotionally present to modify the distress, what was really a transient experience at the beginning of life became a "way of life" informing all of her development.

Clinical Example #2: A Physical Trauma in the Neonatal Period

Ms. B was a 49-year-old woman coming to treatment because of her desire to be a successful musical composer and her inability to do so. She was the youngest of three children, having one older sister and brother. She described her mother as a distant, emotionally flattened person, unaware of and out of tune with her children's feelings. The father was described as an angry man whose outbursts terrified my patient. All three siblings had significant emotional problems. Both the patient's siblings were now married with families, although both had abusive spouses. My patient had never married but had had a series of relationships with very chaotic men who were emotionally unavailable to her.

Ms. B's complaints centered on her difficulties advancing in her career and her inability to form a meaningful relationship. She wrote commercial tunes for a living and gave music lessons to children. She had a background of classical training and at times had been given assignments to assist in writing scores for television and minor film productions. She would, however, become too anxious to finish the assignments, and other assistants were called in to complete production. When she had an assignment other than to write a brief commercial jingle, she would come home in the evening, begin working on her composition, and then smoke marijuana to ease her anxiety. She would then fall asleep, getting nothing accomplished.

In the first month of treatment Ms. B spoke briefly of her birth situation. She had been informed at an early age that she had been born with Incomplete Acquired Intestinal Obstruction, that is, a blockage in the intestines that prohibited food from passing beyond a certain point. Digestion could not take place. Projectile vomiting of all nourishment would ensue. Emergency surgery was performed when she was a little over a month old to repair the problem, thus saving her life.

Two symptoms were particularly evident at the time of the dream that followed within the first six months of analytic treatment. The first involved the patient's difficulty taking on and completing major assignments. The second and related symptom involved Ms. B's anxiety each time she was offered an opportunity to take some steps forward in terms of establishing her career. She was noted by many to have a gift for her work, and from time to time she would be offered various possibilities that would open up new avenues. At these times, as she drove toward the particular audition that had the potential to advance her career, she would have frightening fantasies. For example, she would imagine having a serious car accident in which the cars would crash with such force that the abdomens of the passengers would be crushed. At other times the fantasy would be that an overhead freeway bridge would fall down on her, collapsing her car and crushing her chest and abdomen. She would have to get off the freeway and stop the car because the anxiety of impending catastrophe would become so acute that she could not continue to drive. During one session, while describing a recent anxiety attack as she drove to an interview, she reported the following dream:

Somebody was saying to me, "Everything is in your head."

She had no idea of the location or circumstances of the dream or who was saying this to her, but she took this statement to mean, "All the problems are in your mind; they're not really issues, but the problems you make of them in your neurosis." For example, she explained that a recent large musical composition assignment was making her so anxious that she was now drugging herself with pills and marijuana in order to sleep at night.

I told her that one important rule by which dreams (the unconscious) operate is that they never take up what we already *consciously* know. They take up only what is truly *unknown*—what we are truly out of touch with. We already knew that some of the problems were "in her head," so to speak, a result of her neurosis. So there must be some other meaning to this dream. She had no further associations. I was particularly struck with the emphasis on *all*: "It is all in your head," meaning "exclusively" in her head, not located *anywhere else*. Perhaps the dream work involved a reversal: it was all located *someplace else* besides the head. But where? I recalled that "it's all in your head" was often used in common parlance (the patient herself used it frequently) to suggest that some pain in the body doesn't really exist but is only a product of one's imagination—"It's all in your head; you don't really have something wrong in your body."

My patient's infancy immediately came to mind. I said to her that all her problems at the beginning of her life had been in her body. In fact, she had almost died because her body's digestive system was unable to function properly. A baby, I said, does not know the difference between its mind and its body; it just knows that, when it can't digest, when it is starving from lack of nourishment, when it has a large incision made in surgery and various invasive procedures in the first month of life, it is in pain, and it feels the pain all over.

Ms. B had a stunning reaction to this interpretation. What came to her mind (and she did not know why it came to mind) was that she had had tremendous difficulties reading anything of any length all through her childhood to the present. Although she did extraordinarily well in high school and college, it was a very laborious process. She would mark off a small number of pages between book marks and would work laboriously to get through the pages at one sitting. She would then have to take a rest before going on to the next small grouping. She did not know why she had never mentioned this problem to me before; it just never had come to mind. She went on to recall how she did everything in very small amounts. Her jingles were very brief, like the few pages between the markers. She would also eat very small amounts at any one sitting. Her various boyfriends usually complained about the length of meals because of her need to stop and pause between each few bites of food. She then remembered that her mother had told her that she had had to be fed by an eye-dropper as an infant because she had such tremendous difficulty digesting anything in quantity.

I suggested that perhaps she was also telling me that she had so much trouble digesting that she could take in only a tiny bit of interpretation at any given time. Then we had to rest before she could take in the next small amount, only an eye-dropper full at any given point. She said that she worried that I, like her boyfriends, might wish to complain about the slow pace.

She then proceeded to tell me more about what she knew of her early trauma. Her mother's pregnancy and delivery were normal, but the baby had increasing problems almost from the moment of birth. Her difficulties in digesting led to more and more weight loss until she was literally in a condition of starvation. At first it was not clear what was wrong. Her mother told the patient that she (the mother) did not seem to be aware of the seriousness of the baby's condition. She thought that all babies cry often and often have difficulty adjusting to formula. Thus, her baby's continuous spitting up and eventual projectile vomiting did not, at least initially, seem out of the ordinary. Ms. B's mother had lost her own mother early in her life. She thought that it was important to raise the baby without any help, as she had had to do everything else as a young girl without any help from a mother. She therefore did not call the doctor when problems were evident. Finally, at the end of the baby's first month of life, Ms. B's mother went to the pediatrician in some alarm. The physician recognized a serious problem immediately and rushed the baby into surgery. The problem was repaired when the baby was in a completely deteriorated condition. After the repair, my patient developed normally physically. She was, in fact, extremely bright and capable, although she became an inhibited child with many fears.

The material concerning her disaster fantasies when going to events that would open up new opportunities in her career was taken up in this hour as well. Each new opportunity for advancement stood for a metaphorical "birth." To be born in any kind of way meant to have to reexperience the disaster of her infancy: starvation, pain, surgery, and near-death. These, then, were the disasters she fantasized, the panic attacks each time she headed for something new and creative. The crushing of the abdomen and chest that she fantasized must have been analogous to the real experience of the crushing spasms and pressure in her stomach and esophagus when she was unable to digest and projectily vomited. She must have felt with her "baby feelings" as if she were dying. Ms. B cried at this point and could say nothing. I commented that essentially, all these years, she had had to stay in a state of being "unborn" just in order to survive. This meant that we could not have a psychological birth here in her analysis, nor could she have a birth of any major sort in terms of her life. Such a "birth" would only mean that a disaster would follow.

We had known about and discussed Ms. B's intestinal obstruction a number of times during the treatment prior to this dream, but it was only at the time of the dream that the material regarding her difficulties in doing anything in depth and breadth—anything that would lead to growth—could be understood. It was connected to her infancy, to her very traumatic beginnings.

The following hour, Ms. B reported a dream that she was lying in her bed and awoke gurgling, nearly choking. She recalled descriptions that her mother had given her of her digestive problems. I wondered aloud if perhaps I had not fed her too much the hour before—more than an eye-dropper full. The patient said that she thought that was a possibility but that she had found the understandings very important and had felt these "baby feelings" the entire day. I suggested that perhaps the dream was saying that she was still living in the state of mind of the precarious infant who had nearly choked to death and could not digest. Her ill baby-self had never gone away. I later speculated out loud that perhaps her drug use was also connected to this problem. Drugs were her only means to block out awareness. She would put herself to sleep, as she must have tried to do as an infant, so as not to be aware that she was in pain, starving, and dying. Ms. B recalled many years of childhood sleep difficulties and nightmares.

I proceeded to deal with the transference in more depth. I noted that when I did not understand these terrible problems, so fundamental to her very existence, I must have seemed to her like her unaware, flattened mother, a mother, as she experienced it, completely out of touch, who would just let her starve. Perhaps, then, I was the person saying, "It's all in your head." Ms. B had indeed spent many treatment hours describing her experience of her mother as completely lacking in warmth, emotional holding, and concern. That kind of relationship must have left her feeling all alone, filled with anxiety and terror. In my lack of understanding of her terrifying infancy, I must have seemed like this mother, saying, "Shape up. There's nothing wrong with you; you are just imagining it." How could she put herself to sleep in the face of such a lack of mothering? She could not. Marijuana and sleeping pills were not available to her as a baby; so she could only have anxieties, insomnia, and nightmares. If I was a similar kind of mother, she would feel anxiety here too and would have to try again to put herself to sleep. Two such mothers would be more than a baby could bear.

Ms. B stated that, although she did not consciously perceive me in this light, the understanding had brought to her a sense of calm. I noted that when I seem to understand I must become like her pediatrician, the "aware mother" who could provide holding and understanding and thus initiate the life-saving surgical repair.

Analysis of this early trauma seemed to alleviate some of Ms. B's symptoms. Her panic attacks on the freeway began to subside almost immediately after her infancy situation was understood. Her marijuana and drug use also diminished considerably, and she eventually gave up the use of drugs. Lengthy composition projects have remained difficult, though she did undertake and complete for the first time several major projects within the year and a half following these interpretations. This in itself was a significant accomplishment. She could not, however, do so without considerable anxiety. Her dynamics are complex and other factors are involved in this particular symptom, including her rage at and terror of her father and his seemingly unconscious wishes for her not to exist, let alone succeed. The work on her relation to her father continued for some time.

Clinical Example #3: A Long-Term Strain Trauma Beginning at Birth

Ms. C is a 31-year-old woman who was sent to me for therapy following the suicide of her mother. Her parents had divorced when she was four and a half years old and her mother moved to another state, leaving the patient with the father. The patient visited her mother a number of times during her fourth year, but the visits became so traumatic that she did not resume them until she was 28 years old. At that time, the mother began indicating to the patient that she was going to kill herself. During one visit, the mother brought a display of lethal weapons (guns, rope, pills, knives) to her daughter and asked her to choose the weapon of her (the mother's) destruction.

The mother did eventually kill herself by hanging, and my patient was in a state of posttraumatic stress following her death.

When I first saw Ms. C, shortly after her mother's suicide, she was married with two young children but was in the midst of divorce proceedings. She had been seen in treatment for only a couple of months when she had the following dream, a few days before going to court in the state where her husband lived in order to have the divorce finalized. On the day of the session, as I opened the door, she held up a bag of empty sandwich wrappings from her lunch and asked if she could throw them away in my garbage. She lay on the couch and reported the following dream:

> *I was taking a plane to the East Coast to go to the hearing for the divorce, just as I am planning to do in a couple of days. When I landed at the airport, I went immediately to the home of my cousin. She was having a party. There was a good deal of noise, but I could not hear specifically what people were saying, just the sounds of other voices. I decided to go out for a breath of fresh air. My husband was standing at the door. We looked at each other, and he asked me to go for a cup of coffee. We went to a restaurant and sat at a table, and each had a cup of black coffee. We looked at each other and sat in silence. We really had nothing to say to each other. We just sat and stared, and drank the coffee. Following this, I went to court. It was really a very simple matter. I said I wanted a divorce, and they just stamped it with a stamp, saying the divorce was complete. Very easy. I then went over to the hospital where my children were born to get their immunization records. I got those records, and then I went back to the party. Only this time there was a great big board in the center of the living room. I took an eraser and erased all the things written on the board, and cleaned it up. Then the entire scene from the first part of the dream was repeated. I went outside for a breath of fresh air, there stood my husband, we went for coffee, stared at each other, had nothing to say, and then I took the plane and went home.*

A summary of my questions to her and her responses and spontaneous associations follows:

[Going back East]: I am going to the East in a couple of days for the divorce. I am nervous about it, but I think my husband will cooperate.

[Her cousin's house. Why did she pick her cousin's home to locate where she landed? Did she have any special relationship to her or to the home?]: She was my very closest friend at the time I lived in the East. We got together around our pregnancies. We took prenatal classes together when I had my first child, Lamaze and Taking Care of Baby. We read about and talked about our babies: what they would be like when they arrived; whether or not they could feel what we were feeling. She and I have remained in touch over the years, and I look forward to seeing her when I go back. She is a very decent person and I always enjoyed her company.

[A party at her house; the people she couldn't make out]: She didn't have parties often; neither did we. I was often there for dinner. I'm not much of a party person, in fact. I don't like crowds much. It would be typical of me to go outside for a breath of air when in a room with a lot of people. I didn't recognize any of the people specifically.

[Her husband greeting her at the door]: The situation with my husband at the door was just as it is; we never had much to say to each other. We're there, but there's never been much communication. I don't like coffee. I never drink it. It's bitter. I don't think it's very good for you.

[Going to court to get a divorce; having the paper stamped]: I anticipate what the divorce proceedings will be like. I hope it is as straightforward as in the dream. I don't recall who stamped the paper in the dream—whether it was the judge or a clerk. I couldn't really make out anyone distinctly. I only know the paper was stamped, as I imagine is done, indicating the divorce was granted. I hope this is how it happens.

[Going to the hospital to get her children's immunization records]: I do have to get my second son's immunization records because he is starting preschool. But the records are at the doctor's office, not at the hospital. My stay at the hospital for my children's births went well. There were no particular difficulties. Nothing comes to mind about this.

[The board in the living room]: The board, when I went back to the party, is the most interesting thing. It reminds me of the board where I keep track of all the residents and staff in the adolescent residential treatment center where I work—which room the residents are in, the times and locations of their activities, the staff shift changes, and so on. The board is filled every day, all the time. You know, I've never had any hobbies or interests. My mother was a musician. She played the flute. My father is a biologist. So it was some surprise that I've always had trouble learning in school. All subjects were so difficult for me. But for some reason, I have this board memorized in detail. I know every location, every patient, every activity, and I keep track of them precisely, which is why I have done so well on this job.

[The eraser]: The eraser in the dream was what I use to erase the board at the end of the day. I don't know why I repeated the scene. There was my husband, there was the coffee, there was the staring, and the whole thing happened again.

Where to begin with this dream? It is long and involved. The majority of her associations seemed to center on her impending divorce. Certainly this was her conscious concern over the last few days. So it seemed that the divorce was the day residue. If this was the case, then one part of the dream struck me as truly out of place: her landing at the home of her cousin, to whom her main associations involved experiences with pregnancies and prenatal issues. Why was she thinking unconsciously of prenatal classes and concerns with what went on in the womb at the time of the divorce? I thought of her husband, a man she described as "empty of nutrients" and uncommunicative. Whom could he stand for? Had I been providing her with very little, and was she trying to divorce me? I recalled how disturbing Ms. C's contacts with her mother were and that the mother made little effort to contact her daughter after the father stopped visitation. How does a mother let her daughter go so easily? Her mother was essentially uncommunicative for some 24 years. Perhaps the husband stood for the mother or, in her experience, the mother and husband were emotionally similar. Ms. C was still in a profound state of shock regarding her mother's recent suicide. Beyond the divorce, her mother's traumatic death was still a fundamental preoccupation. I was unclear as to why she was going back to prenatal times in the dream. I felt, however, that we should start here, since this is where she started the dream, as well as her life: at her prenatal times. If I started where she landed, then maybe the rest of the very lengthy dream, which she described almost in the form of a story, would actually tell us the rest of *her* story. Then perhaps the sequence of what had happened to her, or the sequence of at least her emotional experience, would become clear.

I thus took up the "story" in the following way over the course of the hour (the interpretations are condensed here into a single narrative for purposes of presentation). I told her that I thought the key to understanding the dream began where she landed: the home of the cousin with whom she took prenatal classes. I felt that this probably located the situation not so much in the current divorce, although this must certainly be involved, but rather at the time prior to or at her birth. I said that I did not know why she would be dreaming about her birth or her prenatal experiences at this time. (She also seemed unclear at this point as to why.)

I then speculated that the scene at the party, where she could hear the sounds but did not recognize any people, might be her mother's womb, that she was perhaps listening to the sounds from inside the womb. I said that I thought she was telling us a story of her birth and her experiences with her mother and what she attempted to do to cope with these experiences. It appeared that she attempted to go outside for a "breath of fresh air," meaning to get born, and was greeted by a mother who was simply uncommunicative. They only stared at each other, the mother having nothing to say to her. There was no cooing and loving breast milk, but only staring, with nothing to say—black coffee, bitter and empty of nutrients.

I said it appeared from the story of this dream that when she became aware of the nature of the situation with her mother at birth, this empty experience—with no communication, and only staring—she tried to get a divorce. In the dream, it was a very simple matter; she would just get the paper stamped and say, "That's fine, this is not my mother," thus denying the fact that as an infant she could not divorce herself from a mother who did not want her and had no way to communicate with her. When she realized, I said, that she could not get a divorce from her mother, she tried to get "immunized" from the experience. In the dream she went to the hospital to get the immunization records.

How does a baby who realizes it has a mother like this begin to immunize itself against such an experience? It appeared to me from what followed in the dream that the immunization did not work well, so the only way she was able to exist and preserve herself from the awareness of a mother who could not contact her was to erase her mind. The board in the living room represented her mind and everything that was on it, including her experiences with her mother. She felt she simply had to erase it. At one point in the hour I suggested that this might be connected to her learning difficulties in school, and her lack of hobbies and interests. Such activities meant she would have to preserve her mind, the experience with her mother, and so on.

In discussing the repeated breath of fresh air scene, I said I thought that the fact that it happened a second time represented two things. First, she had gone back to see her mother for the second time when she was 28 years old, the emotional experience being identical to the first—nothing had changed. Second, she might feel that I would be like her mother and that she would have to erase the treatment here and my interpretations. She would like to throw away the experience with her mother, as she had asked when she came to the door whether she could dump her garbage into the garbage can in my office. She was worried that, instead of her being able to get rid of it, our attempt would be to understand it and she would have to erase this here too in order not to experience it again.

Ms. C had a striking response to these interpretations. She said, "Oh my God, it was my birthday this week. I always get very depressed at the time of my birthday. I forgot for a moment. (She had erased it.) I never like to think about it because my mother told me that when I was born she thought I wasn't her child because I was so ugly and I didn't look like her. She thought they had mixed up the records in the hospital, and that I was somebody else's baby. She told me she didn't want me when she saw me." I commented that perhaps she had wanted to check the records in the hospital in the dream in order to make sure she was actually the baby of this mother. She then began to recall occasions in which her mother told her of her dislike for feeding and taking care of her as a baby. She remembered how her mother had repeatedly said that as an infant, Ms. C had interfered with or disrupted her mother's life. Ms. C continued with an outpouring of associations to her mother's hatred of her.

When I spoke of her wish to erase all these painful happenings, Ms. C stated that the chemical solution used on the eraser to erase the blackboard was extremely powerful. One had to be careful not to get it on one's hands because it would damage the skin.

She did begin to make efforts toward more significant learning experiences during treatment. She eventually returned to school part time, having become interested in working with preschool children. The theme of erasing me and the interpretations was taken up throughout her treatment whenever painful material emerged that she wanted to forget or actually did forget.

Ms. C's marital situation was of interest. She did not divorce her husband. Over the course of many months of treatment, her husband became sufficiently differentiated from her mother that she began to see more clearly the caring side of him and his desire to continue the marriage and remain a father to their children. She began to feel more warmly toward him, particularly after her identification with the mother who had abandoned her was taken up. It appeared that Ms. C identified with this mother, precipitously leaving a husband who stood for her own abandoned baby-self. She eventually returned to their home in the East and to her marriage. She entered therapy as well as marital counseling in her hometown.

The dream reflects an infant's awareness, from the time of birth, of the emotional deprivation and emotional abuse of a mother who rejects and is unable to care for her. It is certainly a matter of debate, but I do not feel that the dream is a projection backward, that is, that the patient's current state of knowledge was imposed on her birth situation. Rather, I feel that the patient's ongoing experience with her mother, her developing cognitive and perceptual capacities as she grew, provided the means to represent, to symbolize in a dream, that which was known *emotionally* from the very beginning of her life—as her dream's "story," which begins at her birth, tells us. Such an understanding is in line with the research findings of Terr (1988) and the psychoanalytic investigations of Bernstein and Blacher (1967), Schur (1966), Paul (1981), Dowling (1985), and Laibow (1986): Primitive sensory experiences and early mental processes may be "reworked" into new, more mature forms as development proceeds. These forms help to organize emotional experience into verbal forms capable of symbolization. Thus, the capacity for symbolic representation in the dream work.

I believe also that this dream is illustrative of the importance of ascertaining the specific associations to each element of the dream, at all times but particularly in cases of early trauma. Had I not inquired into the details of my patient's relationship with her cousin, the "prenatal" story would not have unfolded. On the manifest content, the fact that she landed at a the home of her cousin, who was having a party could sound like a flight from pain—she was going to a party to get away from the pain of the divorce, or some such understanding. The whole story was understood only because the prenatal detail was ascertained. The patient then confirmed the story in her associations to her birthday—which she had forgotten. It was now clear that the birthday and her terrible situation with her mother from infancy were the primary day residue. Her story would never have been properly understood without this crucial and unexpected, or "out of place," association.

Finally, I feel that this dream is a very important illustration of the "compromise of the mind" that can happen when trauma involves hostile material projections into the infant (Ferenczi, 1932; Fairbairn, 1952; Kahn, 1964a, b; Bail, in Reiner, 1993a, b). Essentially she had to "leave her mind" (to erase it) perhaps, as suggested in the dream, from the very first moments of her life, in order to mute awareness of a parent who did not want her to exist. She could not *have* her whole mind—her whole self—psychologically survive. A product of two intellectually gifted parents, she could not learn, develop emotionally, or grow mentally. Her personality was, in effect, erased.

Clinical Example #4: Sexual Molestation in Infancy

Ms. D, a 47-year-old waitress, came for marital therapy with her husband because of a stormy marriage of several years. Both had prior marriages and several children between them but no children of their own. There was much conflict and resentment regarding each other's treatment of the children as well as quite a bit of tension in the sexual relationship, which they did not specify initially. I was just beginning to get some idea of the history of the couple's marriage and their individual childhood histories when an event occurred just prior to the fourth session of the couple's treatment. Ms. D had been working in the restaurant where she had been employed for the past two years when a customer, obviously having had too much to drink, became quite seductive with her. While getting up to pay the bill, he fondled her on the buttock quickly, sliding his finger near her anal area. Ms. D was taken aback by her intense response to his behavior, since customers had on one or two occasions harassed her before (kissed her or stroked her breast). She had not reacted so intensely at those times. She now found herself very agitated, had some difficulty concentrating, and kept repeating the event in her mind. She had always had sleep difficulties, but since the day of the incident, getting to sleep had become a considerable problem.

When she initially came to marital therapy she seemed most uninterested in talking about her early history. She wanted to focus only on her husband, so that it was difficult to get a picture of her in time and space. She became more open to discussing her childhood only as she felt the need to understand her intense response to the experience in the restaurant.

Ms. D was the youngest of three children, with two older brothers. Her parents had divorced when she was in her teens, although they had had a very conflicted relationship throughout. My patient had been a very withdrawn, timid, and frightened child. She remembered fears of strangers, particularly men, coming in the home. She would cling to her mother. She had a fear of taking baths. She did not know why. She became sexually precocious and more outgoing as she grew.

She recalled attempts to tie her dolls in ropes and place them in bondage positions. In grammar school she was preoccupied with the genitals of animals and would draw pictures of animals with huge genitals. She recalled becoming sexually consumed as an adolescent. She slept with many boys indiscriminately. At one party, she danced naked in front of boys. In her early 20s, she became a topless dancer in Las Vegas for a period of time. She quit, however, feeling the life style was too lonely and abusive.

Since Ms. D's particular distress had been precipitated by the customer's contact with her buttock, I asked if she recalled any early issues in this specific regard. She said that she had been particularly preoccupied with having anal sex as far back as she could remember. In fact, this was an issue in the marital relationship. Her husband did not enjoy anal sex, and she experienced his withdrawal from her as withholding and a lack of caring. She then recalled that she had recurrent intermittent proctitis, a physical condition involving recurrent rectal infection. The condition occurs, she was told, when one has had some damage to the mucous within the rectal wall, often due to old scarring. She had been informed during one physical exam when she was in her 20s that she had traces of scars—really a series of faint diagonal lines or discolorations—in the upper inner thigh area. The doctor had asked her if someone had dug fingernails into her skin.

Ms. D stated that her mother had suggested at one time, in a fit of rage at her father, that her father may have molested her as a very young girl. The father would encourage the mother to take the boys on errands and would offer to baby-sit his daughter. Ms. D had no conscious recollection of molestation.

In the marital session following the incident in the restaurant, Ms. D reported the following dream.

> *I was in the room where I did my topless dancing in Las Vegas. My (at the time) large black boss was there. The room that I danced in was completely dark. There were no tables. Instead of a whole large audience, there were 10 or 12 men sitting around the dance area. There were wooden bars around the whole area. I went to get my records to play in order to do my particular solo dance, but they were stolen. There was no name and no identification in the slots where the records were kept. If I couldn't get the records, I couldn't dance.*

Ms. D's associations to the dream were:

I did topless dancing for several years in Las Vegas, as I had mentioned. Men would sometimes get abusive. I was very young and found it difficult to be away from home in a cold and competitive environment. My boss was rather cruel. He would get very angry if I didn't do things just his way. He reminded me of my father in that way. He intimidated me. The rooms I danced in for the shows were dark, but this room was smaller, had no lights on at all and no furniture around except the chairs the men were sitting in. Usually they serve drinks and food on the tables in Las Vegas. The room doesn't seem familiar. I never saw a room with wooden bars before. Maybe it was like a prison, but I have no experience of prisons except what I have seen on TV. Usually there are audiences full of men and women during the shows. This was exclusively men and only a dozen or so: a very different feeling than the Las Vegas shows with hundreds of people in very large rooms. I used to use particular records when I did my solo dance. I don't recall now what songs were involved or which ones were in the dream. In the dream, it was just that they were stolen. I didn't know who stole them. That never happened in real life. I was never robbed in real life. I had a mailbox with my name on it in the hotel where I danced—but these slots were on a slant in the dream. I don't know what that means. My name was no longer there and the records were gone.

I said that it seemed significant that she had had many sexual experiences, preoccupations, and activities in her life and yet it was this one incident—the fondling of her buttock—that had caused her to *feel* traumatized. I noted that some of her symptoms were those of a traumatized person (i.e., her lack of concentration, sleep disturbance, recurring thoughts of the experience) and that because of this, I had to think that this brief experience stood for something very important. I said that her lifelong interest in anal sex, her preoccupation with the genitals of animals, her doll play, her choice of occupation as a young woman, all spoke of a mind and body that had been somehow filled with experiences with which it simply could not cope. I told her that, from her dream, I suspected that such experiences went back to her earliest years—or at least that she *felt* these experiences from the perspective of a frightened infant. I told her that I did not know if my understanding of this was correct, but that I thought we needed to

address the possibility and see if this understanding resonated with
her in any way. She said that she wished to hear my understanding.

I suggested that if we follow the dream the scene might be an
image of her experience, or how she perceived her experience, as an
infant. The room with no furniture, dark, with wooden bars, would be
a nighttime view of her bedroom from inside a crib. This was perhaps
a scene in which her father (or some man) came to her room in the
night (the large black man). He was large and black because in the
night, to a baby, adults are large and dark. The 10 or 12 men would
stand for the fact that this type of experience had happened many
times over. What she might be saying was that the experience of
repeated abuse as an infant led to the loss of her identity. In other
words, there were no records; her name was gone. The identity of who
she could have been was stolen from her by this experience. In this
sense, I said, if this understanding was correct, then she really had
been robbed—robbed of her infancy, robbed of a chance for her own
mind, her own body, her own personality. Her infancy, her crib, was
a prison.

My patient appeared stunned, almost dazed for a time. She
suddenly remembered that the slots where the records were supposed
to have been kept in the dream were exactly the size and number of
the diagonal marks on her inner thigh. She began to cry profusely.
Images came to mind of her sexual preoccupations, her sexual
fantasies as a topless dancer, how she wanted to please her father by
acquiescing to his demands for her to be with him: "He seemed to be
touching me always."

The next week, the patient came to her marital session looking so
different that I almost did not recognize her in the waiting room. Her
face seemed younger and much less strained. Her eyes were bright
and clear. Her previously unkempt hair was combed and neat. Her
clothing was much less tight-fitting and seductive. Ms. D announced
that this was the first week in her entire remembered life that she had
been able to sleep through the night, and to do so without the light on.

I saw Mr. and Ms. D for only a couple of months of marital
sessions. It was clear that they were both in need of more intensive
individual analytic treatment and that the marital work had helped
them to recognize this need. I referred them each to different analysts,
and they began their individual work. Ms. D did report, however, that
during the course of marital work her preoccupation with anal sex
seemed to have diminished as had the other symptoms following the
incident in the restaurant. She was sleeping better on a regular basis,

and the tension in the marital situation had also decreased to some extent. There was much work left to be done in all areas, however.

Clinical Example #5: An "Environmental Trauma" at Birth

Mr. E is a 32-year-old divorced man who came to treatment because of conflicts in his relationship with his girlfriend and the fact that he had had two unsuccessful marriages in the past. The patient, an extremely intelligent man with many talents, worked as an actor in local theater. However, he never established himself in his career. He was living marginally, being financially supported by family assistance and some inheritance, which financed his treatment. In addition to relationship and career difficulties, Mr. E experienced some agoraphobic symptoms. He also experienced anxiety when attempting to take long walks or to jog around his neighborhood for exercise. He could describe the feeling only as that of being lost and anxious in the open space and needing to return to the comfort and structure of his home.

Mr. E was the youngest of three children, with an older sister and brother. He spent his childhood in a small Southern town. His parents' marriage had been extremely troubled. Mr. E described his mother as quite occupied with the older children and preoccupied with the marital situation during most of his early years. His mother also appeared to him to be a self-involved person who never seemed to "know" him as a person in his own right. Mr. E described his father as relating to him in a very superficial way. My patient's struggles to find himself, to utilize his many talents, and to have meaningful relationships with others clearly were related to the problems involved.

Mr. E was in treatment for a few months when he presented the following dream during the week of his birthday. At this time, he had begun complaining about what he thought was his difficulty in feeling any sense of emotional attachment to me or any connection between us. He saw me as rather detached and businesslike—a person with no real personal interest in him, someone who was just "doing her job." After describing these complaints, he presented the following dream.

I was biking over the canyon, which was a route I would regularly take going from one side of my home town to the other. There was a ravine area which in the dream looked almost like a trench, very long and narrow. But this trench had glass around it like a greenhouse (hothouse). The light was very bright, almost white.

*There were many people who seemed to be lined up on either side of
the corridors. It was difficult for me to get to the end. When I got to
the end I was concerned as to whether the children that were there
would get out because I couldn't find their mothers. I wondered who
was responsible. Was I responsible? Then I realized, no, the children
weren't mine. Finally, at the end, my aunt showed up apologizing
that she was late.*

In association, the patient stated that from the time he was a
young boy he would bike from one area of his town to the other
through this canyon and that the area was sort of a crossroads in
which one could go one of several directions. The ravine, with the
people lined up, reminded him of a hospital corridor. He had had
recent surgeries that were very difficult. He noted that the hospital
corridor seemed crowded in the dream. The people seemed backed up
against the wall on each side. They seemed fine in the dream, he said,
but "I had the sense that there was some devastation, some catastrophe, the result of some war or perhaps the effects of a natural
disaster." He further stated, "A greenhouse is a place where plants
grow. Sometimes greenhouses have special lighting. I don't know
about a bright white light though." Regarding the children at the end:
"There was a question as to whether they would get out, as if
somehow the effects of the disaster would prevent this, as if, in the
commotion and confusion of the disaster, they couldn't get connected
to their mothers and so couldn't leave."

He then said, "I feel like this is very important, as if something
inside is going on but I don't have the words to put to it." He went
on: "I never did feel much connection to my mother. She was
absorbed with my older siblings and her troubles with my father. She
seemed more like my aunt, who never seemed to me to be a very
good mother and did not have much connection to her children. She
was more occupied with her own needs in life. My mother was always
'showing up late' in relation to me and I could never really understand whether this was my problem or hers." There was a long pause
and then Mr. E suddenly remembered that the ravine also reminded
him of the place where his best friend had lived. This too was en route
between one side of his town and the other. He visited his friend
frequently. "This was my friend who died a terrible tragedy. I was
very close to him before he died. He was a wonderful person, so
bright and talented. His marriage worked out very well. He was very
happy when his cancer was discovered. He died at 32. It was a
devastating catastrophe." The patient then noted that this was his own
32nd birthday.

I suggested to Mr. E that since it was his birthday and he had associated to the death of his same-age best friend, the dream might be telling us something about his birth experience. At least that is where we could start in attempting to understand this dream. If this was about his birth, then possibly the ravine with the glass dome that was bright with people lined up against the walls of the sides of the corridor might be the hospital nursery—a place where newborns begin to grow; the lineup of people would then stand for the babies in the nursery. The glass dome might represent also the incubator with its glass warmth and bright lights. I wondered out loud if he had had any "disaster incubator" experience that would bring this imagery to his dream at this time.

He said, starting to cry, that he had had a very precarious beginning. His had been a normal birth and delivery in a hospital. However, he was initially jaundiced and had to be placed under special bright lamps. There was at the time a diarrhea epidemic on the ward, and within the first 24 hours of life, he came down with diarrhea. He was quarantined along with other babies. He became severely dehydrated and was treated with special equipment. He was not allowed any contact with his mother for almost three weeks. Instead, he was taken care of by a single nurse in the nursery. His mother pumped breast milk, which he was fed from a bottle each day. He subsequently was returned to his mother and then was released from the hospital. He remained a somewhat ill baby for the first month of life but gradually recovered and pursued normal development.

I suggested that perhaps we could understand the devastation (the war ravages in his dream) in the light of this experience. They would be the effects of the "natural disaster" in the dream, the jaundice and diarrhea epidemic in the hospital. I felt that he had identified with his best friend, a bright and talented, happy newborn who then suffered a "devastating catastrophe." The catastrophe was such that it was like a crossroads at which one could go in either direction, toward life or toward death. As an infant, he would not have known who was responsible for this terrible experience—he or his mother—or whether the jaundice and diarrhea were just natural occurrences in his body. I said that he must have worried, the only way a baby can worry—with feelings without words, that he would never become connected to his mother with all the commotion and devastation going on in his body. He must have also experienced her as a neglectful mother, represented by his aunt, who was not able to make contact with him for almost three weeks and then showed up late with an apology at the end of the quarantine. Instead of having personal contact with his mother, he had to be taken care of by the impersonal nurse. Mr. E then said that he thought that this might be the feeling that he had not been able to put into words.

I said that I thought that this was the issue currently in our relationship as well—the fact that he felt that he could not make any personal contact with a caring-mother me. I was, instead, the impersonal nurse who was just baby-sitting him, so to speak, during his illness; not his real mother but the hired help just impersonally doing my job. The patient then reminded me that he had initially seen the analyst of a friend of his. He had wanted to see that analyst for treatment, but the analyst referred him to me instead. I was, then, the baby-sitter nurse instead of the real mother. I said that as the baby-sitter-nurse I would have no real personal interest in him, and he would have no real attachment to me. I would be there just to keep him going and clean up his diarrhea, an unpleasant task at best. He must wonder whether he and I would ever get connected in the midst of all this bodily commotion. Would I finally "show up with an apology"? (That is, I must have been missing some very significant connections for at least the last three weeks, if not for the whole course of our contacts.) Would I finally realize and convey to him that this was the problem, that this was what had been going on? Mr. E shook his head affirmatively.

In this hour I also took up his birth experience in relation to his agoraphobic symptoms and, more generally, in relation to some of his difficulties in living. I said that he must still unconsciously experience himself as an ill baby. If so, then he could not really leave the house or take long walks. To go outside was to leave the safety of his home. His home stood for his mother's womb—an "inside place" that was safe. In addition, his home stood for the hospital: a place where he became ill but also a place that was essential for his survival. If he went outside into life, he could risk illness and death. I thought also that he was still living as this precarious baby, marginally functioning in work and still quite dependent on his family, unable to function fully as an independent adult. He told me at this point that his chronic reaction to any stress was to get diarrhea. He noted at the end of the hour that this was the first session in which he had begun to feel some emotional contact with me.

Clearly, many factors other than this patient's birth accounted for his difficulties. Shortly after this interpretation, however, he was able to begin to exercise and take long walks in his neighborhood. His complaint about my impersonal manner and his inability to make contact with me emotionally began to dissipate at this time.

Exactly on his birthday one year later, however, Mr. E returned to the complaint about my impersonal manner. He had a dream that he was a janitor in a park. His job was to clean up outside and inside the bathrooms for the many people that visited the park. I believe he was saying here that from his birth he had been "stamped" or imprinted with the identity of the janitor for all the metaphorical bodily products of his family and those significant others to whom he was connected. His job in life seemed to be to clean up everyone's anxieties, destructiveness, and projections, everyone's diarrhea—that of his family and even that of mine. If I did not understand this problem, I was again just the cold, impersonal nurse. If he had such a job in life, certainly he could not go on with his own job of being a baby who had the opportunity to grow and develop his mind and his own unique personality. Thus, he was still living in his "marginal state."

By his birthday in the third and fourth years of treatment, no such imagery of diarrhea or precarious states occurred in Mr. E's dreams, nor were there complaints about my detachment. He described satisfying birthdays with friends and many warm feelings. Birth material did not appear in his dreams. By this time, he had made substantial progress in his career and was establishing himself as an independent working person. His difficulties in separating from identification with disturbed parental figures continued as the focus of the treatment. I believe the feeling of imminent diarrhea still occurs in situations of acute distress. We can see here the conclusions of Terr (1991) and Lipin (1955): current physical symptoms may actually contain physical "memories" of early traumatic experience.

This material also addresses another important issue in psychoanalytic technique. It has often been stressed that the transference (as opposed to the dream) is the primary vehicle for analytic work (Gill, 1982; Caper's discussion of Freud, 1988). The dream material of my patient, however, was of enormous value in helping to ascertain the specific nature of the negative transference in operation at the time. All the factors involved, both past and present, became evident in depth through the specific associations and interpretations to the dream material presented in this hour. Understanding the dream also helped me to "touch" my patient emotionally in a most profound way, a way I believe would have been difficult to achieve without such an understanding. The transference, then, and my patient, were both reached through the dream.

Clinical Example #6: The Trauma of a Premature Birth

Mr. F was a 19-year-old young man who came to treatment because he could not find any interest, goals, or direction in life. He described himself as suffering an underlying depression and malaise. He had completed high school with great effort, though he was very bright. He began college but dropped out shortly afterwards, finding the work too laborious. He took a manual labor job instead. He preferred to spend his time in his room, sleeping for long hours, watching TV, and eating. He was quite a handsome young man, and girls often called to extend invitations to various parties and events. He had little interest in these social activities and usually declined the invitations. He was the second of two children, with an older sister. His parents had had a difficult marriage and divorced during my patient's early teens. He felt abandoned by his father, whom he rarely saw. His mother was now working two jobs to support the family and to pay for therapy for herself and her two children. It seemed understandable that this young man would be depressed.

In the initial months of treatment, we focused on the patient's feelings and conflicts related to his parents' divorce and his longing for his father's more active presence in his life. Within the first six months of treatment, the patient began feeling better. He had just started running track and had been taking a course at school. He had begun going out with some friends and completing daily chores, tasks that had always seemed overwhelmingly laborious to him in the past. In the session in which he reported these changes, he described the following dream.

> *I was parked in a parking lot garage. I tried to exit but found that the exit was still under construction and not complete. I went down the exit ramp anyway and smashed in the front end of my car in the fall. I was not permanently hurt but the car was dented. A man came up and said, "You're lucky you made it." I returned to school, and I noticed that when I looked down, my feet were bare and I was wearing white shorts and an undershirt. I was told that my history teacher was no longer competent and was being replaced by someone new. The new teacher was a very capable old family friend, Celia.*

Mr. F was puzzled by this dream and had difficulty thinking of any associations. The car was his current Volkswagen. He parked in a garage frequently. He could not associate to the incomplete ramp nor to the exit in which the front of his car was smashed but he was not hurt. He noted that he had had one car accident but that his car had been hit on the side, not the front. He had never been in a front-end crash. He had no association to the man saying that he was lucky that he made it and could not describe the man. He said that such a statement is something a person says to you if you made it through some disaster or some near-miss, life-threatening situation. No such thing had ever happened to him. He did have an association to the bare feet, white shorts, and undershirt: he spent a lot of time dressed that way at home when he was lounging, sleeping, or watching TV. He stated that from his many dealings with his history teacher, she seemed to be a very kind and capable woman who would not be likely to be fired. He found history an interesting subject. His particular history teacher, he said, organizes and manages all the learning activities for his freshman class. He did not know what precipitated the firing in the dream. Celia, the woman who was taking over as teacher, was also a very capable person, a long-time friend of the family's whom he had known all of his life. She had cared for him when he was a baby.

Like the patient, I too was puzzled by this dream. Certainly the bare feet and white shorts and undershirt and his lying in bed seemed to represent his infantile, regressed, "small car" self. The garage and his difficulty exiting certainly also seemed to stand for some aspect of the withdrawn, "inside" state of mind in which he lived: coming out in life and developing as a young man presented some real danger. But what to make of the very specific imagery of the smashed front end of the car and someone saying, "You're lucky you made it"? A car often stands for the self in dreams. If the front end was smashed, then perhaps Mr. E was making reference to a *specific and concrete experience* in this dream, something that had actually happened. It also seemed to refer to a time when he left some place, some "inside" place, before *it* was ready. When he did so, something *specific* happened to his head (the front-end of the car). If he was lucky and made it, then the experience was a "close-call" of some sort. His life might have been in danger. I thought the inside of the garage might be the inside of his mother's body (since he was clearly still living as a baby) and that something of her body (the construction of the ramp) was not complete, although there was no question that *he* was incomplete.

Thus, I suggested, after trying other possibilities, this dream might relate to his birth (about which I knew nothing at the time) because of the form of his dream and the very lack of his associations. I suggested that the lack of associations might indicate that he was describing an experience from a time when he would not have had any associations, that is, any other experiences to relate it to. I said that if this was his birth and a description of his beginnings, then perhaps he was saying that he went down the birth canal when it was under construction and not complete, that he had had a premature birth and was not ready to be born. The reference to the smashed front end of the car might mean that some damage incurred during the birth process. It might have been the doctor or his parents saying how lucky he was to have made it. I said that I assumed that the bare feet, white shorts, and undershirt when he returned to school was a reference to him as a baby in diapers and shirt, but that I did not know the meaning in this context of the dream, if in fact this was indeed a dream regarding his birth.

The patient gasped and said, "Oh this is amazing that my dream could so clearly depict the situation." He then told me that his mother had been Rh negative, and that she had miscarried after the birth of his older sibling and been told by her doctor that it was very unlikely that she could carry through another pregnancy. Mr. F was, in fact, born nearly 10 weeks prematurely. There was a difficult delivery. Apparently there were some significant forceps marks on his head but no permanent damage. He had spent a good deal of time in an incubator. His mother had been extremely ill during her pregnancy and delivery, with complications from the Rh factor. She was unable to care for the baby for a considerable time. A nurse was hired to care for him when he went home and for several months following while his mother recuperated. This woman became a friend of the family's. I told the patient that this must be a reference to the teacher who was fired—a woman who was part of his history, his warm and usually competent mother. She was replaced by the new "managing" and "organizing" nurse—the nurse he had known all his life and who provided the organizing care he needed when his mother was so ill and unable to function for him as a mother. This reference to the new teacher/nurse also appeared to be a reference to me and to his treatment, which now seemed to be providing this managing, organizing, and teaching experience.

I commented that what was striking about this dream was not just that it depicted his early experience so clearly but why it had occurred at this particular time. After a long pause, the patient blurted out with a start: "It's the running track!" I asked what he meant. "It's the fact that I now have energy, that I am doing things, that I'm taking care of myself, and that I'm getting out in life. It's about the change!"

In the next session, Mr. F came in saying that he had thought about the last dream all day and had asked his mother "a million questions" about her experience. (We see here the value of dreams in stimulating curiosity about the mind, in addition to a person's reclaiming his history.) His mother had told him more of what she could remember: her labor had been approximately 36 hours long, and then the baby was induced because it would have been poisoned by the Rh complications in another 72 hours had they not delivered him. His mother told him that he was so tiny when he came home that his parents were afraid to touch or hold him. Perhaps, I said, the dream was expressing his feeling *then,* and perhaps even his feelings *now,* that he needed a new nurse-manager who was not afraid and who would be able to care for and hold such a tiny infant with all its premature parts.

In this hour I speculated that perhaps in the dream of the last session his returning to school barefoot and in diapers and shirt was saying that he had remained living in the state of mind of a 10-week premature baby. In that state of mind, life would simply have overwhelmed him, and he could not have managed the ordinary tasks of life. Certainly school, chores, relating to friends, and so on would be tremendously difficult. In such a state one could only think about the basic functions for survival: breathing, sleeping, eating, evacuating. Beginning to cry, Mr. F responded that his favorite position was to lie in his bed curled up in a fetal position, listening to TV, and eating crackers, and then going to sleep while watching his breathing. He had been occupied for as long as he could remember with watching his breathing: breathing in and breathing out. How does one know that one will take another breath? What insures that a breath will be taken? He said that at times he thought he could not stand to think about things for too long. I said, "How could an almost two-and-a-half month premature infant stand to think? If it had to think, it could only know how difficult and precarious its life was." The patient agreed.

The patient gradually progressed over time. He began to be able to sustain interactions with people. He eventually returned to school part-time while retaining a part-time job. He began dating periodically and engaged in some school athletic activities. He spent progressively less time in his room in a regressed state. In the transference, I took up the contrast rather regularly between who I was when I seemed to understand his infant self (the care-taking nurse, Celia) and who I was when I did not (the Rh negative factor, a destructive force at best).

Of interest was the day residue for this dream. It appeared to be precipitated by a psychological birth in the patient: a true change in his way of feeling and being, the beginnings of a move into a psychological life and a rudimentary self. The dream seemed to serve the purpose of recalling or reviewing for him where he had come from. He was not to forget how this all came about. I would consider this, then, a "change-of-state" dream.

Clinical Example #7: A Double Trauma at Birth and in Infancy

Mr. G, a 29-year-old man, came to analysis because of many unresolved feelings regarding his early childhood experiences. He saw himself as a withdrawn and closed person with an underlying feeling of embarrassment and humiliation about himself. He was chronically irritable and angry and felt needful much of the time. He indulged in some mild drug use on a regular basis. He had difficulties settling on and developing a career and establishing himself in a meaningful relationship some years after a divorce.

The patient was one of three children, with two older brothers. The issues surrounding his beginnings in life were very traumatic. His father had just finished law school at the time of the mother's pregnancy with the patient, and the family was moving from their home in the Southwest to Los Angeles, where the father had obtained a job in a prestigious law firm. Mr. G's mother moved to Los Angeles with the older siblings to set up house while the father was finalizing arrangements for the move. But at this point the father had an acute psychotic break and suddenly killed himself. This suicide seemed to happen, as far as the patient could gather, "out of the blue." My patient's mother, six months pregnant with him at the time, was overwhelmed with the sudden and completely unexpected loss of her husband and remained medicated and sedated for the last three months of her pregnancy. Mr. G was informed over the years that he had been a very difficult baby, crying constantly, and was described by his mother as "inconsolable" from the time of his birth.

Following the father's death, the mother moved into her parents' home, where she stayed with her children until Mr. G was about four years old. Mr. G's grandmother appears to have been a very troubled woman who was preoccupied with bowel functioning and apparently began giving the patient enemas regularly while the mother was at work, despite the mother's request that she not do so. The patient felt that the enemas were administered until he was almost three years old, when his mother was able to persuade the grandmother to cease the practice. The patient had no conscious recollection of the enemas but only memories of feeling very withdrawn and frightened and of retiring to his room in a "state of shock" following what he later learned were the enema experiences. This "later learning" of the enema episodes came about sometime before he began his analysis after seeing a film about a woman with a multiple personality who had been given repeated enemas by her psychotic mother. Mr G had a very severe panic attack while viewing the film; he become overwhelmed, shaky, and frightened during the enema scenes. Inasmuch as he had never had panic attacks before, he discussed the situation with his mother, who then informed him of his early experiences with the grandmother.

Early in the analysis, the patient had a dream of a horse kneeling on a white cloth. The location of this scene was not clear. He could only see the horse and the cloth, and the "camera angle" of it seemed to focus progressively in on the kneeling knees of the horse. The dream appeared to represent his own position as a baby kneeling for the enemas, the white cloth standing for the diaper. It seemed as if he had been metaphorically "brought to his knees" on the diaper in shame, humiliation, and rage as he was subjected to the intrusive and traumatic procedures. Initially, the analysis, in which the patient would lie down and interpretations were made from behind his head, was experienced as a similar "get on your knees" intrusive predicament.

The patient's birthday occurred several months into the treatment, and he had the following dream:

> I was in the forest with my brothers and my older cousin, Allan and his wife, Rebecca. They had brought some trinkets from a trip they had been on which they were giving to my brothers and myself—one of which was my birthstone. The second gift was a wood contraption or structure of sorts in which a bear came out, looked around, made a funny noise—a cry or a grouchy sound, and quickly went back into the structure.

His associations were:

> The structure itself around the bear was very old, rough wood, clearly neglected, clearly not kept up. It reminded me of some of those toys or clocks in which the toy comes out, makes a noise, and quickly goes back. Only this wasn't kept up like a nice shiny toy or like Disneyland where they have these things made to look old but they are kept up very well. This was truly neglected and worn. The bear itself did not seem neglected and worn, just the *casing* out of which the bear came. Allan and Rebecca, my cousins, are a very nice couple. Of my whole family, they are probably the most congenial and

the ones that I would wish to keep contact with. It was as if they were the parents who go on a trip and bring back presents for their children. I always looked forward to that when my mother or grandparents did that on occasion. My birthstone must connect to the fact that it's my birthday. I have always thought of the forest as a nice place to be, quiet and peaceful with nature all around. The bear toy was supposed to be a novelty they found. The scene reminds me of a fairy tale when you're in the woods and there's the bears and animals, except that the casing of this toy bear was so worn. The bear just made a grouchy noise—as you think of bears when they make their noises. We were amused in the dream, but I had the feeling that despite the amusement, it was somehow a very serious thing. Real bears scare me but this was a toy and it did not.

I said that I agreed that the dream might be saying something about his birth, since it was his birthday today and one of the gifts brought to him in the dream was his birthstone. Perhaps the quiet peaceful forest was his mother's womb or body. The couple might stand for his parents, but his parents at an earlier, better time— perhaps at the time he was conceived rather than the time when he was actually born. He might be saying that when he was conceived, he was meant to be like the gift or jewel that was given to him. Mr G said that his mother had told him that he had been a planned and wanted child. He began to cry.

I said that perhaps the very worn, neglected case in which the bear came out stood for his mother, worn down by her trauma and grief, no longer well and not equipped for the birth of a new baby all ready for life. His mother had told him that she had given up at the delivery, that she had gotten to a place in the process in which she could not do any more and they had to extract him with forceps. "My mother said she had nothing left to work with. She was so exhausted from her grief and the emotional pain she was in." I said that he must have felt, in an "infant way," these awful feelings. Perhaps we could say that he came out like the bear, looked around, saw the terrible circumstances, and could only make a grouchy sound (he was told that he was a grouchy, irritable baby) and psychologically go back inside. At least *inside*, he would feel more peaceful and tranquil, like the forest. Perhaps he worried that if he remained outside, he could not be cared for by his mother or would wind up becoming worn and neglected just like her.

The old casing reminded Mr. G of his mother's old robe and messy hair on Sundays, when she would sit for hours, depressed, with the curtains drawn, and would sleep on and off all day long. She too would come out for a moment and then go back inside to her room and to oblivion.

I said that he seemed to still be in this "inside," unborn state and that our problem was how to get him born in his life and in the analysis. He also needed to know, I thought, that I would not be like his exhausted and worn mother, who had given up; rather I would be able to see him through and give him psychological life in a natural way.

The next day Mr. G arrived 10 minutes late (unusual for him) and presented a dream in which he was erasing a cassette tape at the same time that he was saying "Wait, stop, let me see it." He said that he used cassette tapes to record many aspects of his current projects at work. He imagined that the two contrasting states represented his mixed feelings about what we had discussed the day before, his birth. He wanted to erase it and at the same time he wanted to know about it. He went on to say that he had felt very sad and thought that perhaps he didn't want to be born again. I commented that perhaps he couldn't imagine that things could be different from what they had been at the time of his original birth.

He said, "I think things could be different if we could sort out the different factors; but there seems to be a big X over it, as if I'm not supposed to go over it in my mind." I asked why that would be so. He answered, "I always thought that day was one of the saddest days in the world because my father was not there. There was no joy, just get it over with. I was a complication. My mother couldn't attend to me at all. There are no baby pictures of me whatsoever, no baby books, only of my older brothers. My mother needed so much care herself after my father's death. I thought she didn't like me." I said that such an impression must have been the only thing he could make of it at the time, the only way he could comprehend why she was so unable to care for him.

I asked about the tape erasure and his feeling that he was not to go over the birth in his mind. He said, "It was a secret. We were not supposed to talk about it—about my father's illness and his death. It was, in fact, never talked about in the family." I said that his response to my question indicated that he had gotten his father's death and his own birth mixed up together in his mind. He said, "Yes, I got tied with that from the beginning; I think it was just too close. He left; I came. Everything changed. Nothing was the same as it was before.

They never talked about him and never talked about those days, never. It was a taboo subject."

I said, "It would be difficult for you to come here because you are not supposed to talk about your father's death, and you and your father's death are treated as one. So you are not to talk about yourself either. The two things are fused in your mind and shrouded in secrecy and embarrassment."

He said, "Well, that's the way I've always felt, totally embarrassed about my birth and my existence. I do think that way. I have these things connected. I can never think of one without the other. Everyone said, 'He died and then you were born' in the same sentence with the 'and' connecting them. I thought that at times that his dying may have allowed me to be born. Why was I living and not him? Maybe he was angry about this. Certainly, my brothers were mad. They no longer had a father—they just had me."

I said that there must have been so many fantasies and so much confusion for a little person to cope with when nobody would talk about it and help him to sort it out. He said, "I don't want to think about him very much or to think about this. They said, 'Don't ask about it.' But I guess part of me wants to know because in the dream, I say, 'Wait let me see it.'"

I said that the part of him that was erasing the tape was identified with the family, whom he saw as wanting his birth and his father's death erased. The part that was saying "Wait, stop, let me see it" was the part of him that was identified with me and the analysis and therefore wanted to be born and wanted to know about himself and his beginnings. He agreed.

I suggested that perhaps he thought that, if we could understand this, maybe we could put his birth and his father's death into two separate sentences with a period between them, so to speak. Then, he could exist without the shame, embarrassment, and secrecy that surrounded his father's death. He could come out to life and not have to go back inside. He thought that if we could accomplish this, it would be a very good idea.

Now, several years into the analysis, Mr. G describes himself as feeling much less angry and "grouchy" and much more interested in people. He has stopped his drug use. His feelings of shame and humiliation have not been a topic of the analysis for quite some time. He has worked very hard to situate himself in an established and professional career for the first time. This particular goal seems to him to be a truly important achievement in his life and his analysis thus far. He continues to work on the meanings of his mother's emotional absence from him for many of his early years and the loss of the father he never knew.

Perhaps it would be useful to mention an incident that happened with Mr. G's drug use because it illustrated so well how important it is to obtain specific associations to the dream elements. With birth dreams, it appears that associations are not always readily forthcoming (see Pulver, 1987; Williams, 1987). The form of the dream and the symbolism—such as here the forest for the mother's womb, or, in Ms. D's case, the crib for the wooden bars, along with the day residue and the history—bring one to a working hypothesis about the birth or infant experience. Sometimes, however, the symbolism can be misleading.

At one point in his treatment, Mr. G decided to stop using recreational drugs, which he was then taking in small amounts on a nightly basis. He was in the initial weeks of withdrawal, a very uncomfortable time. He had a dream in which his puppy was being strangled by a rope and was drowning in a pool of water. Mr. G himself wondered if this dream was about his birth—if the rope stood for the umbilical cord strangling him at the time of his birth. There was, however, no evidence that such a thing had happened and no reason for his birth to come up as the day residue at this particular time. I asked Mr. G if he had any associations to his neck and the strangling. He recalled that the day before he had been to his doctor, who had told him that all Mr. G's feelings seemed to be located in his neck. The meaning of the dream, as it turned out, centered on Mr. G's being strangled with and drowning in all his feelings now that the drugs he had relied on for so many years could not be used to suppress them. He was completely filled with his feelings, not with his birth. Such are the interpretive pitfalls.

Clinical Example #8: A "Change-of-State" Dream Following a Ten-Year Analysis

This last example is a dream that appeared in a patient after 10 years of a complex and difficult analysis. This patient, Mr. H, is a 45-year-old man who came to analysis because of his despair about his second failed marriage, the failure of other friendships, and career struggles. He was extremely depressed. He was totally preoccupied with the failure of his marriage and his wife's abandonment of him. The situation so consumed him that he found it difficult to think or to work. He had always been a lonely person, finding it difficult to make and retain friendships. He was, nevertheless, not without warmth and generosity despite an overall significant disturbance. Despite having some talent for his work, he seemed to have a great deal of difficulty sustaining his business and holding the various jobs that he acquired over the years; thus he was always "living on the line" and just "barely making it."

The patient was the only child of his parents but had three older half-siblings from the mother's first marriage. The mother was a very narcissistic woman who had been deprived in childhood and used her children essentially as mothers for herself. Mr. H seemed to live, as illustrated in one dream in which he was holding a compact of eye shadow, as literally "the shadow to his mother's I (eye)."

He was a planned child. The parents had been married a number of years and the father had expressed an interest in having a child. The mother had not planned on more children, since she had three nearly grown children, but she acquiesced as a gesture of appreciation for her husband's loving care of her and her three children.

Mr. H was told of his precarious beginnings by both parents at different times. As her pregnancy was described to him, the mother experienced extreme morning sickness for five months; it lasted from morning until night and incapacitated her completely. She vomited constantly, lost a great deal of weight, and had a difficult time leaving her bed. The father apparently felt very guilty about his wife's suffering and suggested an abortion. In fact, he took her to an abortionist and the procedure was initiated. But just as the instruments were about to be inserted into her, his mother asked that the procedure be stopped. She was a compulsively clean woman, according to the patient, and told the father that the instruments in the setting seemed too dirty. She could not go through with it. The father took her home, and she completed the pregnancy without complication. Delivery and the neonatal period were normal. The baby was extremely distressed in his early months, suffering severe colic and crying continuously. The mother was quite anxious about caring for this child, who had been born to her late in life. Nevertheless, she described this to the patient as a very happy time—that she and his father were actually thrilled with having the child. The patient's physical development progressed well, but he appeared to have been a lonely, depressed, and extremely anxious child who had a great deal of difficulty relating to other children.

There was certainly evidence in his unconscious that, despite the mother's protestations otherwise, he was less than truly wanted by her. In the dream presented in his first consultation hour, Mr. H is seated on a grassy hill in a lovely picnic area. A beautiful actress comes toward him. He thinks that she is there to join him for the picnic, but instead she comes to choke him to death. In association, the actress closely resembled his mother. He had been born, expecting a pleasurable, feeding experience (a picnic); instead the attempt was to murder him. He should not exist. He was worried, of course, that he would come to analysis and have the same experience with me. The possibility of new life could only bring a wish on someone's part for his death.

The overriding theme of his analysis was what I would describe as "his precarious state." This was particularly evident in his financial and work situation. Each time he began to do well in his business, things would suddenly and dramatically deteriorate so that he would be "on the edge" financially. His analysis would be in jeopardy. His living circumstances would be in jeopardy, and he would have to struggle to get various jobs just to survive. This pattern was repeated many times in his treatment, and, in fact, his existence, like that of the patient in example #1, was always in a state of "near sudden infant death."

One illustrative dream occurred some years into his analysis. In it, he was at his linen closet reaching for something. At the front of the closet were baby toys and other infant paraphernalia. At the back of the closet were similar baby things. There was a large empty space in between. Mr. H's associations to the empty space involved his having viewed a recent TV science program in which a particular empty space was described metaphorically as a very precarious state between life and death. I think Mr. H was saying that he had lived in such a state from the very beginning of his life, from the time of his infancy, if not from the time he was in the womb (hence the baby items) and this was being reflected in all his difficulties.

It would be impossible to describe here the entire course of a 10-year analysis. Suffice it to say that by the end of 10 years this patient had improved considerably in all areas of his life. He now had a number of enduring friendships. He had a very stable and caring relationship with a woman. His shaky finances and business had improved. His business had not only stabilized for a considerable period of time, but was now growing. In one analytic hour, Mr. H was noting his improvements and the contrast between the richness of his life now and the poverty of his beginnings 10 years earlier. He then reported the following dream.

I was getting married and I was very very happy about it. This seemed to be a much better relationship than the others. We were at the altar and the woman I was marrying had this dull gray metal ring on her finger from a prior marriage. It was important that we get the ring off to proceed with the ceremony. It was very difficult. We struggled. It seemed to be almost cemented to her finger. However, finally, the ring was removed and the ceremony proceeded. I was so extremely happy.

In his associations to this dream, Mr. H stated that he did not know the person he was marrying but hoped that it was a marriage to me, meaning that we were now having a good analytic marriage. He had no associations to the dull gray ring or to the place or circumstances of the wedding.

In associating, he kept repeating how thrilled he was about the marriage. What he meant to say in describing this feeling was, "I can't believe this is happening; I can't believe this is happening." However, what he *actually* said was something slightly different. This difference led me to tell him that I did not think the person he was marrying was me; rather, I thought the person he was marrying was himself. He was surprised and asked how I had arrived at this understanding. In response, I asked him if he had noticed his slip of the tongue when describing how thrilled he was about the marriage. He said "No," that he was not aware of any slip of the tongue. I told him that he had meant to say "I can't believe *this* is happening." Instead, his slip of the tongue was, "I can't believe *I am happening*. I am so thrilled, I can't believe *I am happening*."

The patient gasped in shock. After a long pause, he said, "This means that I am happening—meaning that I can be born. I don't have to be an aborted baby. I can have a life." He began to cry and then suddenly recalled that the gray metal ring on the finger of the bride, the item to which he could bring no association, was exactly the way he had imagined the material of the abortion instruments—dull gray metal instruments that did not look clean. If this "abortion ring," which appeared to be cemented to the bride's finger, could be taken off, then he would not have to be the "almost aborted baby." He would not have to live in the very marginal state in which he could not fully progress and grow. He could be born and live a full life. He could be born in the analysis as well.

Mr. H expressed through his tears that perhaps this was the point of it all—the point of the years of hard work of analysis—one could finally say, "I am happening."

SUMMARY

Infant traumas, as reconstructed from dream material of eight analytic patients, ranged from physical and accidental environmental traumas at birth and infancy to traumas involving the projections of maternal hatreds and disturbances, that is, sexual and mental abuse. What does a baby do with such experiences? Evidence from this material suggests that the experiences "grow" with the baby, organizing and influencing later behavior, thoughts, fantasies, symptoms, and "ways of life." Evidence from this material suggest that aspects of these traumas are lived out as if within a time warp. Life becomes the trauma, and trauma becomes one's life.

10
Conclusion

Our unconscious is our universe, and we have to accord it a vastness we may not be able to comprehend as perhaps we cannot comprehend the vastness of our physical universe. [Bail 1991, p. vii].

TRAUMA AND ITS EFFECTS:
THE FORMATION AND STORAGE OF
VERIDICAL MEMORY AND MEMORY SCHEMAS

B oth my clinical experience and the preponderance of research reviewed in the foregoing point to a stunning conclusion: birth and early infant trauma can have enduring effects and can be encoded in various memory systems such that they can be accessed through dream analysis and other psychoanalytic methods. As noted in the Engel et al. (1985) longitudinal study of Monica, these effects can endure throughout the life of an individual *and* can be passed on through the generations to effect the future of one's offspring. Even if the overall personality is functioning quite well (not the case with many of the patients presented), one can venture to guess that the specific enactive memories for trauma would be embedded *someplace* in the soma, dream life, behavior, fantasy life, or personality style of the person.

The research and clinical evidence presented here support two related findings in regard to memory of infant trauma: (1) memory for infant trauma can be stored veridically and can be indelible; and (2) infant trauma forms memory schemas (Bartlett, 1932; Paul, 1967) or "templates" through which future development is filtered. This latter conclusion speaks to infant trauma as an "organizer of experience" or "organizing principle" (Stolorow and Atwood, 1992) or a "posttraumatic neurotic-like state" (Yorke, 1986).

That such memories are veridical and that they *also* form memory schemas are not seen as contradictory propositions, although that

226

antitithesis is sometimes presented in the literature. Graf and Schacter (1987) demonstrated that schemas help one to *retain* material because they form "meaning networks." If such schemas are based on earliest trauma, a "trauma meaning network," so to speak, emerges. New perceptions, experiences, and objects are filtered through this network. Future fantasies are formed from it. Future stances and perceptions of the world are shaped by it. I believe that perceptions, experience, and objects filtered through such a schema or network would be particularly well "remembered" in the unconscious, particularly ingrained. They have been formed, in essence from a meaning network of trauma shaped by veridically imprinted traumatic experience. Thus, we see enduring residues of such early trauma.

Piontelli's (1988) analytic work with a two-year-old psychotic child whose autistic play was replete with "memories" of fetal experience suggests that such a "memory schema" can begin in utero. Other clinical examples from the literature as well as my own cases provide evidence that such memory schemas for trauma may very well begin during the very first year of life (see Schmideberg, 1950; Lipin, 1955; Robertiello, 1956; Niederland, 1965; Frank, 1969; and clinical examples 2, 5, and 8, in chapter 9). In actual clinical work, these experiences were quite difficult to discern initially. Very detailed analytic work with patients' dreams had to be done to unearth them. Once the traumas were discovered, however, it became clear that they dominated all of life. Rather than it being difficult to keep track of these traumas, one could not get away from them. They appeared to affect the entire manner in which a person lived out his or her life. They were found in somatic reactions, behaviors, symptoms, character manifestations, fantasies (conscious and unconscious), transference manifestations and dreams. Essentially all the components of a person's being demonstrated and lived out the enactments of these experiences in one way or another. Slap (1987) came to a similar conclusion in his discussion of repressed schemas:

> When a patient is analyzed to the point where the repressed schema is understood, it seems that the schema pervades the analytic data. All is seen to be influenced by these core ideas, and the life of the patient can be comprehended . . . as a play or motion picture which is being constantly remade: the plot supplied by the repressed schema; the settings, the props, and the actors keep changing as the patient goes on through the years [p. 639].

Of the nature of infant memory, we have evidence of a much wider breadth and earlier timetable for memorial capability in the infant than was considered previously, even without the "advantage" of real trauma to increase its effects. The studies of Gunther (1961), Liley (1972), Nachman and Stern (1984), and, most significantly, Perris et al. (1990), as well as the infant research literature, all support evidence of at times stunning memory capabilities in the infant. Anecdotal reports of two gifted children (Bernstein and Blacher, 1967; Laibow, 1986) provide evidence that discrete experience may be "known" to infants from the very beginning of life, (including prenatal life, according to Laibow's child). Such experiences, however, cannot be translated by a child into verbal thought until the child has acquired fairly complex linguistic capacities. By that late date, birth and neonatal experiences are usually consciously forgotten by most children, particularly if the experiences were not traumatic (see Winnicott, 1949a). The children of Ann Bernstein and Rima Laibow, however, began speaking at five months of age. They possessed an organized symbolic capacity and the verbal facility to tell us of their birth and neonatal experiences. These children's remarkably accurate descriptions of discrete, structured memories lend support to the experimental and other research findings demonstrating that the mind of the infant is not amorphous and undifferentiated, capable of only fleeting perceptions, sensations, and experiences.

Where are such memories stored? In addition to the soma, however that is subtended by the nervous system, early memories appear to be stored in the amygdala. This structure houses primitive and simple memories, such as the feeling state of fear. One can see confirmation of this neurobiological experimental finding in Gaensbauer's (1982) study, in which an abused child evidenced a fear response toward men at three months of age. Ordinarily, such a response is developmentally not considered feasible until seven or eight months of age. The capacity of the amygdala-thalamo circuits to store primitive affective memories in the first year of life suggests that they would serve as "memory containers" in utero as well. LeDoux's (1989; LeDoux et al., 1989) research lends further support to the existing evidence of fetal memory and to the fact that feeling states can be known, stored, and "remembered" from earliest time.

A third and very important memory storage structure is that of the dream's REM state. The work of Pötzl (1917) and Mancia (1981) is particularly important in this regard. The experimental tachistosopic studies of Pötzl (1917), extended in contemporary research by Fisher (1960), demonstrated that experiences and impressions *outside of conscious awareness* are transmitted *directly* into the unconscious and are processed in one's dreams. Since dreaming begins in utero (Roffwarg et al., 1966), I propose that the experiences and perceptions of the infant—not yet, of course, formulated within the structure of conscious verbal, secondary-process thought—can be processed *directly* in REM states. Because the unconscious is timeless (Freud, 1915b), these earliest experiences can initially be represented in dreams in some primitive sensorial form. They then remain available for transformation and, over time and as development proceeds, are capable of being represented symbolically in dreams. These data become part of an "unconscious catalog of past and present experiences" (Palombo, 1978) from which dreams draws their pictorial representations. Like other later childhood experiences seen in dreams, these earliest experiences may take form as the dream's "means of representation" and thus may be available for translation and reconstruction through dream analysis in adult life.

The hypothesis that infant memories can be stored in REM states supports the hypothesis of Mancia (1981), who postulated a mechanism whereby psychological data from the mother may be transmitted to the fetus. He suggested that such transmission takes place through REM states and may begin the formation of mental representations or "a protomental nucleus" in prenatal life. I suggest that REM states may, in fact, be primary vehicles for transmission of the mother's unconscious to her fetus and baby. If we have REM storage of experiences and impressions outside of conscious awareness, as proposed by Pötzl (1917), then the baby's perceptions and experiences of the mother *in all their forms* may remain with the baby from the fetal period onward. The exchange between the unconscious of the mother—her mental states—and that of the baby may begin before birth.

Recent analytic experimental research from the Anna Freud Center (Fonagy et al., 1993) demonstrating that the mother's self-reflective capacities, as assessed during her pregnancy, accurately predicted the security of her child's attachment in the first 18 months of life, lend credence to the idea that the quality of the mother's mental life has a direct influence on the developing infant. Mothers who were self-reflective about their own early histories when they were three months pregnant had children who evidenced secure attachments at 18 months of age. The mothers' self-reflective capacity provided a containing function. It seemed to "protect" the babies in some way, allowing them the mental space to develop their own inner worlds and selves relatively free of destructive parental projections.

In addition to the particular "locations" of infant memory storage in the soma, the amygdala, and the dream, Mott (1964) suggested that the electrical conductivity through the umbilical cord of the fetus may provide memory imprints from fetal life. What "other places" exist as possible sites for memory storage of birth and infant experience will be known only in the course of future research.

PSYCHOANALYTIC RECONSTRUCTION VERSUS THE NARRATIVE

The possibility of veridical memory of trauma brings to fore the controversy about reconstructive versus narrative technique in psychoanalysis. As noted earlier, Terr's (1988) "behavioral memories" can be considered roughly analogous to Freud's "perceptual image" (Lewy and Rapaport, 1944), and Terr's "verbal memory" might be analogous to Freud's "memory image." The "perceptual image" or "behavioral memory" is available for veridical reconstruction; the "memory image" or "verbal memory" is not. The perceptual or behavioral memory lends itself to reconstructive methods; the memory image or verbal memory is conducive to a narrative approach. The controversy, to at least some extent, hinges on a failure to distinguish between these two very different kinds of memories.

An either/or position may not be entirely necessary. I feel that a reliance on the narrative approach and here-and-now transference manifestations *alone* is not adequate. Certainly, with such an approach one would have great difficulty reaching the precise nature of the infantile traumatic experience, resulting, I think, in a significant loss for the patient. I suspect also that the literature has very few case reports of reconstruction of earliest trauma in part because of a reliance on here-and-now transference methods and a failure to work closely with the details of associations (see Pulver, 1978, in this regard). I also feel, however, that once the veridical nature of infantile trauma and infantile experience is understood, then a coherent story of the patient's experience in narrative form can be very useful. It helps the patient to locate himself in time and space, to know himself as a person in the world, and to understand the continuity of his being. In this way, veridical and narrative meaning can form an important whole.

PATHOGENIC BELIEFS

Another finding, evident although not developed in my own clinical work, lends support to the analytic research of Weiss and Sampson

(1986): infantile trauma creates unconscious pathogenic beliefs. Almost all the patients reported in this book carried the unconscious notion in one form or another that if they took a step forward in the world, some catastrophe would ensue. This was especially evident in my second case example, Ms. B, who suffered a severe anxiety attack when moving to a potential job situation that would advance her life. Moving out in the world seemed a vary precarious process. Such beliefs were evident in the behavior and dreams of many of the other patients as well: Mr. F left his mother's womb and smashed his head. His attempts to move out in life psychologically brought a reminder in his dream of the difficulties involved. Ms. C came out and found a mother full of hate and bitterness. She developed a defense that erased the experience, including the memory of her recent birthday. Neiderland's (1965) patient had to dress for the disaster of his prior frozen infant self that he now anticipated at all times. Monica (Engel et al., 1985) could not hold her babies in her arms lest her arms become tired. And so on. All these patients seemed to respond to their experiences by staying "inside" mentally, which is where they remained until their analyses. In essence, there appeared to be no "psychological birth" in these patients. They were living in this "unborn state," with an "alive" mental life frozen in their traumatic infancies. The task of analysis was to help the patients to "get born" into life and into the analysis, and interpretations had to be made to this effect in virtually all the cases.

SOMATIC MEMORIES

A finding of importance from the clinical material was the presence of physiological memories of trauma (Greenacre, 1945; Lipin, 1955; Terr, 1991). Some of these memories were stunning in the way they had been carried directly from their traumatic infancies, almost as if in a time warp, to the present-day physical feelings. Cohen's (1980) patient experienced the cold room, shivers and chills in a physical memory of her enema experience. Anthi's (1983) patient, in a piece of nonverbal behavior, was still turning his neck exactly as he had done for physical therapy as a baby. My patient (clinical example #5) born during a diarrhea epidemic on the hospital ward continued with a feeling of imminent diarrhea under stress. Rosen's (1955) patient experienced "bizarre bodily sensations" (p. 211), feelings of choking, and unbearable stretching of the diaphragm in identification with his mother's attempted hanging witnessed at three years of age. And, finally, Monica (Engel et al., 1985) was living out her feeding experience in her own handling of her infant girls. The body appears to retain a record of earliest traumatic experience in a very literal way. Such a record remains over time, regardless of future mental and physical development. In my case examples and that of Rosen, the meaning of the physical symptom or somatic behavior became clear through an analysis of the patients' dreams. Other vehicles for accessing this data were noted in other cases.

In some of the cases cited in the literature (Lipin, 1955; Cohen, 1980; Engel et al., 1985), it is suggested that the somatic memories were lived out exclusively in the soma. Cohen suggested that through the treatment process, these somatic responses can be transformed into verbal memories. He may have been correct. It is not clear, however, that in *addition* to somatic enactments, these experiences were processed in dream thought, since dream material was not presented in any of these cases. It is possible that what seemed to be *exclusively* somatic was not and that the somatic enactment was only one of a variety of ways in which the traumas manifest in the personality. Monica (Engel et al., 1985), for example, demonstrated memory of and fantasy for her gastric fistula experience in her doll play. She also demonstrated fantasies about her experience in her first Rorschach response at five years of age; to Card #IV, for example, she commented, "That looks like a bird . . . it doesn't have any mouth . . . because they cut it off" (p. 75). Somatic memories, then, may be organized into more structured symbolic dream thoughts or fantasy formations if one were to look more carefully in this direction.

PRESERVATION OF INFANT TRAUMA
IN THE MENTAL SPHERE

It is clear from the work with my patients and those cited in the literature that traumatic experiences of infancy are retained in some form that allows for understanding, interpretation, and change. It is possible, though, that there are patients, perhaps more psychotic or more fragmented than those presented in the studies in the literature and in my practice, to whom Bion's (1967) concept of bizarre objects— experiences that are fragmented into bits, jettisoned, and dispersed in a projective manner—would be more applicable. These objects would not be amenable to dream and transference analysis. One would find the experiences only in the soma or in some other primitive form. In the cases presented here, the experiences were not dispersed entirely, even though enactments occurred. They presented themselves in dreams and in such a manner as to be amenable to understanding by way of Freud's rules of primary-process, dream, and transference analysis.

It seems evident from most of the clinical examples that these traumas were split and dissociated from the normal part of the personality. In fact, the concrete literalness of the enactments and their aliveness in the mind recalls Breuer and Freud's (1893–1895) original concept of the hypnoid state in which traumas were split off in a particular ego state and then lived out as foreign bodies affecting all of behavior, symptoms, and fantasy formation. Loewald (1955) took up the idea that the hypnoid state represents an infantile state of mind (a traumatic event cannot be associatively absorbed because it is part of the immature or infantile state of the ego—or hypnoid state). Perhaps in the case of the earliest birth and neonatal trauma, these states remain preassociational, so to speak; that is, they did not mentally "come together" in the first place in order to be split and dissociated (J. Gooch, 1992, personal communication). Winnicott's (1945) point is of value here in considering the dissociated nature of these traumas. He considered the dream of particular value in being able to break down the dissociation process. Thus, the patient's *bringing* a dream for processing suggests that at least unconsciously he is ready to consider "associating" this split off trauma into the personality.

INFANT TRAUMA
AND THE ORGANIZATION OF ANXIETY

Another issue of importance is the pervasive experience of anxiety suffered by these patients. Greenacre (1945) suggested that birth trauma organizes the pattern of anxiety. We could extend her statement: early infant trauma as well as birth trauma organizes the pattern of anxiety. In my first case (Ms. A), the anxiety surrounding the birth was projected into the analyst. I was to feel it—holding my breath—not the patient. In the other cases, the patients experienced the anxiety directly. Schmideberg's (1950) patient was constantly anxious about impending catastrophe and the country's inadequate food supply. Anthi's (1983) patient experienced anxiety and helplessness, along with fears of being manipulated and controlled by others. The anxiety crystallized into anxiety attacks in a few of the other cases. Thus, we see Pulver's (1987) patient who experienced an acute anxiety attack at a doctor's office and my patient (Ms. B) who experienced such attacks while driving toward important career objectives. Such primitive anxiety seen in full-blown anxiety attacks may indeed be connected to infantile trauma of some sort.

With such a hypothesis in mind, we could begin to investigate the fantasies specifically related to the attacks, taking them up like an association to a dream. We may find clues to the specific nature of the trauma. For example, my patient's specific fantasies were that her chest and abdomen would be crushed. Investigation into particular fantasies and particular pathogenic beliefs may be quite fruitful: Why do such ideas come to mind? What experiences, if any, have you had where feeling of crushing in the abdomen and chest occurred, etc.? One might in this way begin to reach the early traumatic experience.

FANTASY AND REALITY IN INFANT TRAUMA

Most striking in all these cases was the literal manner in which these traumas were reenacted in dreams, transferences, and behavioral manifestations. Questions arise as to what the literal manner of enactment says about the nature of early fantasy formation and psychic reality. We ordinarily consider psychic reality to be a mixture of fantasy and reality. Early trauma, however, with its direct veridical enactment, does not evidence this mixture in the way we customarily characterize this process. Could it be that literal enactments demonstrate Fairbairn's (1952) assumptions that fantasy formation is secondary to experience and that it is truly the experience with the "bad object" that we internalize? Could it support Stern's (1985) conviction that, from the beginning of life, infants experience reality? From Stern's view, distortion is largely a result of inevitable perceptual or cognitive immaturity rather than wishes and defense such that "reality experience precedes fantasy distortion in development" (p. 255).

I suggest a third possibility. The results of this work indicate that extreme trauma disrupts normal fantasy formation, just as it disrupts normal perceptual and memory functions. As suggested by Kris (1956) and others, normal memories, nontraumatic experiences, and normal fantasy life are worked over, transformed, and layered with development. With early severe trauma, there may be no "evolution" to these processes. Fantasy development in its "rich and variegated way" (Hayman, 1957) is stifled or coarcted. This was particularly evident in Frank's (1969) patient for whom tying up and being tied— fantasies developed from his real experience at eight months of age— dominated his mental space. We saw none of the elaborate, varied fantasies characteristic of children his age. Fantasies developed solely around the trauma and the trauma in its literal form remained at its center.

THE TRAUMATIC TRANSFERENCE

The transference in these cases conformed to the specific and unique nature of the trauma under consideration for each patient (i.e., the cervix that would not hold, the aunt who showed up late with an apology, etc.). This was also noted in the cases cited from the literature (see, e.g., Yorke, 1986; Blum, 1987). My initial lack of understanding of these traumatic experiences did, however, engender a rather uniform response: I was to each patient in his own way the mother who was not in touch with the mind of her baby. In each case, the form in which I was not in touch mirrored the patient's perception of his or her emotional experience with his or her real mother. It was essential to take up my failures in this regard because the patient now had *two* mothers who had failed. The trauma was thereby doubly compounded. On the other hand, understanding seemed to ease the pain and to evoke healing images in the positive transference (e.g., the doctor who did the life-saving surgery). The conceptualizations of Balint (1968), Bail and Reiner (Reiner, 1993a, b) are very important here. The infant's communications must be recognized and understood by the mother, for the infant is unable to defend himself against the mother's misunderstanding. Such is also the case in the relationship between patient and analyst. I believe my patients told me in each of their dreams and transference manifestations how significant my "misunderstanding" of their infant-self was to them.

With regard to the value of one type of interpretation over another (reconstructive versus here-and-now transference), these cases suggest that both reconstructive *and* here-and-now transference interpretations are important and that one cannot be emphasized at the expense of the other. In each case, reconstructive work was essential to the discovery of the specific infantile trauma. Here-and-now transference interpretations were crucial to understanding the impact of the trauma on the immediate transference situation and the patient's unconscious perceptions of the analyst. Furthermore, Gill's (1982) point that reconstructive and extratransference interpretations are more likely to produce "defensive intellectualization" and a "flight from the immediate transference situation" (pp. 122–123) did not seem evident in any of my cases or those from the literature. In fact, the opposite was true. An understanding of the infantile trauma reached the patients in an emotionally affecting way. Affect shifted markedly during the hour, becoming more genuine and alive. The patients seemed to touch their real selves in a way that could truly be experienced in the room.

MATERNAL HOLDING AND INFANT TRAUMA

One issue mentioned in the literature that was not evident in any of my patients was the suggestion of Heimann (1958) that surviving early physical trauma brings somatic memories of both the trauma *and* the fact of being able to overcome it. The latter brings a sense of hope and self-confidence to the personality, according to Heimann. There was no evidence of hope and self-confidence in the personality or character structure of my patients, nor did either seem particularly evident in the patients reported in the literature. The consequences of early trauma for my patients manifested only as repetition, pathogenic beliefs, extensive anxiety, and a sense of a future that offered little. (Similar findings were noted by Krystal, 1978, and Terr, 1991.) Perhaps such consequences were due to the nature of early trauma itself. Perhaps they were due to the significant pathological family factors that surrounded the trauma. A sense of hope may have been evident in those patients whose parents had helped to modify the traumas with very sensitive attunement to the needs of their babies. Such was not the case, however, with my patients or their parents.

This brings us to the role of the real parent in the modification and exacerbation of trauma. In most of my cases, no holding mother was present anywhere. If trauma forms meaning networks that influence later development, we should ask, what makes that meaning network more or less influential? According to my patients' dreams, the role of the mother (or parents) seems to be key. A baby whose mother's mind was very in tune with his or her needs might be able to acquire a "positive meaning" that could help to mitigate the influence of the trauma network. Fonagy et al.'s (1993) research lends credence to this possibility. Terr (1991), however, noted that, with truly terrifying experiences, modification may be difficult regardless.

PARENTAL PROJECTIONS AND
THE COMPROMISE OF THE MIND

What about the type of trauma that comes about because of pathological projections of the mother? Here clinical experience suggests that a compromise of the mind is the most significant feature. The two cases in which an erasure presented as a significant aspect of the dream are good examples of such projections of parental pathology. In clinical example #3 (Ms. C), projections of hate appeared to produce a singular and dominating defense: the patient erased her mind. This singular dominating defense affected all the patient's capacities to learn and to develop mentally. In clinical example #7 (Mr. G), the erased cassette represented the record of his birth, which coincided with his father's suicide. The adoption of such total, all-encompassing defense indicates that projections of maternal hatred and disturbances may be more mentally unbearable for the infant than are traumas of an external nature, even if the external traumas are severe and the parent was not able to detoxify their effects. I would certainly like to encourage future research in this important direction. If this understanding is, in fact, true, then I think that the reason would lie in the fact that such maternal hatred and disturbances can never act like a "circumscribed war neurosis" as Robertiello (1956) describes it. The trauma can never be separated from the person of the mother, because the trauma *is the mother*. Since the infant's very life depends upon his mother, the infant truly has no way out. The only thing left for him to do is to compromise an aspect of his own self, his own mind, in order to continue to exist in such unbearable circumstances (See Reiner, 1993 a, b). Only through the process of analysis can some objectivity and understanding of the mother–infant situation at an *unconscious level* be brought to the patient. Such a process can, I feel, help to differentiate the patient from the traumatic mother and thus begin to bring hope for life to the patient's infant-self.

Could it be that the early traumas in these cases became the dominating, organizing forces of personality precisely *because* the parent lacked adequate "maternal reverie"? I don't think we can know for sure at this point. I think we can only say here that the strength of the parent–child relationship was not sufficient to prevent the traumas from becoming organizers of experience in the cases presented. Birth and infant traumas may serve as organizers or even "nodal points" (Kris, 1956) because they signify or screen a whole lifetime of traumas in the way that a posttraumatic dream can serve a similar function (Lansky, 1991). The earliest infant trauma simply becomes the way the person's mind and body "talk about" mental suffering.

INTERPRETATION AND CHANGE: THAWING OF THE FROZEN SELF

It is clear that analysis of these early traumas led to significant changes in many of the patients. In the literature, the change is especially dramatic in the cases reported by Rosen (1955), Robertiello (1956), Niederland (1965), and Frank (1969). In all the case reports in the literature, reconstructive work with early traumas were characterized as turning points in the treatment, leading to marked alleviation of symptoms, further involvement in the treatment, and progress in the patient's growth and development. This also seemed to be a trend in my cases. Perhaps Winnicott's (1954) concept of the "freezing of the failure situation" (p. 281) is applicable here. Winnicott stated that it is a healthy response for a person to attempt to defend himself against environmental failures. With such a response, "goes an unconscious assumption . . . that opportunity will occur at a later date for a renewed experience in which the failure situation will be able to be unfrozen . . ." (p. 281). Winnicott considered such later thawing an example of regression in the service of healing. In fact, the characterization of "thawing" of frozen defenses was specifically used in the discussion section of two of the case presentations in the literature (Niederland, 1965; Anthi, 1983). There let us note the centrality of reconstruction in this process. It is in the course of reconstructing these "frozen experiences," interpreting them, and thereby making contact with the patient in this way that the enactments ceased and development proceeded.

A very interesting aspect of my cases further attests to Winnicott's view. Most of my patients brought the dreams depicting their traumas exceedingly early in the treatment, usually within the first weeks and months. These early presentations could partially be accounted for by the coincidence that in a number of cases the day residue for the dreams happened to be the birthdays of the patients and that their birthdays just happened to come early on in the treatment situation. One can think of another explanation, however.

We could say that the initial weeks and months of analysis represent a hopeful opportunity. Moreover, in each case I attempted (from the very first session if possible) to analyze the patient's dream material in significant detail. In doing so, I attempted to address the central unconscious anxiety evident in the dream and to provide as coherent a story of the patient's unconscious suffering as could be put together at the time. Could it be that the patients recognized some hope in this—hope of having these traumas understood? They then presented their traumas for analysis at the first appropriate opportunity, for instance, their birthdays, as if to say, can you think about and understand what has been this "unspeakable terror" for me? My being able to decipher the meaning of these unspeakable terrors for these patients led to a shift in their state of mind and an involvement in a now more hopeful process.

It is also interesting that two of the patients (clinical examples #6, Mr. F, and #8, Mr. H) brought the birth traumas in dreams *following* a positive change in ego state. For Mr. F the representation of the premature birth was the first indication of the trauma, indicating that the work of the treatment was already leading to an unfreezing and the dream signified the beginning of a mental resolution of the experience. The birth trauma could be dreamed about and thought about. For Mr. H, the dream referring to a near-abortion came at a time of change of ego state, represented by the culmination of a 10-year analysis. The early trauma was presented in the dream as an indication that the near-abortion of the patient's personality had been an underlying and pervasive source of the major symptoms and pathology and was now finally being resolved.

It is possible that such significant responses in the treatment as described in my patients and in the cases in the literature (see also Fodor's, 1949, dramatic example of the interpretation of the knots in the umbilical cord to a woman with chronic knotting sensations) are due merely to the contact and demonstration of interest, care, and empathy from the analyst. I think such an understanding fails to appreciate the complexity of the process. I believe that the empathic relationship is a necessary but not a sufficient condition for change. In my cases, interpretations of similar material were often made with much care and interest but did not address the central and specific unconscious issue remaining in the mind and enacted in detail in the present. On these other occasions, the patients did not improve. In addition, further material indicated that I was still being seen as an unattuned mother. It was only with the *specific interpretation to the unconscious* of the infantile traumatic experience (or whatever issue was present) that a notable shift in the patient's mental state took place and the patient's perception of me began to change. I think this is a very important finding. To touch the patient we *must* touch the part of the patient that is not yet conscious. As Bail (1993, personal communication) puts it, only when the unconscious mind of the patient is truly understood can his or her life move forward. In turn, deepening the level of understanding brings a true connection between patient and analyst. In my view, this is how the analytic relationship develops at its best.

The work of Frances Tustin (1981) may be relevant here both as to the nature of the trauma and the ramifications for the analytic relationship. It may be that these early traumas create a premature "not-me" awareness (via severe physical pain, separations from the mother during hospitalizations, sexual abuse, etc.) and prevent the "illusion of oneness" with the mother so necessary for the baby's sense of safety, security, and peace of mind. What occurs instead is a premature awareness of a separate bodily self. To deal with the terror of this experience, the trauma becomes encapsulated—preserved whole, and kept within the individual like a mental "autistic" object. This metaphor may be another way of explaining the literalness of the reenactments of these experiences. Perhaps we could say that the analytic work restored the sense of oneness that had been lost so early in infancy. The analyst made contact with the patient's desperate infant-self in such a manner that the premature separation from the mother accompanying the early trauma, and precipitating the premature awareness of bodily separateness and not-meness, was modified.

The understanding of the analytic relationship provided by Tustin's autistic metaphor may also throw light on the nature of the repetition compulsion. Freud (1920a) suggested that the repetition compulsion is instituted in the mind as an attempt to master overwhelming trauma. In the light of the case presentations here, another meaning of the repetition compulsion may be an attempt to find an object of significance—someone who can think about and understand at a deep level what is "not thinkable" for the patient. These traumas were enacted everywhere—in the transference, behaviors, symptoms, fantasies, character styles of the patients. Such an array of manifestations could offer an analyst who is willing to listen a number of avenues to recognize and understand what the patient simply cannot.

Perhaps we should pause for a moment to raise an objection to the findings implied by the data presented. Arlow (1991) takes up as one of the difficulties with preoedipal reconstruction the role that family myth or legend plays in the patients' early recollections: are patients reporting the family legend of what happened to them, and is this what is being reconstructed? (see also Etchegoyen, 1982, for a similar formulation). I believe that the family legend is not the central issue in the cases presented in this study, although the patients had often been told as children about their traumatic experiences. The traumas were reconstructed from dream material and (in the cases in the literature) from detailed enactments in somatic reactions, transference manifestations, symptoms, nonverbal behavior, and the like. The traumas were evident as repetition compulsions and were pervasive throughout large segments of the personality. I do not believe that a family myth alone could have such effects. Terr (1988) makes a similar point: traumatized children must show some evidence of behavioral memories (repetitive enactments) of their traumas, *in addition* to their conscious verbal descriptions, if these traumas are to be considered legitimate rather than a product of suggestion or lying. Further, in all the cases in the literature as well as in my own cases, interpretations about these traumas resulted in some modification, usually some or even an appreciable diminishment, of the repetitive enactments. These factors suggest that what we are seeing here is not simply family myths or legends, but manifestations of actual happenings experienced traumatically by infants.

DREAMS

It is important here to note the value of dreams in reaching these traumas. Dreams are a reflection of the core of the unconscious and remain our most important access to it. As noted in chapter 8, they store earliest experience and can tell us the story of that experience. They also help us to ascertain and follow the most important transference configurations at an unconscious level. The method of gathering detailed associations to dream elements seems particularly useful in the matter of unremembered trauma. Such early experiences are stored in visual rather than verbal form (Terr, 1991) and associations help us reach specific memories encoded in the visual imagery.

As was noted in several of the cases, few associations to trauma-related images were forthcoming. This seems particularly to be the case when the trauma occurred at birth or during the neonatal period. I think that "no associations" may refer to a time—the beginning of life—when, in fact, there was little to associate to, that is, when there were few prior experiences from which to make associations. Although it would certainly not be the case at all times, a possible criterion for determining a very early trauma or experience at birth would be the phenomenon of no associations to many elements of a dream, behavior, thought, or fantasy. In fact, the single criterion suggested in the literature to help distinguish fantasy from reality that regularly appeared in my cases was the one described by Greenacre (1956): the frequent appearance of dreams that exactly reproduce reality events but seem to be without associations. In these cases, the particular form of the manifest representations in the dream and the day residue, as well as knowledge of the patient's history, symptoms, and transference manifestations, help to point to earliest experience.

As noted at the outset of this work, questions could be raised as to whether suggestion or persuasion on my part is a consideration in these interpretations. I raised the question myself in the course of my work. Certainly when I first realized that dreams could take up material from the very beginning of life (clinical examples #1 and #2, Ms. A and Ms. B), I conducted future treatments with this possibility in mind. The particular method I use to work with dreams, however, as well as the interaction between patient and analyst that evolves in relation to the dream, militate against the patient's response being only a product of the analyst's suggestion. In addition, there was only a very small number of cases over the course of more than a decade of analytic practice in which birth trauma or early physical traumas appeared. Many more cases of long-term strain traumas involving misattunements from the parents were seen but not reported here.

In terms of the style of working in the dream, the particular method adopted by me involves an attempt to provide a synthesis of all elements of the dream material and associations. All parts of the dream must fit together as a coherent whole *and*, at the same time, must fit the exact state of mind of the patient (Bail, 1993, personal communication). It is often a daunting task to attempt such a coherent synthesis and one is not always successful. In attempting such a synthesis, I necessarily rely quite heavily on the responses of the patient as we go along.

I often make an initial interpretation as to the meaning of the dream. If it does not prove correct, I suggest other interpretations. The patient and I then go back and forth, following the paths that seem most promising. In Mr. F's case (clinical example #6), for example, I first ventured some other interpretation of the car's having to leave the ramp prematurely and the accident that followed. None of these possibilities seemed to touch the patient. Mr. F either had no response or else responded that something didn't feel right about the understanding.

Often, what doesn't "feel right" can be used as a starting point for further associations: What comes to mind about this? Then we can often get a more precise view of the issues at hand. Thus, I do not hesitate to discard what I consider my incorrect interpretations. The patient and I continue to work together, thinking about the various elements as well as whatever else comes to the patient's mind until an understanding seems to jell. The process is often difficult (which is not entirely reflected in the case reports) and takes a great deal of work on the part of both the patient and analyst. There is, however, an almost palpable difference in the room between times when interpretations address the unconscious correctly and times when they do not. One can see also the furthering of meaningful associations that comes from a correct understanding. The patient's state of mind seems to shift. When I do not understand at least a part of the unconscious meaning in a given hour, I often have a complaining patient at my door in the next. If the patient doesn't complain overtly, often there will be indications in the dream to follow suggesting my failure to understand. Again, I use this information to try to put together a more precise understanding.

This method of working with the patient is a very cooperative one. The patient's associations, thoughts, feelings, and conscious and unconscious reactions are of real importance in our trying to understand together how the unconscious mind has made meaning of experience. (One must, of course, consider that the patient's conscious responses to the analyst's interpretations may not always tell the whole story.) Even with such a cooperative arrangement, however, if I fail to understand what is going on unconsciously, the work falters and we must then take up the meaning of my failure to understand. Thus, I do not have a stake in *which* material provides a correct understanding, only that I arrive at whatever seems to be the patient's unconscious state of mind. For example, in clinical example #7, Mr. G, a conclusion that the puppy was being strangled as part of a birth experience was discarded—even though it would have been a fascinating discovery—because it did not in fact fit the unconscious issues that the patient was dealing with at that time.

Dreams worked with in this way become an important vehicle for understanding at a very deep level for both the patient and the analyst. One could ask, what about patients who do not dream? I find such patients are rare when treatment proceeds in this particular manner, although they may enter treatment stating that they never recall their dreams. It is my experience that once even a small aspect of the unconscious life of the mind is understood—just taking one fleeting dream image or fragment—the unconscious seems to come to life. Patients begin remembering their dreams quite regularly. When the unconscious is not understood, on the other hand, dreaming seems to stop. I think also that a dream presented in a given hour contains what the patient *needs* to know about his unconscious mind and what he is *ready* to know. It is our work to help him know it.

James Grotstein (1991, personal communication) puts most poetically the issues of infant trauma that help us to think of its relevance to dream analysis:

> Does the infant take in the trauma and live it out, or does the trauma "take in the infant," "swallow him up," so to speak, so that he must live inside of it instead of it living inside of him?

Perhaps the dream of this "lived-in" experience must be understood and interpreted by the analyst if the patient is to move to an "outside state of mind" where he may grow and develop. In this way, the patient may begin truly to live in his life rather than in his trauma.

INFANT TRAUMA AND
THE UNIVERSE OF THE MIND

Many fields of study—medicine, psychology, neurobiology, psychoanalysis—will need to bring their expertise to bear before further understanding can advance of how the earliest experiences and mental states are known to the fetus and infant, of the means whereby these experiences and states are retained in the mind, and of how they may be acted on in later development. It is in the detailed work of examination of the unconscious mind that psychoanalysis has a unique place in this endeavor. Theoretically, the capacity for the mind to know and store earliest experience, and the knowledge that the infant's mind is not a vague and amorphous structure, widens the scope of our work and the depth and breadth of our interpretive stance. The clinical data presented here, the results of infant research, and recent neurobiological research all suggest that the "universe of the mind" (Bail, 1991) may be a larger one than we have assumed. As analysts, we need to know this universe—its inner workings and its outer reaches—however far those reaches extend. Continued analytic investigation may help us to go further, assisting us in fine tuning our methods of identifying and reconstructing earliest experience. The work presented in this book does not in itself prove the existence of such early storage and knowledge but, rather, presents some material that opens the door of our minds to its possibility.

I end with a few questions: How are birth and infant trauma lived out in persons with a very well-attuned parent–infant upbringing? Would the results be less global than the pervasive effects we have seen in this work? How, by contrast, are exceptionally *good* experiences at birth and in infancy manifest in dreams and lived out in character? Do they undergo, as Frank (1969) suggests, "a change in function" and become ego strengths, or are they lived out in very specific ways in behavior, feelings, and character traits that are positive and growth-promoting? And, finally, how far back can we go? Perhaps in time we will discover that storage of early experience takes place not just from the beginning of life or from the fourth or fifth month of fetal development, but from the very moment of conception. . .

References

Abraham, K. (1913), A screen memory concerning a childhood event of apparently aetiological significance. In: *Clinical Papers and Essays on Psychoanalysis*. London: Hogarth Press, 1955, pp. 36–41.

Allik, J. & Valsiner, J. (1980), Visual development in ontogenesis: Some re-evaluations. In: *Advances in Child Development and Behavior, Vol. 15*, ed. H. Reese & L. Lipsitt. New York: Academic Press, pp. 2–52.

Altman, L. (1969), *The Dream in Psychoanalysis*. New York: International Universities Press.

Anthi, P. (1983), Reconstruction of preverbal experiences. *J. Amer. Psychoanal. Assn.*, 31:33–56.

Arlow, J. (1969), Fantasy, memory, and reality testing. *Psychoanal. Quart.*, 38:28–51.

———— (1991), Methodology and reconstruction. *Psychoanal. Quart.*, 60:539–563.

Aserinsky, E. & Kleitman, N. (1953), Regularly occurring periods of eye motility and concomitant phenomena during sleep. *Science*, 188:273–274.

Atwood, G. & Stolorow, R. (1984), *Structures of Subjectivity*. Hillsdale, NJ: The Analytic Press.

———— (1992), *Contexts of Being*. Hillsdale, NJ: The Analytic Press.

Bail, B. (1991), *The Freud-Klein Controversies: Los Angeles (1973–1977)—Testing Ground and Final Solution*. Self: Beverly Hills, CA.

Baillargeon, R. & De Vos, J. (1991), Object permanence in young infants: Further evidence. *Child Devel.*, 62:1227–1246.

Balint, M. (1968), *The Basic Fault*. London: Tavistock.

———— (1969), Trauma and object relationships. *Internat. J. Psycho-Anal.*, 50:429–435.

Bartlett, F. (1932), *Remembering*. Cambridge: Cambridge University Press.

Begley, S. (1989), The stuff that dreams are made of. *Newsweek*, Aug. 14, pp. 41–44.

Bernstein, A. & Blacher, R. (1967), The recovery of a memory from three months of age. *The Psychoanalytic Study of the Child*, 20:156–161. New York: International Universities Press.

Bion, W. R. (1962), *Learning from Experience*. New York: Aronson.

———— (1967), *Second Thoughts*. New York: Aronson.

———— (1977), Caesura. In: *Two Papers: The Grid and Caesura*. Rio de Janeiro: Imago.

———— (1979), *A Memoir of the Future, Book Three.* Perthshire, UK: Clunie Press.

Blum, H. (1976), The changing use of dreams in psychoanalytic practice. *Internat. J. Psycho-Anal.*, 57:315–324.

———— (1977), The prototype of preoedipal reconstruction. *J. Amer. Psychoanal. Assn.*, 25:757–785.

———— (1978), Reconstruction in a case of postpartum depression. *The Psychoanalytic Study of the Child*, 33:335–362. New Haven, CT: Yale University Press.

———— (1980), The value of reconstruction in adult psychoanalysis. *Internat. J. Psycho-Anal.*, 61:39–54.

———— (1986), The concept of reconstruction of trauma. In: *The Reconstruction of Trauma*, ed. A. Rothstein. Madison, CT: International Universities Press, pp. 7–27.

———— (1987), The role of identification in the resolution of trauma: The Anna Freud Memorial Lecture. *Psychoanal. Quart.*, 56:609–627.

Bollas, C. (1987), *The Shadow of the Object.* New York: Columbia University Press.

Bower, T. G. R. (1974), *Development in Infancy.* San Francisco: Freeman.

———— (1977), *A Primer of Infant Development.* San Francisco: Freeman.

Braatoy, T. (1954), *The Fundamentals of Psychoanalytic Technique.* New York: Wiley.

Bradley, R. & Stern, L. (1967), The development of the human taste bud during the foetal period. *J. Anat.*, 101:743–752.

Brazelton, T. B. (1978), The remarkable talents of the newborn. *Birth & Family J.*, 5:187–191.

Brenman, E. (1980), The value of reconstruction in adult psychoanalysis. *Internat. J. Psycho-Anal.*, 61:53–60.

Breuer, J. & Freud, S. (1893–1895), Studies on hysteria. *Standard Edition*, 2. London: Hogarth Press, 1955.

Caper, R. (1988), *Immaterial Facts.* Northvale, NJ: Aronson.

Cassel, Z. & Sander, L. (1975), Neonatal recognition processes and attachment: The masking experiment. Presented to Society for Research in Child Development, Denver, CO.

Chamberlain, D. (1987), The cognitive newborn: A scientific update. *Brit. J. Psychother.*, 4:30–71.

Clements, M. (1977), Observation on certain aspects of neonatal behavior in response to auditory stimuli. Presented at the Fifth International Congress of Psychosomatic Obstetrics and Gynecology, Rome.

Cohen, J. (1980), Structural consequences of psychic trauma: A new look at "Beyond the Pleasure Principle." *Internat. J. Psycho-Anal.*, 61:421–432.

Corliss, C. (1976), *Patten's Human Embriology.* New York: McGraw-Hill.

Davidoff-Hirsch, H. (1985), Oedipal and preoedipal phenomena: Some thoughts on their interrelation as manifest in adult analytic reconstructions. *J. Amer. Psychoanal. Assn.*, 37:821–840.

Dayton, G., Jones, M., Aui, P., Rawson, A., Steele, B. & Rose, M. (1964), Developmental study of coordinated eye movements in the human infant, I. Visual acuity in the newborn human: A study based on induced optokinetic nystagmus recorded by electro-oculography. *Arch. Opthalmol.*, 71:865–870.

DeCasper, A. & Fifer, W. (1980), On human bonding: Newborns prefer their mothers' voices. *Science*, 208:1174–1176.

DeCasper, A. & Spence, M. (1982), Prenatal maternal speech influences human newborn's auditory preferences. Presented at the Third Biennial International Conference on Infant Studies, Austin, TX.

Dement, W. (1955), Dream recall and eye movements during sleep in schizophrenics and normals. *J. Nerv. Ment. Dis.*, 122:263–269.

Demos, E. V. (1985), The elusive infant. *Psychoanal. Inq.*, 4:553–567.

De Saussure, J. (1982), Dreams and dreaming in relation to trauma in childhood. *Internat. J. Psycho-Anal.*, 63:167–175.

Deutsch, F. (1947), Analysis of postural behavior. *Psychoanal. Quart.*, 16:195–243.

Dorpat, T. & Miller, M. (1992), *Clinical Interaction and the Analysis of Meaning*. Hillsdale, NJ: The Analytic Press.

Dowling, S. (1982a), Dreams and dreaming in relation to trauma in childhood. *Internat. J. Psycho-Anal.*, 63:157–166.

———— (1982b), Mental organization in the phenomenon of sleep. *The Psychoanalytic Study of the Child*, 37:285–302. New Haven, CT: Yale University Press.

———— (1985), A Piagetian critique. *Psychoanal. Inq.*, 5:569–587.

Dreyfus-Brisac, C. (1968), Sleep ontogenesis in early human prematurity from 24 to 27 weeks of conceptual age. *Dev. Psychobiol.*, 1:162–169.

Dubowitz, L., Dubowitz, V., Morante, A. & Verghote, M. (1980), Visual function in the preterm and fullterm newborn infant. *Devel. Med. & Child Neurol.*, 22:465–475.

Ekstein, R. & Rangell, L. (1961), Reconstruction and theory formation. *J. Amer. Psychoanal. Assn.*, 9:684–697.

Engel, G., Reichsman, F., Harway, V. & Wilson, D. (1985), Monica: Infant-feeding behavior of a mother gastric fistula-fed as an infant—A thirty-year longitudinal study of enduring effects. In: *Parental Influences in Health and Disease*, ed. E. Anthony & G. Pollack. Boston: Little, Brown, pp. 30–89.

Erickson, M. (1941), On the possible occurrence of a dream in an eight-month-old infant. *Psychoanal. Quart.*, 10:382–384.

Etchegoyen, R. H. (1982), The relevance of the "here and now" transference interpretation for the reconstruction of early psychic development. *Internat. J. Psycho-Anal.*, 63:65–74.

Fagan, J. (1976), Infants' recognition of invariant features of faces. *Child Devel.*, 47:627–638.

Fairbairn, W. R. D. (1952), *Psychoanalytic Studies of the Personality*. London: Routledge & Kegan Paul.

Fajardo, B. (1987), Neonatal trauma and early development. *The Annual of Psychoanalysis*, 15:233–240. New York: International Universities Press.

Fantz, R. (1963), Pattern vision in newborn infants. *Science*, 140:296–297.

———— (1965), Visual perception from birth as shown by pattern selectivity. *Annals of New York Academy of Science*, 118:793–814.

Fedor-Freybergh, P. (1983), The maternal-fetal psychoendo-crinologic system. Presented at First International Congress on Pre- and Perinatal Psychology, Toronto, Ontario, Can.

Ferenczi, S. (1913), Stages in the development of the sense of reality. In: *Sex in Psychoanalysis*. New York: Basic Books, 1950, pp. 213–239.

———— (1931), On the revision of "The Interpretation of Dreams." In: *Final Contributions to the Problems and Methods of Psychoanalysis*. London: Karnac, 1955, pp. 238–243.

———— (1932), Repetition in analysis worse than the original trauma. In: *Final Contributions to the Problems and Methods of Psychoanalysis*. London: Karnac, 1955, p. 268.

———— (1933), Thalassa: A Theory of genitality. *Psychoanal. Quart.*, 2:361–403.

Field, T., Woodson, R., Greenberg, R. & Cohen, D. (1982), Discrimination and imitation of facial expressions by neonates. *Science*, 218:179–181.

Finkelhor, D. (1984), *Child Sexual Abuse*. New York: Free Press.

Fisher, C. (1960), Subliminal (preconscious) perception: The microgenesis of unconscious fantasy. In: *Fantasy, Myth and Reality*, ed. H. Blum, Y. Kramer, A. Richards & A. D. Richards. Madison, CT: International Universities Press, 1988, pp. 93–108.

Fodor, N. (1949), *The Search for the Beloved*. New York: Hermitage Press.

———— (1951), *New Approaches to Dream Interpretation*. New York: Citadel Press.

Fonagy, P., Steele, M., Moran, G., Steele, H. & Higgitt, A. (1993), Measuring the ghost in the nursery: An empirical study of the relation between parents' mental representations of childhood experiences and their infants' security of attachment. *J. Amer. Psychoanal. Assn.*, 41:957–989.

Forman, M. (1984), A trauma theory of character neurosis and traumatic transferences. In: *Psychoanalysis*, Vol. 2, ed. G. Pollack & J. Gedo. New York: International Universities Press, pp. 321–345.

Frank, A. (1969), The unrememberable and the unforgettable. *The Psychoanalytic Study of the Child*, 24:48–77. New York: International Universities Press.

French, T. (1970), *Psychoanalytic Interpretations*. Chicago: Quandrangle Books.

French, T. & Fromm, E. (1964), *Dream Interpretation*. New York: Basic Books.

Freud, A. (1951), Observations on child development. *The Psychoanalytic*

Study of the Child, 6:8–30. New York: International Universities Press.

———— (1969), *Difficulties in the Path of Psychoanalysis.* New York: International Universities Press.

———— & Burlingham, D. (1942), *War and Children.* New York: International Universities Press, 1944.

Freud, E. W. (1989), Prenatal attachment and bonding. In: *The Course of Life,* Vol. 1: Infancy, ed. S. Greenspan & G. Pollack. Madison, CT: International Universities Press, pp. 467–483.

Freud, S. (1893), Some points for a comparative study of organic and hysterical motor paralyses. *Standard Edition,* 1:160–172. London: Hogarth Press, 1966.

———— (1896a), Heredity in the aetiology of neuroses. *Standard Edition,* 3:141–156. London: Hogarth Press, 1962.

———— (1896b), Further remarks on the neuro-psychoses of defence. *Standard Edition,* 3:162–185. London: Hogarth Press, 1962.

———— (1896c), The aetiology of hysteria. *Standard Edition,* 3:91–221. London: Hogarth Press, 1952.

———— (1899), Screen memories. *Standard Edition,* 3:303–322. London: Hogarth Press, 1962.

———— (1900), Interpretation of dreams. *Standard Edition,* 4 & 5. London: Hogarth Press, 1953.

———— (1901), The psychopathology of everyday life. *Standard Edition,* 6. London: Hogarth Press, 1960.

———— (1906), My views on the part played by sexuality in the aetiology of neurosis. *Standard Edition,* 7:271–179. London: Hogarth Press, 1953.

———— (1908), Hysterical phantasies and their relation to bisexuality. *Standard Edition,* 9:159–166. London: Hogarth Press, 1959.

———— (1910), Leonardo Da Vinci and a memory of his childhood. *Standard Edition,* 11:63–137. London: Hogarth Press, 1957.

———— (1911), Psycho-analytic notes on an autobiographical account of a case of paranoia. *Standard Edition,* 12:9–82. London: Hogarth Press, 1958.

———— (1912), *Minutes of the Vienna Psychoanalytic Society of 1912–1918,* Vol. 4, ed. H. Nunberg & E. Federn. New York: International Universities Press, 1975, pp. 24–25.

———— (1914a), Remembering, repeating, and working through (further recommendations on the technique of psycho-analysis). *Standard Edition,* 12:147–156. London: Hogarth Press, 1958.

———— (1914b), On the history of the psycho-analytic movement. *Standard Edition,* 14:7–66. London: Hogarth Press, 1957.

———— (1914c), On narcissism: An introduction. *Standard Edition,* 14:73–102. London: Hogarth Press, 1957.

———— (1915a), Papers on metapsychology: Repression. *Standard Edition,* 14:146–158. London: Hogarth Press, 1957.

———— (1915b), Papers on metapsychology: The unconscious. *Standard*

Edition, 14:166–215. London: Hogarth Press, 1957.

———— (1917a), Mourning and melancholia. _Standard Edition_, 14:243–258. London: Hogarth Press, 1957.

———— (1917b), Introductory lectures on psychoanalysis, Part III: General theory of neuroses. _Standard Edition_, 16. London: Hogarth Press, 1963.

———— (1918), From the history of an infantile neurosis. _Standard Edition_, 17:7–122. London: Hogarth Press, 1955.

———— (1920a), Beyond the pleasure principle. _Standard Edition_, 18:7–64. London: Hogarth Press, 1955.

———— (1920b), The psychogenesis of a case of homosexuality in a woman. _Standard Edition_, 18:147–172. London: Hogarth Press, 1955.

———— (1923), The ego and the id. _Standard Edition_, 19:12–66. London: Hogarth Press, 1959.

———— (1925a), An autobiographical study. _Standard Edition_, 20:7–74. London: Hogarth Press, 1959.

———— (1925b), A note upon the mystic writing-pad. _Standard Edition_, 20:227–232. London: Hogarth Press, 1959.

———— (1926), Inhibitions, symptoms, and anxiety. _Standard Edition_, 20:77–174. London: Hogarth Press, 1959.

———— (1930), Civilization and its discontents. _Standard Edition_, 21:87–174. London: Hogarth Press, 1961.

———— (1937), Constructions in analysis. _Standard Edition_, 23:257–169. London: Hogarth Press, 1964.

———— (1939), Moses and monotheism. _Standard Edition_, 23:6–137. London: Hogarth Press, 1964.

———— (1940), An outline of psychoanalysis. _Standard Edition_, 23:144–207. London: Hogarth Press, 1964.

Furst, S., ed. (1967), _Psychic Trauma_. New York: Basic Books.

Gaensbauer, T. (1982), The differentiation of discrete affects. _The Psychoanalytic Study of the Child_, 37:29–65. New Haven, CT: Yale University Press.

———— (1985), The relevance of infant research for psychoanalysis. _Psychoanal. Inq._, 5:517–530.

Garma, A. (1946), The traumatic situation in the genesis of dreams. _Internat. J. Psycho-Anal._, 27:134–139.

Gibson, R. (1965), Trauma in early infancy and later personality development. _Psychosom. Med._, 27:229–237.

Gill, M. (1982), _Analysis of Transference, Vol. 1. Psychological Issues_, Monogr. 53. New York: International Universities Press.

Gislason, I. & Call, J. (1982), Case report—Dog bite in infancy: Trauma and personality development. _J. Amer. Acad. Child Psych._, 21:203–207.

Glover, E. (1929), The screening function of traumatic memories. _Internat. J. Psycho-Anal._, 10:90–93.

Goleman, D. (1989), Brain design emerges as a key to emotions. _New York Times_, August 15, pp. B1, B9.

Graf, P. & Schacter, D. (1987), Selective effects of interference on implicit and explicit memory for new associations. *J. Exper. Psychol.*, 13:45–53.

Graves, P. (1989), The functioning fetus. In: *The Course of Life, Vol. 1*, ed. E. Greenspan & G. Pollack. Madison, CT: International Universities Press, pp. 433–465.

Greenacre, P. (1941), Predisposition to anxiety. In: *Trauma, Growth and Personality*. New York: International Universities Press, 1952, pp. 27–82.

———— (1944), Infant reactions to restraint: Problems in the fate of infantile aggression. In: *Trauma, Growth, and Personality*. New York: International Universities Press, 1952, pp. 83–105.

———— (1945), The biological economy of birth. In: *Trauma, Growth and Personality*. New York: International Universities Press, 1952, pp. 3–26.

———— (1949), A contribution to the study of screen memories. In: *Trauma, Growth and Personality*. New York: International Universities Press, 1952, pp. 188–203.

———— (1952), Pregenital patterning. *Internat. J. Psycho-Anal.*, 33:410–415.

———— (1956), Re-evaluation of the process of working through. *Internat. J. Psycho-Anal.*, 37:439–444.

———— (1967), The influence of infantile trauma on genetic patterns. In: *Psychic Trauma*, ed. S. Furst. New York: Basic Books, pp. 108–153.

———— (1979), Reconstruction and the process of individuation. *The Psychoanalytic Study of the Child*, 34:121–144. New Haven, CT: Yale University Press.

———— (1981), Reconstruction: Its nature and therapeutic value. *J. Amer. Psychoanal. Assn.*, 29:27–46.

Greenberg, R. & Pearlman, C. (1975), Psychoanalytic dream continuum: The source and function of dreams. *Internat. Rev. Psycho-Anal.*, 2:441–448.

———— (1980), The private language of dreams. In: *The Dream in Clinical Practice*, ed. J. Natterson. New York: Aronson, pp. 85–96.

Greenson, R. (1970), The exceptional position of the dream in psychoanalytic practice. *Psychoanal. Quart.*, 39:519–549.

Gunther, M. (1961), Infant behavior at the breast. In: *Determinants of Infant Behavior, Vol. 1*, ed. M. Foss. London: Methuen, pp. 37–44.

Haith, M. (1976), Visual competence in early infancy. In: *Handbook of Sensory Physiology, Vol. 8*, ed. R. Held, L. Liebowitz & V. Teuber. New York: Springer, pp. 311–356.

Hall, C. (1967), Are prenatal and birth experiences represented in dreams? *Psychoanal. Rev.*, 54:157–174.

Hartmann, H. (1950), Psychoanalysis and developmental psychology. *The Psychoanalytic Study of the Child*, 5:7–17. New York: International Universities Press.

Harwood, I. (1986), The need for optimal available caretakers: Moving towards extended selfobject experience. *Group Anal.*, 19:291–302.

———— (1993), Examining early childhood multiple cross-cultural extended selfobject and traumatic experiences in order to create optimum treatment environments. Presented at Sixteenth Annual Conference on The Psychology of the Self, Toronto.

Hayman, M. (1957), Traumatic elements in the analysis of a borderline case. *Internat. J. Psycho-Anal.*, 38:9–21.

Heimann, P. (1958), Notes on early development. In: *About Children and Children-No-Longer*. London: Tavistock, pp. 138–150.

Hill, L., Breckle, R. & Wolfgram, K. (1983), An ultrasonic view of the developing fetus. *Obstet. & Gyn. Surv.*, 38:375–398.

Hobson, J. A. (1988), *The Dreaming Brain*. New York: Basic Books.

Hoffer, W. (1952), The mutual influences in the development of ego and the id: Earliest stages. *The Psychoanalytic Study of the Child*, 7:31–41. New York: International Universities Press.

Humphrey, T. (1964), Some correlations between the appearance of human fetal reflexes and the development of the nervous system. In: *Progress in Brain Research*. New York: Elsevier, pp. 94–133.

Isakower, O. (1938), A contribution to the pathopsychology of phenomena associated with falling asleep. *Internat. J. Psycho-Anal.*, 19:331–345.

Jessner, L., Blom, G. & Waldfogel, S. (1952), Emotional implications of tonsillectomy and adenoidectomy on children. *The Psychoanalytic Study of the Child*, 7:126–169. New York: International Universities Press.

Jones, R. (1970), *The New Psychology of Dreaming*. New York: Viking Press.

Katan, A. (1973), Children who were raped. *The Psychoanalytic Study of the Child*, 28:208–224. New Haven, CT: Yale University Press.

Kernberg, P. (1980), The origins of the reconstructed in psychoanalysis. In: *Rapprochement*, ed. R. Lax. New York: Aronson, pp. 263–281.

Khan, M. (1964a), The concept of cumulative trauma. In: *The Privacy of the Self*. New York: International Universities Press, 1974, pp. 42–68.

———— (1964b), Ego distortion, cumulative trauma, and the role of reconstruction in the analytic situation. *Internat. J. Psycho-Anal.*, 45:272–279.

———— (1974), *The Privacy of the Self*. New York: International Universities Press.

———— (1976), The changing use of dreams in psychoanalytic practice: In search of the dreaming experience. *Internat. J. Psycho-Anal.*, 57:325–330.

Klein, G. (1966), The several grades of memory. In: *Psychoanalysis, A General Psychology*, ed. R. Lowenstein, L. Newman, M. Shur & A. Solnit. New York: International Universities Press, pp. 377–389.

Klein, M. (1975a), *Love, Guilt, and Reparation, and Other Works, 1921–1945*. London: Hogarth Press.

———— (1975b), *Envy and Gratitude, and Other Works, 1946–1963*. London: Hogarth Press.

Kohut, H. (1971), *The Analysis of the Self*. New York: International Universities Press.

———— (1977), *Restoration of the Self*. New York: International Universities Press.

Kris, E. (1956), The recovery of childhood memories in psychoanalysis. *The Psychoanalytic Study of the Child*, 11:54–88. New York: International Universities Press.

Kris Study Group (1971), Recollections and reconstruction: Reconstruction in psychoanalysis. In: *Monograph IV of the Kris Study Group, New York Psychoanalytic Institute*, ed. B. Fine, J. Edward & H. Waldhorn. New York: International Universities Press.

———— (1974), Trauma and symbolism. In: *Monograph V of the Kris Study Group, New York Psychoanalytic Institute*, ed. H. Waldhorn & B. Fine. New York: International Universities Press.

Krystal, H. (1978), Trauma and affects. *The Psychoanalytic Study of the Child*, 33:81–116. New Haven, CT: Yale University Press.

Laibow, R. (1986), Birth recall: A clinical report. *Pre- & Perinat. Psychol.*, 1:78–81.

Lansky, M. (1991), The transformation of affect in posttraumatic nightmares. *Bull. Menn. Clin.*, 55:470–490.

Ledoux, J. (1989), Cognitive-emotional interactions in the Brain. *Cognit. & Emot.*, 3:267–289.

Ledoux, J., Romanski, L. & Xagoraris, A. (1989), Indelibility of subcortical emotional memories. *J. Cognit. Neurosci.*, 1:238–243.

Lewin, K. (1946), Sleep, the mouth and the dream screen. In: *Selected Writings*, ed. J. Arlow. New York: Psychoanalytic Quarterly Press, 1973, pp. 87–100.

———— (1953), The forgetting of dreams. In: *Drives, Affects and Behavior*, ed. R. Lowenstein. New York: International Universities Press, pp. 191–202.

Lewy E. & Rapaport, D. (1944), The psychoanalytic concept of memory and its relation to recent memory theories. *Psychoanal. Quart.*, 13:16–42.

Lichtenberg, J. (1983), *Psychoanalysis and Infant Research*. Hillsdale, NJ: The Analytic Press.

———— (1989), *Psychoanalysis and Motivation*. Hillsdale, NJ: The Analytic Press.

Lieberman, M. (1963), Early development of stress and later behavior. *Science*, 141:824.

Liley, A. (1972), The foetus as a personality. *Austral. & New Zeal. J. Psych.*, 6:99–105.

Lipin, T. (1955), Psychic functioning in patients with undiagnosed somatic symptoms. *Arch. Neurol. & Psych.*, 73:329–337.

———— (1963), The repetition compulsion and 'maturational' drive-representatives. *Internat. J. Psycho-Anal.*, 44:389–406.

Loewald, H. (1955), Hypnoid state, repression, abreaction, and recollection. *J. Amer. Psychoanal. Assn.*, 3:201–210.

Loewenstein, R. (1957), Some thoughts on interpretation in the theory and practice of psychoanalysis. *The Psychoanalytic Study of the Child*, 12:127–150. New York: International Universities Press.

Loftus, E. & Loftus, G. (1980), On the permanence of stored information in the human brain. *Amer. Psychol.*, 35:409–420.

McGuire, M. (1971), *Reconstructions in Psychoanalysis*. New York: Appleton-Century-Crofts.

McLaughlin, J. (1989), The relevance of infant observational research for the analytic understanding of adult patients' nonverbal behaviors. In: *The Significance of Infant Observational Research for Clinical Work with Children, Adolescents, and Adults*, ed. S. Dowling & A. Rothstein. Madison, CT: International Universities Press, pp. 109–122.

MacMillan, M. (1992), The sources of Freud's methods for gathering and evaluating clinical data. In: *Freud and the History of Psychoanalysis*, ed. T. Gelfand & J. Kerr. Hillsdale, NJ: The Analytic Press, pp. 99–151.

Mahler, M., Pine, F. & Bergman, A. (1975), *The Psychological Birth of the Human Infant*. New York: Basic Books.

Mancia, M. (1981), On the beginning of mental life in the foetus. *Internat. J. Psycho-Anal.*, 62:351–357.

_____ (1988), The dream as religion of the mind. *Internat. J. Psycho-Anal.*, 69:419–426.

Martin, C. (1981), Newborns pacified by tapes of their own crying. *Brain/Mind Bull.*, 5:2.

Masson, J., ed. (1985), *The Complete Letters of Sigmund Freud to Wilhelm Fliess, 1887–1904.* Cambridge, MA: Belknap Press/ Harvard University Press.

Mehler, J., Bertoncini, J. & Barriere, M. (1978), Infant recognition of mother's voice. *Perception*, 7:491–497.

Meltzer, D. (1984), *Dream-Life*. Perthshire, UK: Clunie Press.

_____ (1988), *The Apprehension of Beauty*. Perthshire, UK: Clunie Press.

Meltzoff, A. & Borton, W. (1979), Intermodal matching by human neonates. *Nature*, 282:403–404.

_____ & Moore, M. (1983), The origins of imitation in infancy: Paradigm, phenomena and theories. In: *Advances in Infancy Research, Vol. 2*, ed. L. Lipsett & C. Rover-Collier. Norwood, NJ: Ablex, pp. 265–301.

Miller, M. (1951), The traumatic effect of surgical operations in childhood on the integrative functions of the ego. *Psychoanal. Quart.*, 70:77–92.

Mistretta, C. & Bradley, R. (1977), Taste in utero: Theoretical considerations. In: *Taste and Development*, ed. J. Weiffenbach. Washington, DC: U.S. Govt. Printing Off., pp. 51–69.

Mott, F. (1964), *The Universal Design of Creation*. Edinburgh, Scot.: Mark Beech.

Mully, A. (1979), Threat of breakdown in middle life and its antecedents in infancy: Thoughts on pathology at the mother/infant interface. Presented to the faculty of the Canadian Psychoanalytic Society, Ottawa, Ontario.

Murphy, W. (1958), Character, trauma, and sensory perception. *Internat. J. Psycho-Anal.*, 39:555–568.

Myers, N., Clifton, R. & Clarkson, N. (1987), When they were very young: Threes remember two years ago. *Inf. Beh. & Dev.*, 10:123–132.

Nachman, P. & Stern, D. (1984), Affect retrieval: A form of recall memory in prelinguistic infants. In: *Frontiers of Infant Psychiatry, Vol. 2*, ed. E. Galenson & J. Call. New York: Basic Books, pp. 95–100.

Neu, J. (1973), Fantasy and memory: The aetiological role of thoughts according to Freud. *Internat. J. Psycho-Anal.*, 54:383–398.

Niederland, W. (1965), The role of the ego in the recovery of early memories. *Psychoanal. Quart.*, 34:564–571.

———— (1980), Schreber: Father and son. In: *Freud and his Patients, Vol. 2*, ed. M. Kanzer & J. Glenn. New York: Aronson, pp. 251–305.

Norcia, A. & Tyler, C. (1985), Spatial frequency sweep VEP: Visual acuity during the first year of life. *Vision Res.*, 25:1399–1408.

Novey, S. (1968), *The Second Look*. Baltimore, MD: Johns Hopkins University Press.

Obholzer, K. (1982), *The Wolf Man Sixty Years Later*. New York: Continuum.

Osterweil, E. (1990), A psychoanalytic exploration of fetal mental development and its role in the origins of object relations. Unpublished doctoral dissertation, California Graduate Institute, Los Angeles.

Palombo, S. (1978), *Dreaming and Memory*. New York: Basic Books.

Papousek, H. & Papousek, M. (1987), Intuitive parenting: A didactic counterpart to the infant's precocity in integration capacities. In: *Handbook of Infant Development*, ed. J. Osofsky. New York: Wiley, pp. 669–720.

Paul, I. (1967), The concept of schema in memory theory. In: *Motives and Thoughts*, ed. R. Holt. *Psychological Issues*, Monogr. 18/19. New York: International Universities Press, pp. 218–258.

Paul, M. (1981), A mental atlas of the process of psychological birth. In: *Do I Dare Disturb the Universe?* ed. J. Grotstein. Beverly Hills, CA: Caesura Press, pp. 551–570.

Pearson, G. (1941), Effect of operative procedures on the emotional life of the child. *Amer. J. Dis. Children*, 62:716–729.

Peerbolte, M. (1951), The psychotherapeutic evaluations of birth-trauma analysis: A preliminary contribution to Fodor's therapy. *Psychoanal. Quart.*, 25:589–603.

———— (1952), Some problems connected with Fodor's birth-trauma therapy. *Psychiat. Quart.*, 26:294–306.

Peiper, A. (1963), *Cerebral Functions in Infancy and Childhood*. New York: Consultants Bureau.

Perris, E., Myers, N. & Clifton, R. (1990), Long-term memory for a single infancy experience. *Child Devel.*, 61:1796–1807.

Piaget, J. (1945), *Play, Dreams, and Imitation in Childhood*. New York: Norton, 1951.

———— (1954), *The Construction of Reality in the Child*. New York: Basic Books.

Pine, F. (1985), *Developmental Theory and Clinical Process*. New Haven, CT: Yale University Press.

Piontelli, A. (1986), *Backwards in Time*. Perthshire, UK: Clunie Press.

_____ (1987), Infant observation from before birth. *Internat. J. Psycho-Anal.*, 68:453–463.

_____ (1988), Pre-natal life and birth as reflected in the analysis of a two year old psychotic girl. *Internat. Rev. Psycho-Anal.*, 15:73–81.

_____ (1989), A study of twins before and after birth. *Internat. Rev. Psycho-Anal.*, 16:413–426.

Ployé, P. (1973), Does prenatal mental life exist? *Internat. J. Psycho-Anal.*, 54:241–246.

Pötzl, O. (1917), The relationship between experimentally induced dream images and indirect vision. In: *Preconscious Stimulation in Dreams, Associations, and Images*, ed. O. Pötzl, R. Allen & J. Teler. *Psychological Issues*, Monogr. 7. New York: International Universities Press.

Prechtl, H. (1981), The study of neural development as a perspective of clinical problems. In: *Maturation and Development*, ed. G. T. Connolly & H. F. R. Prechtl. London: Heinemann, pp. 198–230.

_____ (1985), Ultrasound studies of human fetal behavior. *Early Human Dev.*, 12:91–98.

Pulver, S. (1987), The manifest dream in psychoanalysis: A clarification. *J. Amer. Psychoanal. Assn.*, 35:90–115.

Purpura, D. (1975a), Normal and aberrant neuronal development in the cerebral cortex of the human fetus and young infant. In: *Basic Mechanisms in Mental Retardation*, ed. M. Brazier & N. Buchwald. New York: Academic Press, pp. 141–169.

_____ (1975b), Dendrite differentiation in the human cortex: normal and aberrant developmental patterns. *Adv. Neurol.*, 12:91–116.

_____ (1975c), Consciousness. *Behavior Today*, June 2, p. 494.

Rangell, L. (1967), The metapsychology of psychic trauma. In: *Psychic Trauma*, ed. S. Furst. New York: Basic Books, pp. 51–84.

_____ (1987), Historical perspectives and current status of the interpretation of dreams in clinical work. In: *The Interpretation of Dreams in Clinical Work*, ed. A. Rothstein. New York: International Universities Press, pp. 3–24.

Rank, O. (1929), *The Trauma of Birth*. New York: Harcourt, Brace.

Raskovsky, A. (1960), *El Psiquismo Fetal*. Buenos Aires: Paidos.

Reider, N. (1953), Reconstruction and screen function. *J. Amer. Psychoanal. Assn.*, 1:389–405.

Reiner, A. (1993a), Becoming light: A quantum theory of psychoanalysis. Unpublished manuscript.

_____ (1993b), Psychoanalysis for the 20th century: The dynamics of the deepest self. Unpublished manuscript.

Ribble, M. (1941), Disorganizing factors of the infant personality. *Amer. J. Psychiat.*, 98:459–463.

Ricoeur, P. (1977), The question of proof in Freud's writings. *J. Amer. Psychoanal. Assn.*, 25:835–871.

Robertiello, R. (1956), The importance of trauma during the first year of life. *Psychoanal. Rev.*, 43:501–503.

Roffwarg, H., Muzio, J. & Dement, W. (1966), Ontogenetic development of the human sleep-dream cycle. *Science*, 152:604–619.

Róheim, G. (1952), *Gates of the Dream*. New York: International Universities Press.

Rosen, V. (1955), The reconstruction of a traumatic childhood event in a case of derealization. *J. Amer. Psychoanal. Assn.*, 3:211–221.

Rovee-Collier, C. (1985), Baby's Memory. *Amer. Psychol. Assn. Monitor*, October, p. 25.

Rubinfine, D. (1967), Notes on the theory of reconstruction. *Brit. J. Med. Psychol.*, 4:195–205.

———— (1981), Reconstruction revisited: The question of the reconstruction of mental functioning during the earliest months of life. In: *Objects and Self*, ed. S. Tuttman, C. Kay & M. Zimmerman. New York: International Universities Press, pp. 383–396.

Rycroft, C. (1979), *The Innocence of Dreams*. New York: Pantheon Books.

Sachs, O. (1967), Distinctions between fantasy and reality elements in memory and reconstruction. *Internat. J. Psycho-Anal.*, 48:416–423.

Sadger, J. (1941), A preliminary study of the psychic life of the fetus and the primary germ. *Psychoanal. Rev.*, 28:327–358.

Sandler, J. (1967), Trauma, strain, and development. In: *Psychic Trauma*, ed. S. Furst. New York, Basic Books, pp. 154–174.

Schafer, R. (1976), *A New Language for Psychoanalysis*. New Haven, CT: Yale University Press.

Schimek, J. (1987), Fact and fantasy in the seduction theory: A historical review. *J. Amer. Psychoanal. Assn.*, 35:937–965.

Schmideberg, M. (1950), Infant memories and constructions. *Psychoanal. Quart.*, 19:468–481.

Schur, H. (1966), An observation and comments on the development of memory. *The Psychoanalytic Study of the Child*, 21:468–479. New York: International Universities Press.

Scott, C. (1975), Remembering, sleep, and dreams. *Internat. Rev. Psycho-Anal.*, 2:253–354.

Sharpe, E. (1937), *Dream Analysis*. New York: Brunner/Mazel.

Sherwood, M. (1969), *The Logic of Explanation in Psychoanalysis*. New York: Academic Press.

Siqueland, E. & Lipsitt, L. (1966), Conditioned head-turning in human newborns. *J. Exper. Child Psychol.*, 3:356–376.

Slap, J. (1987), Implications for the structural model of Freud's assumptions about perception. *J. Amer. Psychoanal. Assn.*, 35:629–645.

Sloane, P. (1979), *Psychoanalytic Understanding of the Dream*. New York: Aronson.

Spelt, D. (1948), The conditioning of the human fetus in utero. *J. Exper. Psychol.*, 38:338–346.

Spence, D. (1982), *Narrative Truth and Historical Truth*. New York: Norton.

Spero, M. (1990), Portal aspects of memory overlay in psychoanalysis: An object relations contribution to screen memory phenomena. *The*

Psychoanalytic Study of the Child, 45:79–103. New Haven, CT: Yale University Press.

Spitz, R. (1955), The primal cavity: A contribution to the genesis of perception and its role for psychoanalytic theory. *The Psychoanalytic Study of the Child,* 10:215–240. New York: International Universities Press.

Stern, D. (1985), *The Interpersonal World of the Infant.* New York: Basic Books.

————— (1988), Affects in the context of the infant's lived experience: Some considerations. *Internat. J. Psycho-Anal.,* 69:233–238.

Tauber, E. & Green, M. (1959), *Pre-Logical Experience.* New York: Basic Books.

Terr, L. (1979), Children of Chowchilla. *The Psychoanalytic Study of the Child,* 34:547–623. New Haven, CT: Yale University Press.

————— (1983a), Life attitudes, dreams, and psychic trauma in a group of "normal" children. *J. Amer. Acad. Child Psych.,* 22:221–230.

————— (1983b), Chowchilla revisited: The effects of psychic trauma four years after a school bus kidnapping. *Amer. J. Psychiat.,* 140:1543–1550.

————— (1985), Remembered images in psychic trauma. *The Psychoanalytic Study of the Child,* 40:493–533. New Haven, CT: Yale University Press.

————— (1988), Case study: What happens to early memories of trauma? A study of twenty children under age five at the time of documented traumatic events. *J. Amer. Acad. Child & Adol. Psych,* 27:96–104.

————— (1990), *Too Scared to Cry.* New York: Basic Books.

————— (1991), Childhood traumas: An outline and overview. *Amer. J. Psychiat.,* 148:10–190.

Trevarthen, C. (1974), The psychobiology of speech development. *Neurosci. Res. Prog. Bull.,* pp. 570–585.

————— (1980), The foundations of intersubjectivity: Development of interpersonal and cooperative understanding in infants. In: *The Social Foundations of Language and Thought,* ed. D. Olson. New York: Norton, pp. 316–342.

Tronic, E., Ricks, M. & Cohn, J. (1982), Maternal and infant affective exchange patterns of adaptation. In: *Emotion and Early Interaction,* ed. T. Field & A. Fogal. Hillsdale, NJ: Lawrence Erlbaum Associates, pp. 83–100.

Truby, H. (1965), Cry sounds of the newborn infant. *Acta Pediatrica Scandinavia,* Supp. #163.

————— (1975), Prenatal and neonatal speech, pre-speech, and infantile speech lexicon. *Child Lang.,* 1975, Parts 1–3 (a special issue of *Word*).

Tulving, E. (1985), How many memory systems are there? *Amer. Psychol.,* 40:385–398.

Tustin, F. (1981), *Autistic States in Children.* London: Routledge & Kegan Paul.

Ungerer, J., Brody, R. & Zelazo, P. (1978), Long-term memory for speech in 2–4 week old infants. *Infant Behav.,* 1:177–186.

Valenstein, A. (1989), Pre-oedipal reconstruction in psychoanalysis.

Internat. J. Psycho-Anal., 70:433–442.

Van Buren, J. (1989), *The Modernist Madonna*. Bloomington: Indiana University Press.

Vaughn, H. (1975), Electrophysiological analysis of regional cortical maturation. *Biolog. Psych.*, 10:513–526.

Verny, T. & Kelly, J. (1981), *The Secret Life of the Unborn Child*. New York: Delta.

Weiss, F. (1964), Dreaming—A creative process. *Amer. J. Psychoanal.*, 24:17–28.

Weiss, J. & Sampson, H. (1986), *The Psychoanalytic Process*. New York: Guilford Press.

Wertheimer, M. (1961), Psychomotor coordination of auditory and visual space at birth. *Science*, 134:1692.

Wetzler, S. (1985), The historical truth of psychoanalytic reconstruction. *Internat. J. Psycho-Anal.*, 12:187–197.

Williams, M. (1987), Reconstruction of an early seduction and its after-effects. *J. Amer. Psychoanal. Assn.*, 35:145–163.

Winnicott, D. (1945), Primitive emotional development. In: *Through Paediatrics to Psycho-Analysis*. New York: Basic Books, 1958, pp. 145–156.

———— (1949a), Birth memories, birth trauma, and anxiety. In: *Through Paediatrics to Psycho-Analysis*. New York: Basic Books, 1958, pp. 174–193.

———— (1949b), Mind and its relation to the psyche-soma. In: *Through Paediatrics to Psycho-Analysis*. New York: Basic Books, 1958, pp. 243–254.

———— (1954), Metapsychological and clinical aspects of regression within the psycho-analytic set-up. In: *Through Paediatrics to Psycho-Analysis*. New York: Basic Books, 1958, pp. 278–294.

———— (1958), *Through Paediatrics to Psychoanalysis*. New York: Basic Books.

Wolff, P. (1960), The developmental psychologies of Jean Piaget and psychoanalysis. *Psychological Issues*, Monogr. 5. New York: International Universities Press.

Yorke, C. (1986), Reflections on the problem of psychic trauma. *The Psychoanalytic Study of the Child*, 41:221–236. New Haven, CT: Yale University Press.

Zajonc, R. (1980), Feeling and thinking: preferences need no inferences. *Amer. Psychol.*, 35:151–175.

Zaragoza, M. & Koshmider, J. (1989), Misled subjects may know more than their performance implies. *J. Exper. Psychol.*, 15:246–255.

Index

A

Abortion, near, reconstruction of, change-of-state dream related to, 184, 185, 221–225, 239

Abraham, K., 37, 246

Abusiveness, brush with, 190

Accuracy, in narrative story, 72

Acetylcholine, 172

Acting out, 80, 81; "life and death," 190; of memories, 119; related to birth trauma, 96–97

Action pattern, 142

Adaptive function, dreams as they represent, 178–179

Adequacy, in narrative story, 72

Adult: impact of early trauma on, 90; sex life, 87

Affect, 136; accompanying traumatic experience, 11; tolerance, capacity for, loss of, 59 (see also Anhedonia)

Affective experience, memories of, 135–136, 143

Affective perceptions, 46

Aggressor, identification with, 56–59, 60, 154

Agoraphobic symptoms, 207, 208, 210

Allik, J., 114, 246

Altman, L., 8, 170, 172, 246

Amnesia: infantile, 36; prenatal, 89

Amygdala, 143, 181, 228, 229; infant memory and, 125–126

Anal material, 61

Anal sex, preoccupation with, 204, 206

Analysis: Rank's view, 88; ten year, change-of-state dream following, 184, 185, 221–225

Analyst (see also Patient–analyst relationship); as baby-sitter/ nurse, 210; equated with surgeon, 60; as placental object, 104; as teacher/nurse, 214; trauma patient's view of, 59; as unattuned mother, 239

Analytic hour, reconstruction of infant trauma from nonverbal behavior within, 151–157

Anhedonia, 59

Anthi, P., 45, 73, 81, 151, 182, 231, 233, 238, 246; case study on reconstruction of infant trauma from nonverbal behavior within the analytic hour and within the analytic transference, 151–154

Anticipation, fetal, 110

Anxiety (see also specific type of anxiety): automatic, 31; at birth, 88; organization of, infant trauma as, 233–234; pattern of, birth as organizer of, 94; preparedness for, 27; traumatic, 132; types of, transformation from, 31; unconscious, 182, 239

Arlow, J., 4, 76, 120, 240, 246; view on preverbal reconstruction, 76–77

Aserinsky, E., 172, 246; research on REM sleep and dreams, 172

Association(s): chain of, 11; synthesis of, 242

Associative thinking, 154

Attachments, child's, 229

Atwood, G., 60, 81, 175, 226, 246

Auditory perception, role in reconstruction of traumatic experiences, 161

Aui, P., 113, 248

Autistic metaphor, 240

Avoidances, 32

Awareness, conscious, 228